Vivid Tomorrows

Vivid Tomorrows

*On Science Fiction
and Hollywood*

DAVID BRIN

McFarland & Company, Inc., Publishers
Jefferson, North Carolina

ISBN (print) 978-1-4766-8338-6
ISBN (ebook) 978-1-4766-4173-7

LIBRARY OF CONGRESS AND BRITISH LIBRARY
CATALOGUING DATA ARE AVAILABLE

Library of Congress Control Number 2021005464

© 2021 David Brin. All rights reserved

No part of this book may be reproduced or transmitted in any form or by any means, electronic or mechanical, including photocopying or recording, or by any information storage and retrieval system, without permission in writing from the publisher.

Front cover: Jodie Foster as Dr. Eleanor Ann "Ellie" Arroway in the 1997 film *Contact* (Warner Bros./Photofest)

Printed in the United States of America

*McFarland & Company, Inc., Publishers
Box 611, Jefferson, North Carolina 28640
www.mcfarlandpub.com*

Table of Contents

Acknowledgments   vi

Prologue: Science Fiction and Cinema: Saving the Future by Believing There Will Be One   1

Part One: A Flickering Light on the World

1. The Self-Preventing Prophecy: How a Dose of Nightmare Might Tame Tomorrow's Perils   9
2. Society and Citizens Are Fools! The Favorite Cliché of Cinema and Fiction   15
3. *2001: A Space Odyssey*: Shining Light on How Far We've Come   27
4. Living in a Science Fictional World: Biology and Destiny and Life 'n' Such   32
5. A Quirky Must-See Guide to Science Fiction Movies   44

Part Two: Admirable (But Flawed) Blockbusters

6. *J'accuse* George Lucas … or Zola Meets Yoda   51
7. *Avatar*. Just *Avatar*.   75
8. *The Lord of the Rings*: J.R.R. Tolkien vs. the Modern Age   89

Part Three: Grinding Axes

9. Roll Over, Frank Miller: Street Kids Are Better Than Those 300 Spartans!   101

Table of Contents

10. *Atlas Shrugged*: The Hidden Context of the Book and Film	107
11. Demigods and "Chosen Ones" … Would It Hurt If Humanity Got to Play, Too?	117
12. Getting Science Fictional About a Better World: Marxists and Feminists and Feudalists and Libertarians, Oh My!	122

Part Four: Heroes and Villains

13. Name That Villain: Bad Guys and Aliens in Sci-Fi Movies	135
14. King Kong Is Back! The Ape in the Mirror	141
15. *The Matrix*: Tomorrow May Be Different	148
16. A Mini-Rant: Why All Those Zombies Mean You'd Better Vote!	159
17. Buffy the Old-Fashioned Hero	162

Part Five: Dark Visions and Hope

18. *Dune*: What This Classic Teaches About "Point of View"	165
19. *The Postman*: The Book vs. the Movie	172
20. Man Against Machine: Surrogates, Clones and Dittos	177
21. *Gravity*: Unbearable Lightness … but Solid Storytelling	198
22. Great Opening Lines from Science Fiction Tales	202
23. From Metaphor to Movie Magic—or Why We're Such Good Liars	205
Chapter Notes	221
Index	225

Acknowledgments

The author thanks those who have critiques the many versions of these variously cogent or ranting essays, over the years. Among those who kindly lent a critical eye during formulation of the book itself were science fiction scholars Stephen Potts and Tom Easton, along with Jonathan Armstrong, Jenna Claver, Stephen Collings, Dr. Joe Miller, Edward Lerner, Dan Kimmel, Mike Gannis, Dr. Andrew Love, Kurt Stammberger, Davif Ivory, Doug McElwain, Dré Person, Dr. Charles Gannon, Prof. Tom Easton, Dr. Ed Lerner, Jonathan Alexander. Dr. Thomas Lombardo, Daniel Kimmel, Pat Scannell, Kurt Stammberger, Michael Halbrook, Bonnie Hartmeyer ... and several others who "know who you are."

Special thanks to Robert Prior for the index. And to Cheryl Brigham for patient support.

Keep exploring.

Prologue

*Science Fiction and Cinema:
Saving the Future by Believing
There Will Be One*

Way back in 1924, Thomas Edison addressed early moguls of the film industry he helped create: "I believe … you control the most powerful instrument in the world for good or evil…. [N]ever let a desire for money or power prevent you from giving to the public the best work of which you are capable." Edison went on to speak of a shared dream for "a prosperous, useful and honorable future."

Does that sound hopelessly dreamy and naïve? Surely, money-and-power are the twin screws propelling modern media. And yet, as we'll see, cinema—especially science fiction cinema—has kept busy exploring, preaching, frightening, inspiring and meddling in our attitudes about tomorrow. The medium entertains, but also clarifies and criticizes, laying down stark warnings about failure modes to avoid. And it can inspire—either our better angels or the darker spirits of our nature.

All of this redoubles when science fiction screen dramas take on *change*, the great, salient defining characteristic of our era. Rapid, disruptive, transformative change—much of it dangerous or disturbing, but also (to a surprising degree) change for the better.

Change is the core, essential topic of good science fiction.

Science Fiction (SF) and movies seem made for each other. From tribal folk tales to the superhero characters of Homer or the Vedas, to the surreal films of Méliès, we do seem drawn to vivid extrapolations—or exaggerations—of the life we know. There are many ways that modern Science Fiction *differs* from all those fantasies of the present and past, and we'll get into those differences. But one shared element throbs across the screen and through our minds:

We are not limited beings. Not always. Not inherently.

In the Biblical story of the Tower of Babel, it is said: "If they continue thus, then nothing will be beyond them."

For well or ill, science fiction cinema takes this lesson to heart.

Nothing is beyond us, the new legends say. *So choose well.*

This collection of essays, published across 30 years, explores many aspects of a complex, multisided partnership: between authors and directors, studios and audiences, cinema and society, sci-fi and the future. And hence, let me beg the reader's indulgence! I have tried to reconcile and reduce the number of repetitions, but you are sure to come across points that I re-state—an inevitable outcome of the years that separate some of these pieces. Also because so many tropes and clichés are copied and re-multiplied in Hollywood, by producers, directors and authors who "think they invented" notions like Suspicion of Authority.

In Chapter 1, "The Self-Preventing Prophecy: How a Dose of Nightmare Might Tame Tomorrow's Perils," we'll look at some of the very best and most valuable dramas—like *Nineteen Eighty-Four, Soylent Green, On the Beach, Dr. Strangelove, Silent Spring* and *Gattaca*—delivered to us by dour prophets who seared our souls by making us dwell (for a time) on dark destinies. Stirring millions to take action, these effective warnings show that there is no better medium for social criticism and corrective action than science fiction film and literature.

It's not too "out there" to suggest that contemporary science fiction writers are to the cyberspace era, what Charles Dickens, Upton Sinclair and Elizabeth Gaskell were to the Industrial Revolution, illuminating the impacts of technology on society and human nature. Their novels changed the way citizens viewed everything from child labor to tainted food and treatment of the mentally ill. Today's issues span a far wider spectrum, e.g., surveillance, the environment, tolerance, economic justice and the way that boundaries of gender start to blur when examined, plus existential threats that range from nuclear or biological war to unfriendly, or too-friendly, artificial intelligence.

If Criticism Is The Only Known Antidote To Error (CITOKATE), then good SF novels and films play vital roles in discovering mistakes in time, perhaps making it across the minefield into better days.

Alas, there are chasms of difference between an effective dire warning and the flood of hackneyed dystopias that make up a majority of sci-fi films. In Chapter 2, "Society and Citizens Are Fools! The Favorite Cliché of

Cinema and Fiction," I dissect why your typical Hollywood apocalypse flick tends toward mindless repetition of standard villains and set-piece plots—the sort of lazy drivel that demoralizes audiences, instead of inspiring them to act. It turns out that the source of this plague of unimaginative sameness is something banal, and completely avoidable.

On balance, which of these trends will prevail? Both of them, it seems. For while our new myths (sometimes) stir us to do much better, they also make nearly all of us strangely reluctant to admit *that* any progress has happened. Hence the theme of our third essay, "*2001: A Space Odyssey*: Shining Light on How Far We've Come," in which I share the disappointment expressed by so many future-fans at the turn of the century that we aren't further along in our exploration of space. Only then I also show that there are compensations. A contrast best displayed in film.

After those three sober contemplations of serious matters, we'll finish Part I with some fun: my quirky "best-of" list, proposing a few dozen great (and near-miss) sci-fi films for your consideration. The capsule reviews in this piece (one of the most popular I ever posted online) are brief. Still, they may make you go "Huh!" and maybe even appreciate better the vast range of brilliant creativity in this strange genre of entertainment.

Part II will dive into some wildly popular and lucrative franchises of Science Fictional film. We'll explore dark underpinnings of the superficially ebullient Star Wars movies, especially why their early promise devolved into something both dismal and betraying. My infamous denunciation of George Lucas' downward storytelling spiral—published in *Salon* magazine—stirred so much controversy that it led to a fun book, *Star Wars on Trial*, in which two dozen strong-willed authors thrashed out every complaint against and every defense of this popular, influential epic.

The essay on *Star Trek*, by contrast, shows what is special about the one SF franchise that decidedly *believes in us*, pondering the slim possibility that—perhaps—our descendants might actually learn from our mistakes and do better. *Trek* may be rare in this trait, but audiences have supported more hours of produced material from this one cosmology than *all* other major dramatized series combined.

And where would a book on sci-fi cinema be without a piece on James Cameron's *Avatar*, a work that seems to stand midway between *Star Wars* and *Star Trek*. Earnest, preachy, fun, vivid, well-meaning ... but ultimately (alas) a near-miss failure at delivering its heavy-handed message.

Part III offers up what may be the chief reason that some of you purchased this book. This is where I stashed some of my angriest rants! Not quite at the volcanic level of my dear-departed friend Harlan Ellison, but still pretty darn pointed. And yes, there are filmmakers out there who deserve denunciation! Where George Lucas let us down in the *Star Wars* saga by drifting into vapid carelessness, others have sought to undermine our confidence, as a matter of deliberate design! In "Grinding Axes," I use my soapbox to cry out against a passel of ingrates, who seem to have no other purpose in life than to bite a civilization that gave them wonderful lives. Their common theme? That citizenship and civilization are futile. That average folk, or even above-average, will never matter. That only demigods and "chosen ones" deserve the future. And while, yes, that theme is an ancient one, filling many epics of the past, it is today both vile and undeserved.

And yes, SF applies to every branch of *politics*, which I'll discuss provocatively in "Getting Science Fictional About a Better World: Marxists and Feminists and Feudalists and Libertarians, Oh My!" Can small press ruminations about the effects of science fiction serve to counterweight such powerful propagandists out there? The answer: for sure. *You*, after all, are important and your gift of curiosity is the reason that you are reading these words right now. Together, we can defeat poisonous memes.

Which brings us to Part IV. Some of these essays were written for the SmartPop series by Benbella Books, an amazingly cool publishing endeavor that occupies a unique market niche: Whenever the editors see a trending bit of popular culture, like *Twilight* or *The Matrix*, they quickly commission (cheap!) a bunch of wits, halfwits and scholars to pen sagacious essays about why (for example) *Buffy the Vampire Slayer* is both cool and *deep*! I have already mentioned one of those SmartPop books, *Star Wars on Trial*.

Hence, in Part IV, let's have some fun with an essay about King Kong, that bit about Buffy plus other dollops of SmartPop culture.

And yes, in Part V, surprise, surprise, I do have a few opinions about *The Postman*, the 1997 epic directed by and starring Kevin Costner, based (generally) on my novel. And what would a book about science fiction novels-into-film be without a discussion of the adaptation(s) of Frank Herbert's *Dune*?

We'll round out Part VI with a review of Alfonso Cuarón's *Gravity* (2013), set much closer to our own time and planet, yet in some ways one of the most daring science fiction dramas ever made. Then our final section will be a catch-all, enabling us to briefly encompass the exciting realm of television, wherein far more boldness can be found than in the cinematic side of Hollywood. Here, also, we'll put some *short takes* and *recommendations*, plus a final essay about where we might be heading, toward a future of both danger and hope—guided, at least a little, by our vivid imaginings.

◇ ◇ ◇

Just to clarify, I'm *not* claiming that science fiction saved the world, or that it can. The conversations that it promotes are important, yet they aren't helped by efforts to cram everything into a prescribed pattern—that storytelling should always be like this or like that.

I'm especially wary of literary templates, like those influentially proclaimed by Joseph Campbell, in popular works such as *The Power of Myth* and *The Hero's Journey*, based on earlier, more scholarly efforts like *The Hero with a Thousand Faces*. Campbell did present a very entertaining survey of human folklore (he was far from the first to do so) and highlighted some strikingly similar motifs that span many cultures and eras. These arcs often would present a challenge to the gifted-but-reluctant son of a chief or king or god, supply him with a mentor, then offer up a series of tests or villainous opponents. After overcoming each trial or obstacle, the hero becomes more confirmed in his "chosen one" status and divine duty to rule. We are all enriched by studying the thoughts and ways of our ancestors—the countless generations who struggled with nature and luck and each other, in order to get us here.

And yet, in his famous PBS interviews with Campbell, Bill Moyers never once interrogated the *dark side* of that hoary pattern—what may very well have been the main reason for pervasive repetition of the same constrained motifs, over and over again.

Oh, sure, that standard arc is dramatic! It does resonate with the listener-reader-viewer. And such myths can stir cohesion, even courageous loyalty from a tribe. But above all, such endlessly similar themes served the purpose and interest of the ruling chiefs, lords, kings and priests, helping to maintain existing pyramidal social structures, upholding aristocracies—or toppling some powers in order to replace them with other, more deserving ones.

When you watch epics like *Star Wars*—or another "Campbellian" story that I respect much more, Tolkien's *Lord of the Rings*—let yourself notice the simplistic extremes of good and evil, light and dark, all featuring demigod "chosen ones" whom you know to be good guys because they are pretty and because the villains leer and give speeches and have red, glowing eyes. That romantic view of storytelling may rouse your customers, but it inevitably dehumanizes. You'll note, for instance, that in both *Star Wars* and *Lord of the Rings*, none of the Enemy's henchmen—whether robot soldiers or clone warriors or orcs—have *faces* that could complicate things with emotions like empathy, or even curiosity. By implication, they have no families or mothers to mourn the thousands who are mown down (much to the audience's delight) by Luke or Aragorn and their doughty band of heroes. (And if you do a modern reversal of this cliché as Disney has admirably done lately—e.g. in *Frozen* wherein the handsome prince turns despicable—both the visage and musical background of the villain still veer, at that very moment, toward ugly.)

These storytelling tricks make it easy to cultivate hatred for the "other," as our parents and grandparents were taught to jeer bucktoothed cartoon caricatures of Japanese during World War II. And yet, even so, many of our soldiers knew in their hearts that the men they were fighting had mothers, wives and children. They still fought—but refused the temptation to dehumanize. Not so in fantasy, or simplistic sci-fi, where perfect, demigod heroes and inherently vile foes are basic grist.

Hey, I am not proclaiming this storytelling motif always to be vile. Frankly, I like Tolkien. And sometimes an enemy truly needs to be fought *as if* everything decent in the world depends on the outcome. Nazis come to mind, of course, and note that they were the most romantic of all romantics. (Try listening to Wagner!) The most Campbellian, in every way. No group ever took the "demigods vs. subhumans" schtick more earnestly and passionately.

Yes, these storytelling methods are part of us. Yes, we can continue to enjoy them. But it may also be high time that we developed *awareness* of them—the dark side, as well as the good. And perhaps a bit more skepticism toward the deeply human, and deeply seductive, storytelling tropes that you see in cinema.

After all, it's one thing to convey these themes as entertainment, as Peter Jackson did brilliantly, filming Tolkien's novels. It is quite another thing to let such stories preach to us (as George Lucas has done, *ad nauseam*) how to live our own lives and how to run an advanced and complex civilization.

You'll find that hard, complex and choice-ridden search for useful wisdom in the better science fiction novels. Those of Nancy Kress, Octavia Butler, Kim Stanley Robinson, Greg Bear, Ursula LeGuin and Michael Chabon. And yes, this book is about SF cinema, but go to books when you feel like exploring the deep end.

◆ ◆ ◆

One final (introductory) note about storytelling.

Throughout most of human history, nearly all cultures believed that there was once a *Golden Age* in the deep past, when people were better, more moral, more upright. When they were closer to the gods. They knew more. But inevitably they fell from this state of grace due to some act of arrogance, of hubris. The Garden of Eden is a prime example and yes, the Tower of Babel. You'll find this concept throughout mythologies in the Americas, Europe and the Middle East into Asia and Africa.

Things were better at some glimmering peak long ago.

Ours may be the first civilization to ponder the possibility of a Golden Age *in the future*. Not some long-ago, god-ordained paradise that we clumsily and culpably shattered, but something mighty that we humans might construct by steadily increasing knowledge, skill and good will. That we might earn by working through some of the flaws in our own hearts, and above all by making new generations better than our own.

This notion of a *reversal of the time-flow of wisdom*—aimed forward instead of toward a romanticized past—is a core element of the Enlightenment, perhaps even more important than its other prime innovations: equality and science. The very idea would have been deemed heretical in most cultures of the past; indeed, many neighbors in this very day despise the Look-Forward view! Not just conservatives, but also literary academics who insist that *eternal human verities* must always stay the same.

Is it impudent to suggest that children can learn from the mistakes of their parents? Or from cautionary tales that they read in books or viewed on a silver screen? That they might take our hard, contemporary fights for granted, accept the fruits of our labor … and move on?

It implies that the world is improvable—perhaps gradually, amid many painful lessons. That we might not only rail against fate, but alter it—at least for our descendants.

Or else, if we *fail* to learn or to change course, then the outcome will be our fault—not the gods'! A *chosen* tragedy, more searing than any portrayed by Greek tragedy, or mapped in Aristotle's Poetics.

That notion of a *hard struggle to be better* can be a more meaningful mythical system for humanity. It has already taken us much farther than all those generations of repetitiously cloned "journeys."

But judge for yourself. A journey of our own awaits. I don't promise to convince or change you. But you might be amused by some new ways of viewing cinematic science fiction! And thus, not only this world, but myriad others, may never be the same.

Part One: A Flickering Light on the World

1

The Self-Preventing Prophecy

How a Dose of Nightmare Might Tame Tomorrow's Perils[1]

> I've lived through some terrible things in my life, some of which actually happened. —*Mark Twain*

What will the future be? The question is much on our minds, and not just because we've embarked upon a new century.

Our most-human quality—anticipatory imagination—keeps us both fascinated and worried, using special organs called the *prefrontal cortex* to probe tomorrow's murky realm. Through these neural clusters we envision future actions and possible consequences, noticing some errors, evading some mistakes. Since before the Neolithic, humans have applied these mysterious nubs of gray matter—sometimes called "lamps on our brows"—to future-pondering.

What's changed is our effectiveness using them. Much of the modern economy is devoted to predicting, forecasting, planning, investing, making bets or preparing for times to come. Which variety of seer we listen to can be a matter of style. Some prefer horoscopes, while others heed advisors in Armani suits. Some even consult science fiction authors. Each of us hopes to prepare, and possibly improve our fate across the years ahead. This trait may be the most profound distinction between humanity and other denizens of the planet.

And yet we should remember that a great many more things *might* happen than actually do. There are more plausibilities than likelihoods and more likelihoods than actual events. What *doesn't* happen is just as important as what does.

One of the most powerful novels of all time, published 70 years ago, foresaw a dark future that never quite came to pass. Oh, the terrifying oppression portrayed in George Orwell's *Nineteen Eighty-Four* keeps threatening to arrive! A vast majority of past nations were pyramids of privilege and power, so it's scary to envision what any of those oligarchies—or so many of today's tyrants—would do with 24/7 surveillance, media-controlling, psych-conditioning, killer drones and all the rest. (There are contemporary societies that aim for just such a party-dominated, citizen-squelching rule.)

If some billions have (so far) escaped that dire destiny, turning enough light back upon the mighty to prevent that age-old pattern, then that blessing may be owed in part to how Orwell's novel, and its movie versions, affected millions. Tens, even hundreds of millions who then girded themselves to fight Big Brother to their last breath. In other words, by inoculating us, Orwell may have helped make his own scenario not come true.

Is this the highest use for science fiction? Certainly we owe, to some degree, our surviving the nuclear confrontations of the '60s, '70s and '80s to the frightening warnings of *Dr. Strangelove, On the Beach, Fail-Safe* and later films like *Testament* and *War Games*, each of them portraying a different failure-mode that retired officers now admit changed actual procedures! Or take warnings like *The China Syndrome* and *The Hot Zone* whose worrisome vividness propelled vigorous discussion, and thus helped block their own scenarios from coming true.

What other "self-preventing prophecies" (SPP) rocked public awareness, in possibly world-saving ways? Rachel Carson foresaw devastation if we ignored environmental abuse—a mistake we may have somewhat averted, thanks to warnings like *Silent Spring* and Harry Harrison's novel *Make Room! Make Room!* along with John Brunner's *The Sheep Look Up*. Affecting many more were films like *Silent Running* and the movie version of Harrison's novel, re-labeled *Soylent Green*. All of these recruited millions of new environmentalists, possibly helping tip a crucial balance.

Often mentioned in tandem with *Nineteen Eighty-Four* is *Brave New World*, a scenario that seemed more abstract, nerdy-speculative and equivocal than Orwell's wallow in raw terror. But time and progress have made Aldous Huxley's tale about genetic control and mental conditioning seem evermore plausible. Cinema versions emphasize how elites might rule via manipulative pleasure, rather than thuggish pain.

Huxley certainly provoked plenty of discussion, but did his tale actually *prevent* any of the errors it portrayed? One could argue that our current populace, popping Xanax, Prozac, Adderall and opiates along with endless chunklets of YouTube and cable news fomentation, are well on their way.

Likewise, New Wave authors Ellison, Zelazny, Ballard, Brunner and

1. The Self-Preventing Prophecy

Farmer explored drug culture, with stirring effects on individual readers, but not much evidence of profound social outcomes, at least not until those readers aged into influence, helping to end parts of the insane War on Drugs.

Later, the cyberpunk genre issued plenty of warnings about everything from rogue AIs and crypto-crime to masses transformed into screen zombies. Novelists William Gibson, Bruce Sterling, Pat Cadigan and Rudy Rucker built on earlier speculations by Isaac Asimov *et al.* to stir discussion of an era that's become one of befuddling complexity. (I contributed too, in novels like *Earth.*) These reflections are studied by thousands of folks working in academia, government and commerce, who often credit science fiction with sparking fresh ideas. Of course, a much wider public was stirred—even possibly alerted—by films like *Blade Runner, Rollerball, Existenz, Johnny Mnemonic* and *Ex Machina.*

But stirred to do exactly *what,* other than fear what's coming? Dread is not prevention, or a viable survival plan. The two overlap some, but they aren't the same thing.

Or take another genre of dire warning, popular novels and films about resistance to monstrously sadistic authority. Recent examples range from *The Hunger Games* and *Divergent* to *Westworld* and *The Handmaid's Tale,* a tradition going all the way back to Heinlein's *Revolt in 2100*. While superficially similar to *Nineteen Eighty-Four,* these dark dramas differ, because almost none of them (except Heinlein's) offers a convincing case that the depicted dystopia could actually emerge from our present world, without slaughtering the 90 percent who would oppose it.

But that's not the point. Implausible or not, each holds up a particular type of villainy for dauntless characters to oppose and overcome, a pattern we'll discuss in Chapter 2. And in each case, despite lurid exaggeration, there *is* some *core danger*—a particular kind of malevolence or injustice—that the audience is urged to *prevent.*

If judged according to sheer numbers of readers and viewers riled up against misogyny and cruel, macho tyranny, then sure—Margaret Atwood gets a medal for SPP.

Only then, one can argue that the mightiest self-preventing prophecy of all was *Das Kapital* by Karl Marx! In the East, he was a mythical seer whose incantations only wound up painting revolutionary gloss upon age-old paranoias. But in the West, his scenarios were read as *plausible failure modes,* so vividly credible that many of the rich felt impelled to back Franklin Roosevelt and negotiate a more-fair deal with workers, if only to make the scary Marxian scenario go away. And hence, by the standard of self-prevention, Marx may be the greatest SF author of all.

◊ ◊ ◊

Whether any of these literary or cinematic works made a crucial difference can never be proved. That each motivated large numbers of people to focus on specific dangers can't be denied. And indeed, as we see in this era of ongoing crises, all of our victories against doom scenarios might only have been temporary! Kicking the can down the road.

Might a better term than *self-preventing prophecy* instead be *self-forestalling?*

In a more general sense, research has shown that science fiction's totalitarian-dystopian subgenre can affect real-world political attitudes in compelling ways. Across three experiments that included carefully designed control groups, Calvert Jones and Celia Paris found evidence that exposure to dystopian media made people more willing to justify radical—and particularly violent—forms of action against injustice perpetrated by political elites.[2]

As for Big Brother, Orwell showed us the pit awaiting any civilization that combines panic with technology and the dark, cynical traditions of totalitarianism. In so doing, he armed us against that horrible fate. Contrast the sheep-like compliance displayed by subject peoples in *Nineteen Eighty-Four* vs. the "rebel" image that has taken charge of our shared imaginations, targeting every conceivable power center, from governments and corporations to criminal and techno-elites, with Hollywood's relentless theme: *suspicion of authority*. (We'll talk about this, and other common movie memes, in the next chapter.)

Many authors rail against the cruelty and oppression of despots. But Orwell's portrayal—like Vladimir Sorokin's brilliant update, *The Day of the Oprichnik*—focused also on the banal *stupidity* of tyranny, depicting how the oligarchs of Oceania grind their nation into brutalized poverty by keeping the masses ill-educated, by whipping hatred of scapegoats and with brainwashing. And above all, by eliminating criticism—the only known antidote to delusion and error—they repeat the long saga of errors called *history,* because kings across all eras did those things to preserve their short-term status, guaranteeing long-term disaster for their nations.

That is, until we stumbled onto a solution. One that hasn't saved us yet, but at least keeps us in the game … and that might save us yet.

The solution of many voices.

An Aside: How We Prophesy and Prevent

Each of us may stubbornly ignore our own mistakes. But in an open society, others will notice them for us (while ignoring their own). We all

1. The Self-Preventing Prophecy

hate irksome criticism, but the four great secular institutions that fostered our unprecedented wealth and freedom—*science, democracy, markets and the justice system*—function best when all players get to know, compete and create without fear. One result: the "pie" we're dividing up keeps getting bigger. In other words, elites actually do better—in terms of *absolute* wealth—when they cannot conspire to keep *relative* differences between rich and poor too great, an ironic truth quashed by past aristocracies, obsessed with staying as far above the riffraff as possible.

How have we done with Orwell's warning? Today, cameras are smaller, cheaper and even more pervasive than he imagined, but their swarms haven't had the despotic effect he prophesied, not yet at least, or at least not everywhere, perhaps because—forewarned—we act to ensure that many lenses point *both ways*. The cop-cams carried by police are answered by the cell-cams wielded by citizens.

Yes, would-be despots have learned new ways to blind the populace. Not by restricting light, but filling every space with noise and lies. That problem will be discussed later.

Still, we are left with a key point. That this knack of holding the mighty accountable—our culture's unique achievement—was partly propelled by the warnings of science fiction.

Is government the chief enemy of freedom? Aristocrats? Corporations? Criminal gangs? Technological elites? Is the problem human nature, which E.O. Wilson described as "*Neanderthal emotions, medieval institutions and god-like technology*"? A nature that propels many of us to seek mastery over others ... or else to deeply fear being mastered.

Most of our modern political tussles aren't over *whether* to dread Big Brother, but *which* direction each of us feels oppression might loom out of. Orwell's initial portrayal of a Stalinist nightmare-state begat a science fiction mythos that encompasses all worrisome accumulations of influence, authority or unreciprocal transparency. Can anyone justify exemption from accountability?

Technological advances like the Internet may amplify this trend or squelch it, depending on our choices in the next few years. Soon human cognitive powers will expand; memory will access vast, swift databases; vision will explode in all directions. In such a world, only fools will depend on the ignorance of others. If they don't know your secrets now, someone will pierce your veils tomorrow. Can you be sure it hasn't already happened?

Though informed, fact-based criticism is the best antidote to error, leaders of past cultures reflexively crushed it, a trend Orwell depicts brutally enhanced by technology. And hence, in part thanks to Orwell's warning, ours may be the first civilization to systematically encourage *sousveillance,* or looking back at the mighty. Perhaps it's just another delusion, but we think Orwell's dark future can't come true if confident citizens have a habit of seeing and knowing.

Take the tragedies of September 11, 2001. Most of the video that recorded the event was taken by private citizens. Private mobiles spread word quicker than official media. Volunteers swarmed in. And the sole effective action to thwart terrorist plans was taken by private citizens aboard United Flight 93 … a topic we'll take up elsewhere.

I can't prove that any of this was driven by the inoculative effects of cautionary fiction like *Nineteen Eighty-Four*. But at least this is a different way to look at the effects and importance of novels and films! Scholars aren't used to considering the pragmatic fruits of fictional *gedanke*n-experimentation. Perhaps it's time they started.

Are we unique because of our technology, or our changing society? In a later chapter we'll consider the Stanley Kubrick film *2001: A Space Odyssey*. When it appeared, in 1968, two monumental projects transfixed the people of the United States: conquering outer space and tackling injustice to achieve a more honorable society. Who would have imagined, back then, that colonizing space would prove such a grindingly slow job, yet by the real year 2001 we'd take for granted so many advances in tolerance, decency and accountability?

This is not the path prophesied in *Nineteen Eighty-Four*, which envisioned a bitter society, exploiting every opportunity to stoke hatred and division among the ruled. One where commonfolk are harried sheep, ignorant, disempowered and unable to imagine another way. And yes, there *are* forces trying hard to achieve those very things that Orwell warned against! We seem to be teetering between destinies. But at least those who read science fiction can't be accused of lacking imagination.

And clearly, there are reasons to believe we have a chance.

Do we owe this fact, in part, to anti–Cassandras like George Orwell, whose warnings, once they were heeded, thus were forestalled? Indeed, as we'll soon see, our tendency seems never to rejoice over what's been accomplished, but always to criticize whatever injustices remain. That alone shows how deeply the lesson has been learned.

The worry that Orwell and others ignited in us still burns. It drives us on, far more effectively than any vague, utopian promise of a better world.

We daren't let up, because we've been shown the alternatives. The worlds of failure that Orwell and other dark seers present are too scary to ignore. Ironically, that may lead us on a path to better days.

2

Society and Citizens Are Fools!

The Favorite Cliché of Cinema and Fiction[1]

As we saw in the previous chapter, Science Fiction (SF) books and films have been less about spaceships and machinery than about humanity's confrontation with change.

This shouldn't be surprising. Only a fraction of SF authors have strong backgrounds in physical science, while nearly all of us study *history*. By extrapolating the human saga—from historical reconstruction to futuristic projection—we offer some perspective, and the present surrenders its illusion of self-importance. Our best tales dwell less on the gimmickry of change than how people may react to it, either by rising to meet new challenges or dismally repeating past mistakes.[2]

This trend grows more pronounced as we leave behind the 20th century's fixation on physics, entering an era when *biology* may test human wisdom as harshly as did the atom bomb. Challenges may include lifespan-extension, self-altering, cloning, cyborgism, artificial minds, synthetic plagues, ecological (mis)management, gender-different utopias and human transcendence. Science Fiction has a lot on its plate.

So why are countless stories, novels and movies repetitiously banal?

In Chapter 1, we looked at the most *effective* SF thought experiments, whose frightening depictions of failure motivated millions of readers and watchers to take action (or at least keep their guard up); movies and books that earn renown as *self-preventing prophecies*. Perhaps one of the explanations for the apparent effectiveness of tales like

Nineteen Eighty-Four, *Doctor Strangelove* and *Soylent Green* is that they treated their clients—viewers and readers—with respect. As people who *might* enact change.

Now, alas, we turn to a far more common kind of modern storytelling, spotlighting a trait that SF regrettably shares with every other genre: the widespread tendency for writers and directors to *scorn* the wisdom of their fellow citizens, and to deride the shared project called civilization.

This thread seems to reach across politics, personality and gender. Science fiction authors from Samuel Delany to Philip K. Dick, from Robert Heinlein to Frank Herbert, from N.K. Jemison to Cory Doctorow … all have insulted their readers' intelligence at one time or another. The reflex to "dumb down" is even more prevalent in cinema, from George Lucas to James Cameron to Peter Jackson. Only a few filmmakers (e.g. Spielberg and Zemeckis and Nolan) avoid the "stupid-trap" with any consistency.

What gives?

Your modern reader or viewer pays for a fantasy experience, identifying with some bold hero or heroine. Hence, directors and writers offer a flattering illusion of personal superiority or special insight, or at least some eccentricity that distinguishes the main character as "different." Significantly, *institutions*—the basis that empowered our functioning civilization to accomplish so much—seldom function and often go unmentioned.

Recall how ethno-historian Joseph Campbell described a common pattern in the tales of so many tribes and nations; periodically, sages and mystic guides would appear before the hero, offering well-timed bits of wisdom. While the protagonist strives against powerful forces, he or she hardly ever questions the authority of these Olympian advisors, or the legitimacy of the hierarchies they represent. Likewise, in "modernist" Soviet-era fiction, *organizations* were the central problem-solving entities.

In contrast, *today's* dominant storytelling technique generally portrays one or two protagonists confronting difficulties *without* useful support from their school, the police, any government or non-governmental agency or even family—certainly not the neighbors. The "problem" might be a town gossip or alien genocidal-invaders. A schoolyard bully or a zombie plague. Perhaps some massive cultural error … or else an abusive boss. But one thing you can count on: almost never is there any recourse to meaningful help from village, city or nation. More often than not, society itself is a malignity to be combatted.

Of course, these scenarios mesh well with the intimate, thought-following style of point-of-view storytelling, and that's fine. But modern cinema and fiction often go a step further. It seems that, when in doubt, a writer is best served by assuming the worst.

Hey, we don't create scripts to be accurate. They are commercial products, with certain ineludible requirements. The most basic is: *Thou shalt keep thy hero or heroine in pulse-pounding jeopardy for 400 pages ... or ninety minutes of film.* If you succeed in keeping the audience tense and riveted, then all else is secondary. And that, alas, requires adherence to one of the Great Rules of Drama:

A storyteller must separate his or her hero from meaningful help.

In crude form, this is called *the idiot plot*. We'll see four tricks writers and directors use to get this idea across:

1. No institution works.
2. Focus on demigods.
3. Hoard the wonder.
4. Despise your neighbors.

Never Trust "The Man"

Some intelligent commentators like James Fallows blame news media for declining public trust in our institutions. But when reporters target mistakes by the political or wealthy castes, or bureaucracy, or swarm like flies toward the stench of corruption, they are only doing their job. Moreover, during emergencies they do show public servants skillfully re-knitting the web of services we depend on.

It is we in fiction who show no respite or mercy, relentlessly depicting civilization as feckless, stupid or morally bankrupt. If movies and novels were our basis for judging, then no institution can be trusted. Cops won't answer when you call. Or they'll arrive late. Or if they come in time, they'll prove inept. Or if not inept, it means they'll turn out to be in cahoots with the bad guy.

Ironically, most writers and directors don't really believe society is that awful. Most things work. When the traffic lights (rarely) go out, drivers mostly negotiate passage with courteous aplomb. If we find ourselves in real-life trouble, we dial 911, expecting skilled professionals to leap to our aid. We'd sue and make a real stink if they prove as inept as in movies. And yes, the exceptions—sometimes horrific, as in what happened to New Orleans, during Hurricane Katrina—merit corrective criticism! But is it accurate or even helpful for Hollywood to portray *everything* failing, *all* the time?

Wait a minute! By now you know that I'm a big fan of cautionary tales. As we've seen, *Brave New World*, *On the Beach* and *Nineteen Eighty-Four* served up chilling warnings that helped prevent (or at least postpone) their own dire scenarios. Films ranging from *The Post* and *All the President's Men* to *Erin Brockovich* and *Valkyrie* extol those who confronted malignant power. But this doesn't explain the ubiquity of contempt that seems to fill most contemporary novels and films: depicting our fellow citizens as stupid, portraying lifelong public servants as evil, debasing the very word "civilization." While the dire-warning agenda can be admirable, far more often writers do this for one reason: *laziness*.

A single plot assumption lets an author or movie director keep her protagonist in delicious danger until that final satisfying explosion sets the credits rolling: *The assumption that nothing works.*

◊ ◊ ◊

We've all seen this phenomenon in B-grade movies: a dozen spoiled teenagers enter a haunted house. The lights go out. Someone screams. Then the inevitable: "Hey, gang. I know! Let's split up!"

Why do the stupidest thing imaginable? Because if our characters behave like intelligent people who pool resources and march out of there with skirmish-order caution, the author might actually have to exercise some creativity to keep the kids in jeopardy for the requisite 90 minutes. But if you start by assuming stupidity, the script almost writes itself, proceeding from one decapitation to the next.

Take your typical John Grisham book or film adaptation. At a predictable point, the heroine cowers in a motel room, hiding from Uzi-armed villains who watch the train depot, the bus station and the airport. She's trapped! Somehow it never occurs to our stalwart young protagonist simply to *walk out of town*! Lace your sneakers and just hike a few miles, by sidewalk, to some nearby suburb where cops have an honest reputation. *Why* doesn't it occur to her? Because the story would be over on page 80, and we can't have that now, can we?

Have you ever read a Michael Crichton novel or seen one of his movies in which the hubristic scientist pauses to declare: "Hey, science shouldn't be done in shadows! If I keep this new thing secret, I'll probably do something gruesomely stupid. But if I discuss this innovation with hundreds of peers, some of them will catch my mistakes and things won't get out of hand."

It's the reasonable incantation that any sensible tech wizard—and legions of scientists—recite every day (at least to themselves). But never in a movie.

Here's an example that all sci-fi-ers know well: In *The Force Awakens*, J.J. Abrams faced a problem. The empire had been defeated. How could he put the Rebels back into exactly the same condition they were in, back in *A New Hope*—the film he was exactly copying? Simple! Send out a super-duper Death Star beam to destroy the Rebels' only source of help, the Galactic Republic. (Say what, *all* of it? A bazillion worlds, across a whole galaxy, fried in an instant? How convenient.)

Yes, we want the solitary hero—or pair of them—to prevail through grit and fortitude, against all odds! Too much professional assistance would be a buzz-kill. So? Coming up with an *original* and *plausible* way to separate your protagonist from meaningful help … that's a sign of creative storytelling!

Quick, name a cop movie where the captain or supervisor isn't a blithering idiot. Oh, it's been done. *The Fugitive, The Silence of the Lambs, Fargo* and *In the Heat of the Night* all show institutions and public officials functioning well, as have space adventures like *Apollo 13* and *The Martian*—all of them big hits, and certainly not lacking in action or tension. In fact, these exceptions stand out as excellent dramas *precisely* because the writer decided to work for a living, using imagination to depict credible characters, people in stark jeopardy with problems to solve, who nevertheless are members of a society not (totally) filled with crooks and fools. Indeed, the plot of *The Fugitive* revolves around society's very competence! Its skilled, admirable specialists provide the central obstacle for mistakenly convicted Dr. Kimble to overcome.

One of my favorite examples is *Sleeping with the Enemy,* in which Julia Roberts' heroine realizes that her crazy husband will not be restrained by any of the institutional tools society might use to help her—not because those institutions are ineffective, but because her husband is so diabolically clever and monomaniacally determined. She's on her own for strong narrative reasons, as is Mel Gibson's character in *Ransom*. In those popular films—like *Thelma and Louise*—the protagonists must *evade* skilled and sincere professionals, at least some of whom are eager to assist.

So yes, it can be done, crafting heart-thumping peril with wit and realism. But how much easier it is to just go with the Idiot Plot! Authorial laziness tempts every writer to say, "Forget you're part of a civilization, one with problems but also millions of smart citizens striving hard to solve them. Forget it, because that makes it easier for my hero to blow up lots of stuff."

The Übermensch Effect: *Focus on Demigods*

In occidental fiction, the individual protagonist is supreme. It's all about her or his drama and journey to overcome challenges. Nor am I objecting to that! But what began as a healthy defense of eccentricity and freedom has all too often metastasized into solipsism: a rejection of all but the most intimate social bonds. A spurning of mutual social obligation that's so complete, it would make Ayn Rand proud.

This is not a new phenomenon. Take your typical comic book hero, a figure harkening back to more ancient traditions, like *The Iliad*. One point made over and over by Homer is that *you do not question the existence of gods and demigods*. When Achilles slashes 500 Trojans in *The Iliad*, the prescribed response is neither repudiation nor envy, but awe. So it is in colorful comics with slack-jawed citizens staring upward as superheroes battle supervillains over the fate of Earth.

A branch of SF has always been enamored of this *Übermensch Effect* where the hero of a film or novel towers over ordinary mortals. Famed 1950s author A.E. van Vogt showed the way with his Slans, Silkies and the omnipotent Gilbert Gosseyn. John W. Campbell and L. Ron Hubbard catered to those wanting to identify with Nietzschean, genetically superior characters who can outsmart every foe or pathetic ally. Today this torch is carried ably by the brilliant prose stylist Orson Scott Card, whose godlike protagonists ponder deeply and movingly on the sad loneliness of their inborn superiority. More subtle than their demigod predecessors, Card's characters mourn the obdurate stupidity of average men and women, who (alas!) cannot be trusted with a burnt match, let alone control over their own lives.

Now, to be fair, this subset of the Idiot Plot varies a little. Demigod-worship isn't quite as universal as contempt for civilization. In cinema there's a spectrum running between supremely godlike protagonists and those who are merely way above average. The first category includes not just superheroes, but spies in the genre of James Bond, *Mission: Impossible* and *Our Man Flint*. In contrast, the *Die Hard* series character John McClane is an endearing, and bruise-enduring, everyman. Later, we'll zoom in closer to this topic and compare the force-midichlorian Jedi gods of *Star Wars* to the diametrically opposite heroes of *Star Trek*.

I find non-demigod protagonists more compelling, more tense and interesting; but you can see the appeal of the *Übermensch Effect*. By identifying with a superior protagonist, countless readers can enjoy imagining *they too* are greater beings than the countless, vexing others who surround them. Of course it's pandering and contradictory to everything that makes our civilization great. But it works, and as a writer I myself found it irresistible at times.

So, I took a *Superguy Abstinence Vow*:

> UNLESS THE STORY IS EXPLICITLY *ABOUT* SOME ASPECT OF BEING A SUPERMAN, I WILL NEVER PEN A CHARACTER SO FANTASTIC THAT HE OR SHE COULDN'T BE REPLACED BY A CAREFULLY CHOSEN TEAM OF MAYBE 20 HIGHLY SKILLED PROFESSIONALS.

It sounds like a modest stricture—roomy enough for any writer. Consider how many novels or films would be more interesting if this temperance oath were commonly maintained. How much more human the stories.

But would they be moneymakers? Would they sell?

In fact, I believe so.

Hoard the Wonder

Let's take the archetype *übermensch*, *Superman*. Egalitarian science fiction would treat the mighty Kryptonian differently than comics do. Envision the Man of Steel swooping down, returning to Earth triumphant after defeating invaders from Brainiac Seven. In a true SF flick, society's leaders would greet him with gratitude and a medal, but then add two insistent demands:

1. "Please explain why we started having super-villains only *after* you showed up."
And—
2. "Kindly roll up your sleeve so we can draw blood. Yes, the first needles will bend, but we'll keep trying 'til we find out how you tick. Then we'll bottle your powers and give them to everybody."

You can see why these possibilities are seldom mentioned. They're even dismissed outright at the end of *The Incredibles*. How do you write a movie or novel in which everyone is super? Or even one where average citizens can travel around the world, get information in seconds, converse with minds thousands of miles away … oh, yeah, we have *those* godlike powers already, with more on the way. But seriously, how seldom do we see fictional future people dealing with wondrous advances by universalizing them? Providing cheap miracles for everyone to use?

More often, futuristic advances—from cloning to cryonics—are shown as tightly clutched treasures, guarded by some secretive cabal or an oligarchic class, as in *Elysium, The Hunger Games, Blade Runner* and any number of dystopian films. True, greedy aristocrats are often depicted as bad guys. Still, the filmmakers' own, latent elitism is obvious. A refusal to depict tomorrow's wonders being shared.

Indeed, these directors and authors have a point. How much more romantic would the world seem today, if flight weren't cheaply available to all! Imagine the thrill of staring up at rickety cloth wings and frail spinning propellers while whispering in awe, "There goes a flying man!" Or suppose only a few of us had the power to make light spring forth with a twitch of our fingertips. Such capabilities were once the province of gods, but today infants think nothing of running through a house, flicking on brilliant bulbs, turning night into day. And wonder is lost.

Would the moon landings have been more cherished if news came first to an aristocratic elite, then trickled to amazed masses below? (As it was when Columbus reported back from his first voyage, long before scientists began insisting that photos of distant worlds go instantly on the web.) Is it human nature that we take for granted whatever is shared by all, and revere what is rare?

Despise Even Your Neighbors

We've covered three out of four methods commonly used to perpetrate the Idiot Plot: *No institution can function, focus on demigods, and hoard the wonder.*

A final theme is *contempt for the masses.* It's not enough for institutions to be useless and for the protagonist to be a demigod. Everyone surrounding the hero or his team must be pathetic or useless.

Consider. If you were in dire trouble, and calling 911 failed, wouldn't you turn to your *neighbors* for help? Ring five doorbells—at least two will bring forth someone who is both willing and able. Then why do nearly all films, and most novels, portray your fellow citizens as sheep?

I'll not bore you with a litany of examples, since disdain for people is almost a religious catechism in so much of cinema and fiction, especially sci-fi. Even when everyone does partake in some new wonder, they are portrayed using it as stupidly as possible,[3] as in the Bruce Willis flick *Surrogates*, where the brilliant invention of remote robotic surrogacy is used by the masses only to *look good*. All right, sometimes the shared fault is satirical fun, as with the overfed passengers in *Wall-E*. But far more often it can be a polemically preachy lie, as in *The Circle,* where all of the educated, sophisticated employees of a leading web company can only think of using their hi-tech devices to brutally bully nonconformists. Talk about a jaundiced view of your fellow citizens.

Later in this collection, I'll discuss two storytellers who take this contempt to deliberate extremes, railing against a civilization that's been very good to them, in works ranging from *300* to *Sin City* to *Ender's Game.* But more often, creators assume a society-gone-stupid for a much simpler reason, offering strawmen-demonic villains or contrived social oppressions the heroes can oppose. For example, *The Hunger Games* (2012), *Equilibrium* (2002), *Divergent* (2014), *THX 1138* (1971) and *The Giver* (2014) all suppose that society would inexplicably and oppressively try to squelch emotions or stop human beings from being human.

Though Some Do Celebrate Us

Oh, there are also films and books that celebrate citizens and/or civilization. One tasty recent flick, *The Secret Life of Walter Mitty* (2013), offered a joyful impression—in the background—that civilization is adapting with some degree of wisdom. It's a sense you also get from Luc Besson's optimistic action flick *Lucy* (2014), and from the mellow-thoughtful *Her* (2013). *Monuments Men* (2014), set during World War II, offers plenty of villainy and peril, but civilization gives the museum rescue team the means they need to protect great art from the Nazis.

Some filmmakers tend to that side of things. Robert Zemeckis has proved capable of stirring suspense and danger without Idiot Plot cheats. Steven Spielberg, whether in *E.T. the Extra-Terrestrial* (1982), *Minority Report* (2002) or *Jurassic Park* (1993), casts heroes into jeopardy while displaying hints of gratitude toward a civilization that enabled him to make wonderful movies. Alas, as we'll see later, Spielberg's friend George Lucas did the opposite in his *Star Wars* films, portraying even the idea of a democratically competent civilization as completely absurd. (Foretaste: Name one moment when the Republic, or even the Jedi Council, makes one correct decision or does anything right.)

Other examples that celebrate civilization, even while keeping their heroes in peril, include *Europa Report* (2013), *Mission to Mars* (2000) and especially *The Martian* (2015). Bad things have happened that propel protagonist jeopardy, yet humanity is there for them. Colleagues, institutions, friends and family. They're just too far away.

So, which take on the Idiot Plot correlates with reality? Rebecca Solnit, in *A Paradise Built in Hell,* shows that time and again our fellow citizens show pluck and guts in any crisis, as happened on 9/11, when 80 average folks rose up against hijackers aboard Flight 93. On a less heroic level, a 2019 study in Holland showed that bystanders by and large do step in or engage, in order to resolve problems erupting nearby, refuting the notion that neighbors or strangers won't help during situations of danger or conflict.

I tried to apply this notion of active citizenship in my novel *The Postman*, a theme that Kevin Costner successfully conveyed in his film adaptation. For all its many faults (see Chapter 19), Costner's film kept true to my core message: that civilization's miracle will never be preserved—or restored after any breakdown—by some lone hero. Its only chance will be a collective and widespread revival of faith in ourselves.

Other directors and writers buck the cliché and show average people doing well. Vernor Vinge, in *Rainbows End*, portrays near-future citizenship propelling tech-empowered art in a society that's getting better all the time. And yet, drama is not killed.

One of my favorite exceptions can be seen in those Spider-Man flicks that were *not* woven into the rest of the Marvel universe (*Spider-Man: The Trilogy* and *The Amazing Spider-Man*). They are not highbrow or classy. But despite their corny fluffiness, there appears to be a little-noticed tradition. Sure, in all of the first three films, Spider-Man repeatedly saves New Yorkers from harm. But there is always a moment of brief role-reversal, when normal people, regular New Yorkers, step up and *save* Spider-Man! It happens in all three, so it must have been deliberate.

Indeed, when I watched the fourth one, a reboot, I had to start by quashing sadness over Hollywood's craven inability to ever try anything new. Still, there came a moment, near the end, when—once again and with style—average citizens stood up for their hero. And I felt a thrill.

A Range of Villainy

Summing up. Many messages relentlessly pervade modern films and novels. They are generally in plain view, blaring at us, lecturing and finger-wagging, yet they seldom draw comment or notice.

Some of them, like *Suspicion of Authority,* propel a plot while also helping us stay free, keeping us alert against oppressing elites … though lately Suspicion of Authority has been cynically manipulated against us, a matter we'll discuss later.

Other common Hollywood memes, like *tolerance, diversity* and *eccentricity,* are values that you and I appreciate, in part because those messages *succeeded.* Watch any Marx Brothers or Judy Garland or Preston Sturges movie, to see how far back all of these themes go. And thank you, Hollywood.

Certainly it's healthy that films and books also keep sniffing toward potential errors. That, too, can drive plot, while tuning the public to notice a failure mode—and some of these tales actually divert destiny, earning glory as self-preventing prophecies.

But there are other messages that seem almost as ubiquitous, yet express no higher value, nor shine light on error. These variations of the Idiot Plot saturate far too many of our modern myths, for no other reason than laziness.

No institution can function.
Focus on demigods.
Hoard the wonder.
Despise your neighbors.

Now let me reveal one last secret: one factor that often controls how far the writer or director feels a need to crank up the Idiot Plot. It starts with a simple question: *How powerful is the adversary?*

If your antagonist is a regular person, say a romantic rival, a bully, an abusive husband or a common criminal, the writer must work hard to separate the protagonist from meaningful help. Authorities don't believe her. Or they work too slowly. Or they're bigoted or corrupt. Or the phones are out. Or there's a ticking clock and no time to wait for the (adults/cops/neighbor/sister/friends) to intervene. If the reasons for no-help isolation are inventive and make sense, then the writer has done solid work! And you'll notice that such well-wrought tales get a boost—even if it's unconscious—from the audience.

So what happens when you crank things up? Now the villains are increasingly formidable. We've all seen stories (e.g., *Die Hard*) where bad-guy cleverness is the *reason* why a call for aid goes unanswered. Or why professionals misunderstand the situation and blame the hero. Or first responders, hurrying to help, fall into a trap. Notice how at this level, institutions are not so much *stupid* as they are *outmatched*. In fact, the director or author may even want to portray the cop/teacher/neighbor/helper as *competent*, because that then enhances the villain's awesomeness.

Look back across the films you've watched over the years and keep your eye open for a *sliding scale of scoundrels*. For example, in *Batman* flicks, the Joker is so clever and terrifying that the director allows the Gotham City Police to act professionally ... just so they can fail, propelling the Dark Knight towards the real confrontation. (Later we'll discuss *henchmen* ... how seldom it's ever explained why anyone would choose to work for an evil mastermind who wants to gas a whole city, and we'll return to discuss some surprising villains.)

As the adversary grows in power, society is allowed to seem just a bit more competent. The 1998 film *Armageddon* has a skilled civilization, with NASA and a functioning government, because the impending threat is so huge. But their sole purpose is to get Bruce Willis and his team of roughneck drillers to the comet where they can overcome the mistakes of professional astronauts and have their team adventure. In *Pacific Rim* (2013), technologic civilization exists only to make giant robots so that the individual characters can fight for us, like demigods.

As you move along this scale, notice how institutional competence rises just enough so that it *fails*—barely—to keep up with the enemy. The overwhelmingly powerful alien invaders of *Independence Day* are so badass that the United States government and military are allowed to be *both* capable and good, just so they can serve as a launching pad for a classic pair of buddies to do the actual heroics.

You don't even need a literal bad-guy for the adversary-scale to be blatant and all-controlling. I've mentioned stories where the adversary isn't villainous intelligence but Nature herself. If the environmental threat is just a shark cruising hungrily offshore, the writer and director need some rationale for the failure of city and state to send in professionals. In *The Last Place on Earth*, distance and isolation do the job for you, as in the excellent film *Moon*.

In *Apollo 13* and *The Martian*, nature seems so realistically implacable that you can show brilliant teamwork by hundreds of skilled folks and even institutions, yet still it takes a hero (or three) to seal the deal. In the exceptional *Deep Impact*, our entire civilization must rise to a supreme challenge, showing so much competence that it even shares some of the credit.

Of course, this scale-effect leads, ultimately, to superhero films, in which every episode of the Marvel or DC combo universe has to up the ante, one more time. When each hero acted alone, it was possible for him or her to exhibit some near-fatal flaw that a merely powerful enemy might exploit, in plot-driving ways. But when all of the Avengers join forces, multiplying their power and compensating for each other's weaknesses, then the foe must be a literal god.

Followed in the next sequel by a *super*-god … followed by an *uber-super-duper-I-really-mean-it-this-time* god. (Always seeking to collect all six or nine or twelve cosmic-magic dinguses, in order to become a giga-times googolplex-truly-unstoppable god.)

And where—lost in all this dazzling CGI glory—is humanity? Our science, our spirit, our rare ability to stand as citizens? All the brilliance that enabled us to craft wonders? (Wonders like movie CGI?)

Where does it leave civilization? Have we come full circle, back to the helpless Greek and Trojan soldiers in *The Iliad*, whose sole purpose is to be mowed down by awesome Achilles? Seriously?

By that standard, I have more respect for Michael Bay's *Transformers* series. For all of its bubblegum triteness and cartoony dialogue, at least humanity at large gets to play a role in each of those garishly joyful and stunningly silly romps. (See Chapter 11.) We, and all that we've accomplished, get to matter just a little.

Oh, I'll watch those superhero flicks, every one. Who can resist all the lavish fun? In them, you can see every meme and theme of this chapter played out to a manic, predictable conclusion. But hey, I'm from the '60s. I can flick switches in my head and get back into the chemistry of that decade, at will.

And so, I watch them stoned.

3

2001: A Space Odyssey
Shining Light on How Far We've Come

Many of these chapters appeared across the last 25 years as essays in periodicals. Most were revised for this book, updating to the world of 2020. But in this case, it seemed a sin to alter the period pertinence of an article written in 2000 about the coming year, a landmark for all who think about tomorrow.

The beginning of the millennium got me thinking. Where are all the flying cars, antigravity belts, immortality pills and space liners to balmy Venus we were promised? What about the muscle pills? Robot butlers? Teleportation? The future's here, and the most science fiction thing around seems to have been our recent, weird U.S. politics.

Oh, there are so many aspects to this looming milestone that we could talk about. But let me focus on just one, the cardinal numeric figure of the year: 2001.

What does "2001" mean to you?

Why of course, it's a movie! One that, remarkably despite its age, still shines some amazing sparkles of perspective on our time. I'd like to use it in that vein right now, to point out a few things about the surprising world we're living in. A world that's even more amazing than Arthur C. Clarke imagined.

Yes, yes. Of course the book and film influenced me. How could they not? I was 17 years old. *Star Trek* had been canceled and Norman Mailer was grousing that NASA engineers had achieved the impossible—by somehow managing to make Project Apollo boring. Few of us guessed that the space program was about to deliver its most important product—not the moon landing itself, but rather the greatest *art work* in history: the image of Earth floating as a blue oasis in the desert of space.

That gift wouldn't arrive 'til the end of 1968. Meanwhile, just about the only images that seemed to offer anything like promethean vision were contained in *2001: A Space Odyssey*.

I could go on and on about mixed messages in the film. Its love-hate relationship with technology, for example. Or the story's ambivalence toward the notion of artificial intelligence. Or the quaint combination of optimism and pessimism that we saw repeated over and over again in the works of Clarke and Isaac Asimov—leading visionaries of their era—both of whom worried that humanity might be far too snared by the sticky fibers of an aggressive Neolithic heritage ever to break free on its own.

Strangely, for one known as an idealist, Clarke seemed to be saying in *2001* (and in other works like *Childhood's End*) that we have no hope of transcending the mire of the past all by ourselves. Transcendence must come from without, via some kind of external intervention. Many felt that way during the turbulent '60s—a time when it seemed Western Civilization might all too easily destroy itself with the very brightest of its shiny new tools. If such intervention wasn't coming from old-time religion, it seemed possible to hope for delivery by kindly creatures from the sky.

Yes, I might talk all about that notion, which in the years since has become a grindingly tedious cliché: "Oh, save us from ourselves, kind aliens!" Or else I could switch levels and describe how exciting the film *2001: A Space Odyssey* was to a teenager like me! Especially a teen whose brain seemed better tuned to stories and images than the torrents of ecstatic music that sloshed over contemporary culture during those years—the era of the Beatles, Doors and Rolling Stones.

There were millions of us, you know, though we tried to hide our deviancy. Oh, we liked the music just fine. But guys like me also felt just a bit alienated from the frenzied ardor that our peers devoted to rock'n'roll. All those songs were mere sounds, after all, and what was sound compared to light!

We hungered to be fed through the eyes, and through those flashing-cerebral prefrontal lobes. We wanted to be turned on by images, preferably active ones, supple, changing and McLuhan-cool, not lying dead on some canvas. Today there is a veritable feast of manic color, a full-spectrum orgy! But in the '60s we had little more than sardonic Warhol, some cartoony psychedelia ... and science fiction.

During such a time, for visual-junkies like me, *2001* seemed to fall like manna in the desert. I came to watch again and again, staring for hours at Kubrick's voluptuously gray-blue-modern imagery, with those added touches of *faux* realistic grime.

Oh, I might wax effusive about how the film affected and inspired me, perhaps helping motivate my career in science. But how many tributes of that kind have you already read?

So let me shine a final beam from this epochal artwork in quite a different direction. There is yet another perspective ... one that just occurred to me a few months back, while watching *2001: A Space Odyssey* for about the fourteenth time.

Consider the following two hoary old clichés:

"Isn't it a shame that human decency and justice haven't kept pace with our technological progress?" and "No past era featured as much cruelty and misery as this one."

In spite of their vogue, both of these oft-parroted passages are patently false. It's incredibly easy to disprove them!

Over half of those alive on Earth today have never seen with their own eyes war, starvation or major civil strife. Most never went more than a day without food. Only a small fraction have seen a city burn, heard the footsteps of a conquering army, or watched an overlord brutalize the helpless. Yet all these events were routine for our ancestors.[1]

Of course, hundreds of millions *have* experienced such things, and terrors continue at unacceptable levels across the world. Our consciences, prodded by the relentless power of television and other media, must not cease demanding compassion and vigorous action.

Still, things have changed since humanity wallowed in hopelessness and horror, during the middle years of the 20th century. Look in places that were festering maelstroms back then—from Tokyo and Kuala Lumpur to Warsaw and Istanbul. From Alabama to South Africa. The ratio of humans who now live modestly safe and comfortable lives—or at least better than their parents—has never been greater.[2]

As for contrasting technical and moral progress, there's no contest. Technical advancement has been small potatoes by comparison! For example, while I truly love the Internet, its effects on real life have so far been vastly exaggerated. Telephones and radio had far greater immediate effects when they entered the home![3] Yes, we have fancier autos and sleeker airplanes, and more of us get to work from home. But people still pack their kids in a car and fight traffic to reach the airport in time to meet Grandma's flight from Chicago, as we did when I was seven. Life's tempo has quickened, but the basic patterns differ little from 1958.

It is our *attitudes* that have undergone a transformation unlike any in history. All kinds of unjust assumptions that used to be considered inherent—from racial, sexual and class stereotypes to ideological oversimplifications—have been tossed onto the trash heap where they long deserved to go, in favor of a generalized notion of tolerance, pragmatism and eccentricity that seems to grow more vibrant with each passing year.[4]

Where does *2001: A Space Odyssey* come into all this?

When the famous Stanley Kubrick film appeared, two monumental projects were transfixing the people of the United States: conquering outer space and overcoming deeply ingrained social injustice. This juxtaposition is clear in the film, and its sequel *2010*. Both movies portray the scientific and manipulative power of humanity far outstripping our wisdom.

But is that, in fact, what happened?

Consider those wonderful toys. The "wheel" space stations, rotating to Strauss waltzes. Or those marvelous moon cities. Or vibrant, argumentative and fully sapient computer minds like HAL 9000. We have none of them, alas.

Now recall the human political hierarchies portrayed in *2001*—rigidly pyramidal, officious, patronizing and relentlessly white-male. Remember the film's basic plot premise? Every tragedy arose from obsessive *secrecy*, as aloof bureaucrats like Heywood Floyd contemptuously concealed information from the public—and even from professional astronauts—out of fear that their poor, sheep-like minds would suffer "social disorientation."

What horribly disorienting information were they protecting people from? An archeological dig on the moon?

Oooh!

Now don't get me wrong. That scenario seemed plausible then. The predictions—both technical and social—appeared to be so on-target.

But they weren't. And that's where it gets so interesting.

Who would have imagined that colonizing space would prove so grindingly slow—and yet, by the real year 2001 we'd refute so many cruel bigotries that were once taken for granted, way back in 1967? We still don't (again, alas!) have the fancy space stations of *2001*, but today our astronauts come in all sexes and colors. And kids who watch them on TV feel less fettered by presumed limitations. Each may choose to hope, or not, without relentlessly hearing you can't.

Nowadays, an officious prig like Heywood Floyd would be haunted by whistleblowers. And if an expedition like that were sent to Jupiter today, at least one crew member of Discovery, being *female*, might actually *listen* to poor HAL instead of bullying the poor conflicted machine into feeling cornered and lashing out.

This is not a criticism of *2001: A Space Odyssey*! The film did a great job in the context of its time and it remains terrific art. Indeed, it is not the top job of art—even sci-fi—to predict![5]

Especially in science fiction, the best art offers perspective. This venerable Kubrick-Clarke collaboration still does that, even where the forecasts proved wrong.

Alas, instead of acknowledging any progress we've made, overcoming our worst evils, cinema has gone fetishistically in the opposite direction, shifting from the brash "We're going to conquer space" assumption of *Destination Moon* and *2001* to "We're all gonna be dodging radiation and mutants in ruined cities," in films too numerous to mention. This may be one reason for the persistence of the cliché that social progress lags far behind technology. Optimism doesn't offer as many options for drama!

The movie *2001: A Space Odyssey* can, and should, make you think. About all the fancy toys we were promised, but don't yet have. (Though we're getting others.) And about a society that Clarke feared would stay recalcitrant—but hasn't.

I think that may be the most important thing to notice, as we turn away from the past and face the future. The road ahead remains long, hard and murky. Our achievements often seem dim, compared to imperfections that are left unsolved, and complacency would seem the worst option of all. Yet, at this rate, who will bet me that a woman or person of color won't preside in the White House long before the first human being steps on Mars?[6]

Progress doesn't always go the way we expect it to.

It is sometimes wiser than we are.[7]

4

Living in a Science Fictional World

Biology and Destiny and Life 'n' Such[1]

All right, our first few chapters about SF and cinema took on *big-picture matters,* like self-preventing warnings, attitudes about society, the most relentless Hollywood "messages" and dismal clichés of storytelling. Now it's time to stop evading, and admit the obvious. Science fiction is also about technology and science!

There are so many topics. So this time we'll stick to *biology*. And let's start with a core obsession of fantastic literature since Gilgamesh: how to deal with—and possibly avoid—Death.

Many cultures offered tales of an "undying man who paid an awful price." Others portrayed death as prophetically ordained, or else some fateful, outside force might capriciously intervene to lengthen or snip short a character's life. (My novella "The Loom of Thessaly" incorporated the three Fates in a modern context.) One of the best ruminations on this wide-ranging topic emerged not in literature, but in a thoughtful film, *The Man from Earth.*

Something *has* changed in today's mythology about death. While our lament against extinction remains just as human-hot, what's different is the power that's at work—no longer mystical spells or prayers or incantations, but the kind of technological interventions that might be wielded by normal, flawed or arrogantly daring human beings.

Life extension, immortality and cryonics offer excellent grist for SF explorations, raising issues like: Will our brains burst from all the memories? (*Blue Mars* by K.S. Robinson.) Can even loving relationships last

4. Living in a Science Fictional World

without an expiration date? (*The Nine Worlds* by John Varley.) And will creativity stagnate if generations don't get out of each other's way? (The *Instrumentality* tales of Cordwainer Smith.) Will immortals have to fight against ennui? (Robert A. Heinlein's *Time Enough for Love*.) All of it leading to the classic worry: Will this new thing be hoarded by those with power, turning themselves into gods?

It's a dire concern depicted in the Pohl-Kornbluth novel *Gladiator at Law*, with variations like *Holy Fire* by Bruce Sterling and *Chiller* by Gregory Benford. For thousands of years, the influence and vast fortunes gathered by kings and moguls might get recycled—at least somewhat—by the passing of generations. But what if death is vanquished, and that recycling process ceases? Joe Haldeman's *Buying Time* suggests that a price of life extension should be the surrendering of all wealth, starting over with a youthful body—but poor—to begin creating and earning all over again. In *After Many a Summer Dies the Swan*, the inimitable Aldous Huxley ruminates on Leonardo da Vinci and immortality and eternal youth, then stuns the reader into realizing, on the very last page, that it was a science fiction novel all along.

Alas, such thoughtful contemplations are rare. Most films and stories about immortality suggest that aristocrats will hoard it, and wield the power of ancient oligarchs, even deities, as exemplified by *Zardoz*, *Highlander* and *Elysium*. Of course, that image is justified by nearly all of human history! So writers portray oppressive hierarchies in films like *The Hunger Games* and *Divergent* with such lurid exaggeration as to be of little actual use. Such storytelling laziness may help explain the paucity of tales exploring another possibility—as does the film *Mr. Nobody*—that we might all *share* such breakthroughs ... resulting in more complex and interesting problems.

To be clear, this chapter is long enough, just viewing from many angles the way life and immortality, etc., are treated in science fiction cinema and literature. We aren't here to discuss matters practical and factually scientific, though these are in a perpetual dance with science fiction. I have found myself thrust into debates on that side of things as well,[2] asserting a widely unpopular view that human beings are already the "methuselahs of mammals," getting three times as many heartbeats as mice and elephants, for example. To achieve the lengthy lifespan that allows us to raise neotenous children, *Homo sapiens* likely has already plucked the "low-hanging fruit" of longevity. Science may yet concoct interventions that greatly extend the 100-year (or so) "wall." But those methods won't be anything as simple as a magical nutrient or diet plan.

But we'll discuss all that elsewhere. For now, let's get back to the fun that sci-fi has, just exploring implications and extrapolating ideas.

Cryonics offers a special subgenre about life extension, building on the ancient tradition of the "returning castaway" seen in *The Odyssey, Gulliver's Travels, Robinson Crusoe* and *Rip Van Winkle.* H.G. Wells in *The Sleeper Wakes* and Robert Sheckley in *Immortality Incorporated* (filmed as *Freejack*) used this trope to comment on society by revealing extravagant future outcomes to a 20th century everyman. Or it can be a more-than-everyman, like the reanimated *Captain America.* Richard Morgan's *Altered Carbon* novel and TV series throw such a "time suspension" traveler into situations of extreme adventure violence. Taking themselves less seriously were *Sleeper, Futurama* and the zany *Idiocracy,* showing how wide is the range of topics that can be explored with this device, including even a modest story of romance, as in *Forever Young.*

A sub-category would be tales about rousing *another* kind of time-suspended traveler, like *The Mummy,* or a myriad "what have we stirred?" flicks about Lovecraftian horrors wakened from the past.

At the opposite end of thoughtfulness, Steven Spielberg's *Minority Report* revolves around the bizarre notion that *potential* criminals automatically get dunked into liquid nitrogen without getting even the due process of a hearing, an unlikely device whose sole purpose is to propel the story. One can envision Spielberg agonizing over that, seeking some alternative in a film that otherwise beautifully evades the Idiot Plot, before finally throwing up his hands and concluding, "Who will notice?"

Seldom asked in any of the Suspended Traveler stories is this question: Why would any future culture *want* to revive frozen ancestors? Surely not because our frozen stiffs earn compound interest in a bank account. John Scalzi's *Old Man's War* suggests that such "corpsicles" will be put to work serving the future's needs, rather than the other way around. This also happens in the fluffier *Demolition Man.* Sorry, cryonics zealots, you have no idea how future folks might put you to use.

There have been stories—some light and others deeply moving—about human brains incorporated into robotic machinery, for example. Among the earliest and best was *The Ship Who Sang* by Anne McCaffrey. Keith Laumer's *A Plague of Demons* put the head of a man into a cyber-tank, as did the later *Bolo* series … a trope that's now standard in many video games. And there's *Mayflies* by Kevin O'Donnell, in which a human-brained generation starship must deal with one after another of the brief humans in his charge.

4. Living in a Science Fictional World 35

Likewise, the topic of *self-altering* is commonly depicted as something bizarre, an excuse for stories of perversion, as promulgated by Ellen Datlow in her series of anthologies about nightmarish alien sexuality, or the even more perverted and violent crush-blending of man and automobile in J.G. Ballard's *Crash*.

Or else some solitary protagonist tries an experimental drug, or a secret mind-enhancing experiment goes terribly wrong. We've seen examples ranging from *Dr. Jekyll and Mr. Hyde* to *The Fly* to Neal Asher's *Polity* series of novels, along with all sorts of superhero clichés. In *The People of Sand and Slag* by Paolo Bacigalupi, self-altering is treated as a stage of evolution. In a famed *Outer Limits* episode, "The Architects of Fear," Robert Culp's character volunteers to be altered into a fearsome alien, hoping to frighten humanity into uniting against an outside threat.

I'm More Than I Was!

Of course, in most cases the aim is to become like a god. In fiction, it seems there are four classic ways to gain mighty powers, whether as hero or villain:

1. Come as an alien from somewhere else, as in *Superman, Thor* and *Wonder Woman*.
2. Get born a mutant, then come into your might as an adolescent. The *Übermensch Effect* goes way back to the ancient myths Oedipus and Perseus (*Clash of the Titans*), with many modern variations (e.g., *Harry Potter* or *Guardians of the Galaxy*), as we saw in Chapter 2.
3. Get mutated and transformed by massive chemical or radiation doses—e.g., the Joker in *Batman,* or *Deadpool,* or many of their adversaries.
4. Do it with technology—and some karate—then keep it all to yourself, like *Batman* and his ilk, or K.W. Jeter's *Dr. Adder,* or *The Six Million Dollar Man*.

Almost never is the process portrayed taking place the way science actually works, in cautious steps, as part of a group effort, open and accountable. That would still leave room for lots of potential stories about unforeseen outcomes or dire consequences. Alas, it takes more work to write a scenario in which danger rears up *despite* smart and decent behavior. Far easier to have it happen because the protagonist is surrounded by conspirators and fools.

Self-altering is done with more nuance in the thought experiments of Lois McMaster Bujold, whose "quaddies" are humans modified permanently to live and work in space, by the simple expedient of turning their legs into another set of arms and hands. Bujold does not shrink from exploring how this might affect sex. My own *Elepents*—elephants with grabber hands for feet and prehensile tails, armored for vacuum—are built upon her concept.

Nancy Kress' *Beggars in Spain* considers a simple superpower: What if some self-altered humans learn to do without sleep, getting vastly more productive hours? The Shaper-Mechanist stories of Bruce Sterling depict a war between those who seek deification-powers through genetic and biological alteration vs. their rivals using cyborg-machine enhancements.

Of course, the best form of self-altering is one we've been engaging in for generations. *Simply stop wasting talent.* It turns out that great effects are achieved just with remedial measures to end poverty and injustice. And preventing deleterious substances like lead from stunting young brains. Ensuring that ever-increasing fractions of human children get enough to eat, stay healthy and have minds nourished by education and free self-expression. By that simple though ponderously ambitious project, we've accomplished more wonders than all previous generations combined.

What accomplishments? Why, so much science that it now pervades all our fast-adapting myths, turning most music, art and storytelling toward SF! So much music that we've used up all the melodies (see Spider Robinson's famed short story "Melancholy Elephants"). So much art that Rembrandt-level talents don't even stand out from the rising tide, but must slave away depicting vibrant scenes for popular video games. (Tragic!)

It's an era of superpowers, at least by the standards of our poverty-stunted ancestors; but powers so widely (if still imperfectly) shared that few stand out from the vast crowd of similarly empowered beings around them. It's hard to rise far above, when the average also rises, as the Flynn Effect reveals typical IQ scores climbing for several generations, everywhere that most kids get food, health, education, freedom and encouragement.

It's a deeply flawed, incomplete revolution … and unquestionably the greatest thing that's ever happened. And hardly anyone remarks on it because, unlike our vivid stories of screen and page, it's not Campbellian-elitist. It's not romantically about a lonely demigod. Because the good thing—the mighty accomplishment—is shared so widely that it became kind of… kind of *boring* … the way justice ought to be.

The most magical thing about it is … it's fair. And that fairness means it makes for boring fiction. And hence, it's not *Magical*.

You Are More Than You Were!

Self-altering leads naturally to *other*-altering—transforming other people or beings, either against their will or for their own good. Early examples range from *Pygmalion* to *Frankenstein*, from *The Island of Dr. Moreau* to Cordwainer Smith's *Instrumentality* stories. Typically, a secretive Mad Scientist creates pitiable monsters to enslave. Naturally, everyone suffers for this hubris, both the arrogant creator and his creations. In each case, the underlying assumption is that everyone—the mad scientist, plus colleagues and cousins, all the way down to the local constabulary—has the combined foresight and compassion of a stone.

Don't get me wrong; I believe such tales—mining the rich story-ore of human hubris, righteously punished—have helped us with their wagging, cautionary fingers. Would *our* society long put up with the situation depicted in Pierre Boulle's *Planet of the Apes* series, where humans create intelligent animals simply to beat them in cruel servitude? I would give very long odds against it. Don't forget that we were all raised by those odd tales! We learned a thing or two, as those storytellers wanted.

If you would fight against such cruelty, don't you think your neighbors would, as well? Or at least enough of them to give justice a fighting chance?

Obsessed with otherness, we won't see the uplifting of animals to sapience as a chance to exploit a new servant class, but as a nifty way to give us other minds to talk to. In my *Uplift* universe, I try to depict what Californians and their ilk might do with such powers—say raising the intelligence of dolphins and chimpanzees—then apologizing profusely for having intruded on their cultural sovereignty! In other words, I find it more interesting to explore what the future might be like if our fellow citizens *aren't* complete fools. Won't there be interesting problems, anyway?

One novel which took this approach, John Brunner's *Stand on Zanzibar*, depicts a world in the next century where people, institutions and science have all become a bit better, smarter … though barely fast enough to stay ahead of accelerating troubles. It was original, chilling, realistic and tremendously fascinating.

I won't demean *Frankenstein* or *Planet of the Apes*. I was raised by them. Taught by them. Chastened and roused by their self-preventing prophecies. Schooled to evade the traps they warned against, so that *I* get to warn against others.

The lesson was to question everything, especially your own assumptions. The lesson was not to give up moving forward.

Genetics and Reproduction?

Again, some fine exceptions stand out from a morass of simple-minded exaggerations. Take *Star Trek II: The Wrath of Khan*, brilliantly written and directed, in which Gene Roddenberry's characters truly came alive. This gorgeous film threw down the dreary *Frankenstein* ethos and stomped it flat, as audiences viewed an entire solar system that human beings made, and recognized this usurpation of godlike power as a good thing. A beautiful thing.

How did *you* respond to the end of that movie? According to my informal poll, nearly everyone left the theater feeling good, ennobled, empowered ... and a little more determined to make a better tomorrow. What was the moral lesson? If we fight hard for the future—if our efforts lead to descendants who are much better people, perhaps even as good as those in the *Star Trek* universe—then they may get to pick up God's tools, as young apprentices, and do great work. Making solar systems. Making life. Making worlds!

What a message. What defiance of the *Frankenstein* Idiot Plot!

Ah. So, what did they do with the next film? *Star Trek III: The Search for Spock*? It was as if someone had pulled out a *Frankenstein* checklist!

Oh no, we humans should *never* stick our noses where they don't belong! We arrogated God's powers, so this false creation (the new solar system) must be garbage. (It falls apart! Of course, Spock comes back alive from this garbage stew; so what's he made of?) Moreover, the monster-mutant planet kills its creator, Kirk's son—a betrayal of faith with the audience that was only exceeded when David Fincher began *Alien 3* by murdering the little girl we all rooted for in *Aliens*.

Alas, the makers of these dismal films probably followed their checklist by rote, out of unconscious habit. Their natural conclusion, once again, was that you can't lose by assuming everyone is stupid.

Nothing raises the hackles of authors more than the mere possibility of improvements in mental health. And with some reason, given how often in history the word "insane" was used as a synonym for "unconventional" or "eccentric," or holding opinions that threaten the power of elites. Many past human civilizations—perhaps most—went out of their way to quash anyone who seemed abnormal. And since SF is largely a genre by, for and about eccentrics, it's natural to see cautionary tales warn against psychological homogenization, preaching acceptance of the peculiar, the extraordinary and even the downright strange. Examples range from Kurt Vonnegut's "Harrison Bergeron" to the *Divergent* films and *THX 1138*, along with maybe half of all *Twilight Zone* episodes. Fredric Brown's "Come and

Go Mad" portrays an insane asylum filled with people who Knew Too Much, as does Thomas Disch's *Camp Concentration*.

Even a civilization with good intentions might drift toward crippling sameness. In his story "Madness Has Its Place," Larry Niven asks whether future humans might regret it, if they soothe and smooth away all the rough qualities that enable us to fight when we have to—a theme also explored in my own *Out of Time* series.

Alas, to a large degree today's fiction often seems obsessed with battles that were old and clichéd even before H.G. Wells and Jules Verne. From highly touted works, like William Gibson's "The Gernsback Continuum," all the way to silly movies like *Demolition Man*, a reflexive dread is expressed toward the very concept of "sanity," portraying it as inherently oppressive. Or else it is an impossibly fictitious concept, absurd on the face of it, as depicted in any and every tale by Philip K. Dick.

Seldom is it ever pondered that a progressive society might *define* sanity to include an appreciation of diversity, along with a willingness to live and let live. A kind of sanity that is ethnically neutral, independent of averages, loosely structured, and yet useful at encouraging the kind of diverse, responsible, tolerant, quirky adulthood we'd like to share with over seven billion others on this teeming globe. These authors seem to think that mere people would abuse such a tool for decent living, and so we would all be better off without any standards of mental health at all.

Ooh! Story idea! What if in the future, you are deemed defective if you are *too much like others*? Not contributing enough to diversity. Diametrically opposite to that famous *Twilight Zone* cry against conformity, "Number 12 Looks Just Like You." Kind of like the Pauli Exclusion Principle, for you physics geeks. If taken to extreme, that could be oppressive, too!

But then, didn't Harlan Ellison perform this reversal in his quirky-impudent story "The Crackpots"? An agent comes to spy on a city where "insane" nonconformists are sent. He discovers this was done to create a fertile breeding ground for new ideas, which the observing agents send back. The "insane" nonconformists are aware of this, kind of like the brilliant TV series *Eureka*. Then there were the islands in Huxley's *Brave New World*, where dissidents are sent as "punishment" to tropical leisure, and given copious opportunities to think.

Ah, wisdom.

Genes Determine

The science fictional implications of biology proliferate like mad, in all directions. For example, when we attain true powers of genetic engineering, manipulating the human genome at will, shall we then let individuals or couples tailor their young? Grow feathers on their babies, if they choose? Or will we banish the techniques entirely, and thus forbid the human race tools for improving itself? Generally in SF, especially film, any thought of intrusive gene-meddling is treated with reflexive, Frankensteinian loathing that (alas) will have little effect where it's needed most—secret labs in Xinjiang and Siberia, I reckon.

To be sure, genetics and reproduction are sometimes handled with intelligence in science fiction. A century from now, Robert A. Heinlein may be best known for a few offhand suggestions about biological policy he dropped into *Beyond This Horizon*. With advanced tech, future parents might be shown models of all possible combinations of the husband's sperm and the wife's ova, choosing *which* natural pair to unite. (This Heinleinian option was shown briefly in a memorable episode of *Black Mirror*.) Hence, the child you get is one you *might* have had anyway, by old-fashioned chance. One result: Increased health and intelligence across the human population, without arrogant "designer" meddling in the natural genome. And note that Heinlein suggested we give this power to everyone, not just some elite. Above all, he demonstrated that SF can be more than simplistic warnings and polemics, but about offering practical suggestions as well.

This kind of thoughtful rumination doesn't have to preclude drama and tension, as we see in the highly lauded film *Gattaca*, where we get to see layers. The foreground story is about a lonely protagonist pursuing his ambition, overcoming all obstacles to flying in space. His single-minded pursuit is admirable in its own right, though with disturbing implications. Seldom noted is the layer below, that's implied in many scenes, telling of a society that's *not* evil, but aware of its faults (in this case prejudicial misuse of genetic profiling) and seeking—awkwardly—to confront them. I will continue to discuss *Gattaca* in a later chapter.

<> <> <>

Which leads us back to how *evolution* is handled in science fiction, traditionally on three different levels.

Least discussed in novels and films is Type #1, *natural selection*, the kind we know from Darwin, with traits modified by quirks like sexual selection. I think this area is ripe for many interesting tales! But storytellers are likely deterred by the long time scales involved.

Type #2 is *guided selection*, as in animal husbandry, or my own process of Uplift. We have already seen that stories about this kind of evolution nearly always assume widespread individual and/or social stupidity, plus cruelty, amid preachings against hubris.

Type #3, *fated destiny*, is something most scientists consider completely spurious, a mistake that lures in so many, also called "teleology." Nevertheless, it used to be a very powerful theme across science fiction, as in Olaf Stapledon's *Odd John*. We already mentioned A.E. van Vogt and Orson Scott Card, who pushed the idea that evolution has some preordained destination, some inexorable direction. Just the sort of tall tale we saw in the fervid wish-fantasies of Marxism.

A favorite example of teleology in sci-fi, the *Outer Limits* episode "The Sixth Finger" stars David McCallum as a coal miner who is experimentally transformed, sent plunging up the "future evolutionary path of humanity," developing a prodigiously expanded brain. In a kind of reverse-recapitulation, he first uses his new mental powers for revenge, only then (in the nick of time) forward-evolves past such petty grudges.

More generally, the *Übermensch Effect* still panders to this impulse by saying to the reader (often some nerdy kid without friends), "Psst! Have I got a fantasy for you! What if *you* are the vanguard of the next stage of evolution? Or a lost star-prince (as in the gaudy flick *Jupiter Ascending*)? Or a psychic adept who hasn't quite discovered his powers yet (*The Flight of the Navigator*)? Would that explain why others are mean to you? Hey, buy this fable and picture what they'll think, when they discover you're a god."

Which leads us to "transcendence."

Deities "R" Us

Transcendence of *what*?, you ask. The individual? Society? Humanity? All of these have been covered movingly in science fiction, with Vernor Vinge's much touted "Singularity" among the best recent examples, though the science fiction versions date back to Olaf Stapledon's *Odd John*, and even earlier, obscure tales by Robert Duncan Milne and Edward Page Mitchell.

Here we're not talking about "teleology" or something fore-ordained or even evolved, but perhaps a gift much like the fruit of the *other* tree in Eden. The one Adam and Eve were prevented from eating: the Tree of Life. (Taking us back around, full circle, to *immortality*, perhaps?)

Or maybe it's transcendence of the general sense that we saw a few pages later, in the same science fiction novel, at the Tower of Babel, only this time with all of humanity aiming to climb boldly beyond Heaven? Or else the kind, *enlightenment* transcendence offered by millennia of mystics, conveyed to western contemplation by tales like Hermann Hesse's *Siddhartha* and *Lord of Light* by Roger Zelazny. The varieties seem innumerable.

In fact, it's a surprisingly common theme in films and TV. The very first Captain Kirk pilot, "Where No Man Has Gone Before," featured Gary Lockwood as Kirk's friend who gains prodigious abilities, a theme *Star Trek* revisited time and again, not always with disapproval, but with healthy skepticism and worry about abuse of power, as in confrontations with the "higher" beings of the Q Continuum.

In just about the only other generally optimistic TV future, *Stargate*, Dr. Daniel Jackson transcends (temporarily) in ways that explore many implications, without necessarily calling such ambitions evil. In the film and TV series *Limitless*, the notion of expanded mental capacity is treated as it should be; good or bad outcomes will depend upon the morality—and accountability—of the user, a notion also portrayed in Luc Besson's excellent *Lucy*. Such tradeoffs and responsibilities of transcendence are core issues in the meta-comic and movie versions of *Watchmen*, as in the anime world of *Akira*. (And yes, the topic is one that I frequently explore, in fictions like "Stones of Significance," "The Crystal Spheres," *Kiln People* and *Heaven's Reach*. And though I strive to evade the clichés that I've noticed, I'm sure I invented my own.)

Would you say "Flowers for Algernon"—the famous story about a mentally handicapped man rising all too briefly to genius level—falls into this category? Or the John Travolta film *Phenomenon*? Or might most vampire stories be about transcending human normality, since some of the victims certainly do rise up to greater understanding and power, though not virtue?

Would such a listing be absurd without mentioning the Star-Child at the end of *2001: A Space Odyssey*? The dire warnings like the horrific Kwizats Hadderach monster of Frank Herbert's *Dune*? (In other chapters, I discuss both works, along with the related topic of the *Übermensch Effect*, a tendency of many authors to habitually worship demigods.) Other tales explore ambiguity, like the 2014 Johnny Depp vehicle *Transcendence*, which left you puzzled over whether to be glad or fretful that desperate agents of our protective state failed in their mission to stymie a new cyber-god.

More akin to that first *Star Trek* episode, and a vast majority of sci-fi dire warning flicks, is *The Lawnmower Man*. Both Stephen King's book and the marginally related film portray the unleashing of a mad and angry god, without attaining the saving insight of "The Sixth Finger."

In a strange way, transcendence is rather easier for writers to portray than one might think. The topic is so cosmic, so vast and utterly disruptive of normality, that it doesn't matter much whether society is depicted as stupid or not. In Poul Anderson's classic *Brain Wave*, the main characters face trials because *everyone* in the world is getting terribly smart at the same time. In *City*, Clifford D. Simak depicted masses of humans intelligently choosing among a wide diversity of higher paths.

4. Living in a Science Fictional World

Transcendence of what? As Pat Scannell points out: We are social creatures, each of us a congress of selves, nested within cultural constructs. Uplifting the cognition of one may be great, but may put us in conflict or friction with the collective.

On the other hand, the "Gaia/Galaxia" vision that Isaac Asimov skillfully displayed in *Foundation's Edge* posed a transcendence that's handed to humanity on a platter by devoted robot servants—who have motives that Isaac hinted at and I explored in *Foundation's Triumph*. As in Arthur C. Clarke's *Childhood's End*, it is an elevation via *deus ex machina* that few if any humans are asked to comprehend or deliberate upon. For the most part, we are seen as too stupid to be consulted, even over matters of our own survival and long-range destiny. I'm glad that Isaac hinted strongly at a new solution—a wider, more cognizant and diverse kind of human-chosen transcendence that I was able to convey for him.

◊ ◊ ◊

This survey of sci-fi tales (primarily film and TV) about biology (and more) was never meant to be comprehensive. You'll get longer lists from Wikipedia, the *Science Fiction Encyclopedia* and David Hartwell and Kathryn Cramer's *The Hard SF Renaissance*. Rather, I used this tour to shine some light on patterns, the habits or impudence with which science fiction explores our paths of possible change. Ways that things may not stay the same. We'll get to non-biology sci-fi later on.

What we've learned is that some SF explorations of humanity's future seem inherent, or noble or shocking, while others have appeared in film and literature so often as to become repetitive, hackneyed, even clichés. That doesn't automatically lead to poor art! But, as we'll see in the next chapter, the finest works of SF cinema do seem to have some elements in common.

One of these shared elements is simple.

Try to be joyously and extravagantly different.

5

A Quirky Must-See Guide to Science Fiction Movies

Let's take a breather for some fun. As we've seen, science fiction is multi-dimensional along every spectrum of topic, meaning and storytelling craft. Hence, no one criterion can be used to determine a best-of list. And yet, the temptation is overwhelming. Besides, this is a book about "Sci-fi and Hollywood," and hence, several times in this volume, I will offer *lists*.

Herein, I'll divide my favorite SF flicks into categories, including runners-up and tragic misfires. And yes, each choice would be worth many paragraphs of explanation. But you already know some of the axes that I grind, so I'll try to be concise.

Hey, in this topic, above all other topics, everything is subjective. So expect to fume and argue and disagree! Or throw this book out the window in rage. Then buy another copy.

Movies for Grown-ups

I wish there were more of these—films where the director and writer cared about deep implications of their visual thought experiment, their deliberate departure from reality. Works where creators paid heed to logical what-if and (while delivering tasty action, plus biting social commentary) eschewed lazy Idiot Plots, like the assumption that civilization is automatically worthless. Some institutions function! Adversaries have plausible motives. And no red, glowing eyes! Protagonists aren't "chosen one" demi-gods but merely above-average people who find themselves in a jam for logical reasons, with difficult challenges to overcome, in part, by using their heads.

By those standards, the Christopher Nolan film *Inception* (2010) works harder than any film I ever saw. There's not a scene that wasn't clearly worked out with excruciating attention to detail and impressive consistency with every other scene. True, the movie can be overbearing, especially with that aggressive musical score cranked up to levels that you feel through the soles of your feet. But I've never seen a director juggle so many edgy intricacies as Nolan does in this successful tour de force.

Film awards should have difficulty multipliers, like gymnastics and figure skating. And by that standard, *Inception* should have won them all.

Gattaca (1997) and *Primer* (2004) are much simpler films that still tease your mind into real thinking.[1] As we've already seen, *Gattaca* isn't as dystopian as some lazily presume. In fact, the protagonist is a self-centered jerk ... but a true hero nonetheless, whose triumph is largely one of character and mind and steel will. Moreover, that triumph, if successful at the end of his mission, will change society for the better.

A jewel-like time travel puzzler, *Primer* is a delight of logic and an example of what can be done when very smart people have a filming budget of about 85 cents. All of the very same things can be said about the nifty one-actor space yarn *Moon* (2009).

Another successful time travel set-piece—expanded very nicely from Robert Heinlein's classic story "All You Zombies"—was *Predestination*. The detective mystery overlaid perfectly and I reckon that Heinlein would have been pleased. (In polar opposition, poor Poul Anderson heard how awful was the shoddy production of his wonderful novel *The High Crusade*. He and his wife Karen actually had the willpower never to watch their only film adaptation. I doubt I'd have the strength. But as you'll see, I had more nuanced feelings about Kevin Costner's version of *The Postman*.)

James Cameron gets a couple of mentions here, including a whole chapter later on, about *Avatar*. But his film that's intended for grown-ups—*The Abyss* (1989)—gets only this one sentence. I liked it. Yeah, sure, the ending was ... well, I don't care ... and that's two sentences. No three. Four?

The movie *2001: A Space Odyssey* (1968), discussed in detail elsewhere, was epochal—it helped make me who I am. It remains a mind stretcher—though suffering a bit under close examination. So don't.

I rank Stanley Kubrick's other wonder even higher. Arguably the best motion picture ever made, though only marginally science fiction, was *Dr. Strangelove, or How I Learned to Stop Worrying and Love the Bomb* (1964). And yes, I do think it is the very best and most important film of all time. Not just because it likely prevented accidental war, not just because of the wit and humor and great performances. I am also awestruck by how

Kubrick created massive audience cognitive dissonance. Amid all the silly-strutting man-boys who Kubrick mocks at the Air Force base and the War Room, there are just five *adults* in the film—the crew of a B-52 bomber, whose skill and professionalism makes you proud, while you pray they all will die, so that the world may live. That's art.

Honorable mentions in this category would include *Limitless* (2011) which, despite some self-indulgences, explored with verve and a gram of optimism our glimmering hope for self-improvement. And *Interstellar* was so sincere. It tried so hard. I wish I could meddle with just five minutes of … but sure. Let's put it in this category.

The grown-up in me says thank you.

Joyful Slumming

At the opposite end of the high-quality spectrum are films that I could only watch by tuning way-down my "dials" before entering the theater. Cranking IQ and science and logic to "popcorn" levels, without sacrificing standards when it came to deeper values, like beauty, esthetics and ethics. Admit it, some of *your* brains must be left outside the theater too, in order to enjoy most flicks, and that's fine. It's okay to appreciate as if stoned a simple, stupid movie-movie. Hey, I'm from the 1960s. I can enter a stoned state at will. And I'll do that, if the flick is way-successful at delivering fun.

Noteworthy: All the fantasies are here. Show me one fantasy film that's for grown-ups.

Conan the Barbarian (the original from 1982) is simply the most successful film ever at delivering exactly what it promised, while never promising what it couldn't deliver. A perfect gem. Every scene is filled with visual and musical beauty amid a tale that hearkens to the deeply non-modern and joyfully brainless parts of you and me, a demigod adoration reflex that goes back to the Iliad and Gilgamesh and the caves.

I speak of romanticism many times in this book. And while I'll fight—unto death—to prevent all that king-overlord-feudalist lunacy from ever again running civilization, it is far too lusciously fun to banish from our hearts.

Likewise, *The Fifth Element* (1997) is the single most *joyful* work of art I ever saw. Luc Besson's sheer pleasure at making this film leaps onto your lap like a great big, floppy-dumb retriever and licks your face for 90 minutes, punctuating all the jubilantly eager action with … *an aria*! I adore it. Millions do. And it adores us.

Avatar (2009) … well, James Cameron would demand that we put *Avatar* in category number one or even number three. Sorry. Nice try. It is beyond brilliant in the popcorn category, but keep those neuron dials turned down. And then murmur ... "wow!" (I'll get back to this epic later.)

In contrast, the *Back to the Future* trilogy comes *that* close to vaulting into category three. It's fantastic fun. Big-hearted, unabashedly logical and darn near perfect. Truly. It only belongs in this category because I feel my face thoroughly licked again by that floppy retriever. It made us all happy. It's at home here.

Lord of the Rings (2001) ... all right, Peter Jackson delivered a superb work of art and it definitely was not "just popcorn." I have great respect for Tolkien's complex world-building craft and Jackson's fealty to the original material. Still, neither the books nor the flicks bear adult scrutiny. So turn down the "adult" dials. Be a kid and enjoy. I know I did! Then turn to Chapter 8 if you can stand seeing the Tolkien universe analyzed from a sober, science fictional perspective.

The Whole Package

Rarest of all: films that take us beyond our familiar horizons on adventures that simultaneously satisfy every age you contain within yourself, from awestruck kid to sober grown-up to mystic dreamer ... all the way to your mightiest inner being, *citizen*.

Star Trek II: The Wrath of Khan (1982) delivers from beginning to end. Not only a terrific motion picture but a love ode to the brash, Faustian, unbridled adolescent hopefulness that only *Star Trek* ever gave us, amid today's grotesque tsunami of grouchy-clichéd dystopias. Elsewhere, I talk about this wonderful work of art, and how it was systematically betrayed by its sequel ... but that happened a lot in those days. (See below.)

Blade Runner (1982). Of course. Nothing need be said. Except that the sequel, *Blade Runner 2049* (2017), tried so hard ... so very hard. And there was a lot to like. But the standard could not be met.

Runners-Up

There are so many films that came close, or just missed. Dozens were enjoyable and I'd have been proud to be associated with most. Only nitpicking kept them off the top tier.

Contact (1997) was well worthwhile and inspiring, if a bit preachy. And the aliens should be put under hot interrogation lamps.

Gravity (2013). I expect this one may challenge its way into the Top Ten, with time. Exquisitely done, even if Alfonso Cuarón depicts Low Earth

Orbit (LEO) as roughly the size of L.A. County. (See Chapter 21 about this work.)

Things to Come (1936). My kids were bored, but I am moved almost to tears by its paean to the civilization we might (with difficulty) make, if we overcome the worse sides of human nature. Maybe it's a generation thing.

James Cameron's well-crafted *Aliens* (1986) is the best film about motherhood, ever. And *Terminator II* (1991) was even better than the first one. Alas, both were betrayed by their "third movie" sequels, as happened to *Wrath of Khan*.

In fact, all through the '80s and '90s, there appeared to be a "third movie curse," in which the wondrous second film of a trilogy was utterly betrayed by the final opus. Count 'em up! It happened to *Star Trek, Star Wars, Terminator* and especially the *Aliens* series. But not *Back to the Future*, somehow.

I'm not done! So let me roll off some of my favorites that fall just outside the top lists, each one funky and unique and different in its own way:

Forbidden Planet (1956), *Rollerball* (1975), *Dark City* (1998), *Europa Report* (2013)—plus weirdnesses like *Brazil* (1985), *SteamBoy* (2004) and *Solaris* (1972)—illustrating the fantastic range and breadth and wondrous opportunities for creativity that science fiction offers to those who think bold.

In television, *The Man in the High Castle* has been near perfect, so far. I forgive *The Expanse* for logical flaws, because it shines. Too bad *Extant* was canceled, and likewise *Firefly*. But that sadness extends across decades of lost opportunities all the way back to *The Starlost*.

Stargate was relentlessly exploratory, inquisitive and stunningly logical, while daring to join *Star Trek* in critically wary optimism. (Though I kept asking: Why keep it all secret from citizens of Earth, first that they are at war with a galactic empire and then later that they won?) No one needs to defend *Star Trek,* of course, though I go into detail, next chapter.

And there's more. Much later in this tome, I'll add another list of short takes on many more flicks and TV series that have poured from science fiction's fecundity, a gift to civilization.

Special Category: Faustian SF

I especially like stories that buck a cliché. And I deem the worst cliché of all to be hopeless gloom. A few—a bold few—express confidence in us, in our ability and righteous right to go beyond what we were, and in our children to be better than us. Call these *anti–Crichton tales* that declare the opposite of Michael's endless chiding: "Don't touch that!"

Examples mentioned already include *The Wrath of Khan* and *Inception*. Also expressing a rebel sense of belief-in-us:

Ghostbusters (1984), *Brainstorm* (1983), *Altered States* (1980), *Dark City* (1998), *Quatermass and the Pit* (1958) and *eXistenZ* (1999). And may I give a hint at Chapter 19? Kevin Costner's *The Postman* (1997) was harmed by some nonsensical or uneven scenes—and it might have benefited from even five minutes of talking to the original author. Still, large swathes of the film were terrific. It features some of the most gorgeous cinematography in the history of film. Its heart—if not head—was pure and brave and it belongs in this category.

Still. Compare to the book.

Special Mentions

Surprisingly, no single Steven Spielberg film made my top ten sci-fi films. But almost *all* Spielberg films would rank in my top 50, while *Close Encounters of the Third Kind* (1977), *War of the Worlds* (2005) and *Minority Report* (2002) skate much closer. Spielberg and Zemeckis are the most consistently skilled storytellers of our age, and fiercely loyal to civilization. Nolan and Cameron, while more uneven and less disciplined, did make it onto the top list. *Vive les différences.*

As for harbingers of the future: The recent films *The Martian*, *The Arrival* and *Annihilation* turned excellent novels and stories (by my friends Andy Weir and Ted Chiang and Jeff VanderMeer) into wonderful cinema for tens of millions. Sure I'm jealous! And inspired. May they indeed be harbingers.

And finally....

Tragic Misses: What Might Have Been—If Only...

The Empire Strikes Back is a fine film in its own right, and it shows what a wonderful epic we might have had, if George Lucas stuck to his strength as one of the greatest of all visionary Hollywood producers. If only he *hired* great writers and directors for his other films, the way he did in *Empire*—the same way he hired terrific artists for all the other *Star Wars* flicks. (Their one, consistent strong suit was endlessly voluptuous visuals.) Alas, his decision to ignore advice and try to *write* became our tragedy, as we'll see in the next chapter.

The Day the Earth Stood Still might be listed by some as a "self-preventing prophecy," since it guilt-tripped many into thinking harder about peace. An arguable case. Still, I find the chiding smugness of Klaatu off-putting. Where were you for the 10,000 generations when our ancestors struggled with ignorance and poverty? The whole concept could have been more fascinating if it were more even-handed. Alas, its smarmy preachiness prevented adding another layer of potentially really interesting *counter*-preachiness. How tasty if one human—even just one—stepped up and said to Klaatu, in a Pee-wee Herman voice: "I know we aren't all that … but what are you?"

How I'd love to do that, in a remake.

Total Recall … you're kidding me, right? You can be this creative—in *both* versions (1990 and 2012)—yet still timidly shy away from the central challenge of that story? How about getting all Philip K. Dick on us and persuading us to fret that the entire adventure might *actually* be a bummer recall-trip. You couldn't do that? Why? I mean, why not? It would have been so easy and so cool. Dang. Near-miss.

Dune (1984) … actually, I have no major complaints. Despite his detractors, Dino De Laurentiis was faithful to Frank Herbert, conveying the complex world and characters in a limited run time. Alas, lo and behold, the silver screen made clear what most readers of the novel—captivated and immersed—fail to notice. That every single character in the story is loathsome and ought to die. Yes, the "good" guys, too. Please. As quickly as possible. I hope to convince you of that, in Chapter 18!

Tron was fun and innovative for its time. Alas, in both the original and its sequel, Jeff Bridges' character might have made his crucial moves by actually *coding*, using the skill he's so proud of, instead of waving his arms and invoking magical "user power." And yes, *The Matrix* did the same thing. Neo is supposed to be a whiz of a hacker, but his talent as Chosen One turns out to be in mystical stare-downs and virtual martial arts. Cool when you watch it the first time! But less respect-worthy, as time passes.

E.T. the Extra-Terrestrial (1982) was way-fun and all that, pushing all our buttons for wholesome things like hospitality, charity, courage, suspicion of authority and *otherness*. Terrific, and Spielberg seldom misses a beat. But. Um. Did it ever occur to you to ask who the *real villain* of the story is? Spielberg makes clear that it's not who you first think. (See Chapter 13.)

And so it goes. We'll have more opinionated lists, later in this tome. Meanwhile, let's all hope that there will be great new films in the next decade that outshine all of the above!

Speaking of which, here's a pitch: *"Dolphins … in space!"*

Eh? Who could possibly beat that?

Part Two:
Admirable (But Flawed) Blockbusters

6

J'accuse George Lucas ... or Zola Meets Yoda

Salon magazine published my essay dissecting faults of the Star Wars universe. Not complaints about Ewoks or Jar-Jars or childish dialogue or cringeworthy notions of romance, but core matters of consistency, values, and keeping faith with the audience—vexations that crept into *Star Wars* during those dark years between *The Empire Strikes Back* and the takeover by imperial Disney. Of course, there was another factor. In those days, online zines actually paid really well! And boy, did this one bring in readers, eager to argue, mostly in fun. (The death threats I got were few, and neither plausible nor original.)

Then SmartPop called with a book offer. Let it be decided in a *courtroom*, they proposed! Under supervision of a neutral droid judge!

The result was *Star Wars on Trial: Science Fiction and Fantasy Writers Debate the Most Popular Science Fiction Films of All Time.* As "Prosecutor," I called a dozen eminent writers and philosophers as witnesses. One of George Lucas' *Star Wars* novelizers, Matthew Woodring Stover, was terrific as "Defense Attorney," cross-examining my witnesses and calling rebuttal testifiers. Between chapters we shouted objections amid much suspender-snapping, the droid judge fining Matt and me for stupid human behavior. It's way-fun, even though serious matters were afoot.

Bear in mind that this was written after George Lucas finished his prequels, like *The Phantom Menace,* but before Disney commenced its more coherent and wholesome—if stunningly unimaginative—final trilogy.

The Prosecution Lays Down Its Case!

Nobody, on either side of the coming argument, contends that the fate of civilization will hang upon a literary analysis of the epical and epochal *Star Wars* series—which deserves respect at many levels, if only for the marvelous artists it employed and the raw pleasure that it's given hundreds of millions.

In fact, let me say I never interfere when my children demand the newest *Star Wars* merchandise. A Lego Death Star or Darth Vader mask? Another Obi-Wan Happy Meal? I only grit my teeth a little over the cash flow going to an empire that (in my opinion) could have been a lot more meaningful, a lot more curious or helpful in making a better world. Certainly, my protective instincts don't get all fired up, eager to shield vulnerable young minds from inimical memes!

Why not? Because what youngsters—and millions of others—mostly see in these movies are simple surfaces. The top layer of lavish, goofy, earnestly preachy and even somewhat noble-minded fun. Outnumbered heroes bravely taking on the odds. Going with your feelings, tossing logic aside and blasting away! It is the innocent spirit of the first movie (*A New Hope*) that seems to have spread and captured millions of hearts, young and old.

If you ask them about the "moral messages" of *Star Wars*, most people tend to recall that—

Mean people suck.
It's good to be brave.
Mean people become yucky-looking.
Defend your friends.
Watch out for mean people playing tricks and telling lies.
Don't let nasty old mean guys goad you into losing your temper.

Hmmm. Well, there may be some problems even at this level. In fact, entirely on their own, my kids mused skeptically at the details (e.g., "If something happens to my looks, will I turn into a bad person?"). Still, for the most part, children can take all this in without much harm to their values, or souls. Anyway, who am I to spoil their fun, by yattering on about deeper meaning and symbolism?

But that's the point. I have no intention of spoiling *their* fun at all.

Yours, on the other hand … well, you already paid for this book. So don't pretend you're not interested. After all, there are many levels other than the superficial, and George Lucas would be the first to say so! Following the teachings of mythology maven Joseph Campbell, Lucas claims that storytelling is a central ritual that both describes and helps to shape the way that people picture themselves in relation to society. So, shouldn't we take him at his word?

Many of the trends we see in *Star Wars* have manifested elsewhere in a changing society. Take the rise of feudal and magical fantasy, once considered an offshoot of science fiction, but now pushing its hi-tech cousin off the bookstore shelves and Amazon lists. Even within sci-fi, stories seem increasingly to feature "chosen ones" or demigod-like heroes, and are often set in structured, aristocratic cultures. (See Chapter 2.)

Destroying Our Self-Confidence

How often do you see tales that portray society functioning, perhaps helping the protagonist, or suggesting solutions that arise from collaborative effort? Maybe even offering hope that hard work and goodwill might bring better days? Do cops ever come, when called? Are the hero's neighbors ever anything other than hapless sheep? Does scientific advancement ever come to the rescue, instead of causing more problems and provoking lectures about how "mankind shouldn't meddle"? Do ambitious undertakings or team efforts ever hold a candle to the boldness of the single, archetype hero?

Are we being taught, gradually but inexorably, to turn away from the whole modernist agenda? Or that there was once a good idea—to replace arbitrary leader-worship with democratic institutions that we can all hope to share? What about the notion that any of us regular people—not just mutant chosen ones—can be the hero, if we're ever called upon?

Hey, stories like that can be told. Take the films of director Steven Spielberg. From *Saving Private Ryan* to *Schindler's List* to *Close Encounters of the Third Kind*, these are often stirring stories about people who are only a bit above average, but who achieve great things. Sometimes these characters are deeply flawed. They slip up, or get angry, or even do bad things. Only then, they do the unexpected. They stand up. Taking responsibility for their mistakes, they set things right. And sometimes civilization even helps them a bit. All told, Spielberg's central ongoing theme seems to be unswerving gratitude to a society that—in all honesty—has been pretty good to him.

So how did the diametrically opposite message wind up pervading the biggest, most lavish, most expensive and most-watched series of modern times: the *Star Wars* epic?

Some of the critical "prosecution witnesses" in *Star Wars on Trial* will talk about matters like these—plumbing deeper meanings and messages. Others poke at ways that plot, story and character consistency gradually fell apart (alas) as the series declined into grumpy middle age, then entered crotchety senescence. And of course, Matt Stover's witnesses for the defense will answer back, fiercely!

This should be loads of fun. So let's begin.

It Starts with the Littlest Things…

My own disenchantment began early in my first viewing of *Return of the Jedi*.

Recall how Luke Skywalker shows up at the palace of Jabba the Hutt, calling himself a Jedi Knight? Thrilling! He then offers a bag of gold in exchange for the life of his carbonite-frozen friend, Han Solo. It was a great moment. Filled with high hopes after *The Empire Strikes Back*, I leaned forward in confident expectation that great things would follow, combining vividly creative action and effects with solid plotting, plus a little decent thoughtfulness for those grown-up parts of the brain. (Isn't that what happens in the best art? You get something for the adult and something for the child. There is no need to completely eliminate one, in order to serve the other.)

All right, anticipation was running high, as Luke approached Jabba's fancy desert hut. My own instant theory? Frankly, I expected Luke's offer to be backed up with a threat!

"As you can see, Jabba, from the circle of X-wing fighters surrounding your residence, I am also a high commander of the second most powerful military force in the galaxy. So if you don't comply…"

I mean … duh? Isn't that what anybody would try first, if they were in Luke's shoes?

Oh, sure, that's no fun, *so it can't work*! But this logical plan is an obvious opening move. It doesn't make for great adventure, thrills, spills and escapades, so let it *fail*. Have the Empire arrive and chase away all the rebel ships, leaving Luke in the lurch. Jabba grabs Luke and the fun can begin! Ninety extra seconds, so that the next half hour might make sense.

Look, I'm not saying it had to be that way. I only pose that scenario as an example of how easy it would be to get every part of the opening scene that is already there, with hover-yachts and spider trap creature tentacles— the whole schmeer—while still giving a passing nod to common sense. All the leaping and slashing and narrow escapes that we see in *Return of the Jedi*'s first act could have been the *backup plan*. Because only complete bozos would walk into an obvious trap—with escape utterly dependent upon all of the bad guys being lousy shots! At least not without having a better scheme to start with.

6. J'accuse *George Lucas* ... or Zola Meets Yoda

Okay, I admit that's kind of picky. But the infuriating aspect is how little attention to detail it would have taken, to continue the kind of plot consistency and plausibility we saw in the brilliant Leigh Brackett–Lawrence Kasden script for *The Empire Strikes Back*. A few words, inserted here and there. Then, every subsequent vivid laser bolt and explosion might proceed as planned. Would that have been too much to ask?

A small hole, true. But through it, more nagging thoughts began to fly. Faster than a little ship can dive inside a big ship, shoot the reactor and then run away just ahead of the blast wave. (Yes, that happens *five times*, across this epic franchise. I mean ... really?)

The Allegory of the Ship

Which leads us to the first of what will be many comparisons between *Star Wars* and its chief competitor for the hearts of science fiction fandom, *Star Trek*. A comparison that illuminates two very different views of fiction, civilization and the meaning of a hero.

Consider the choice of which kinds of *ship* are featured in each series. Ponder and contrast the Air Force metaphor vs. one that hearkens up images of the Navy!

In *Star Wars*, the ships that matter are little fighter planes. Series creator George Lucas made liberal use of filmed dogfight footage from both World Wars, in some cases borrowing maneuvers like banking slipstream turns, down to the last detail. The heroic image in this case is the solitary pilot, perhaps assisted by his loyal gunner—or Wookie or droid—companion. It is the modern version of knight and squire. Symbols as old as Achilles.

In contrast, the Federation starship in *Trek* is vastly bigger, more complex, a veritable city cruising through space. Its captain hero is not only a warrior-knight, but also part scientist and part diplomat, a plenipotentiary representative of his civilization and father figure to his crew ... any one of whom may suddenly become an essential character. While the captain's brilliance and courage are always key elements, so are the skill and pluck of several crew members. People who are much closer to average, like you or me, yet essential helpers, nonetheless. And possibly even—when it is their turn—heroes themselves.

The ship, *Star Trek*'s *Enterprise,* stands for something, every time we look at it. This traveling city *is* civilization. The Federation's culture and laws, industry and consensus values—like the Prime Directive—are all carried in this condensed vessel, along with the dramatic diversity of its crew. Moreover, all those things are *topics* and even plot drivers. In every adventure, the civilization of the United Federation of Planets is tested through its proxy, the hero-ship. And when the *Enterprise* passes, often with flying colors, so too, by implication, does civilization.

Compare this to the role of the Old Republic, in the Lucasian universe. A hapless, hopeless, clueless mélange of bickering futility whose political tiffs are as petty as they are incomprehensible. The Republic never perceives, never creates or solves anything. Never even *does* anything. Not once do we see any of its institutions actually function. How can they? The Republic, decent institutions, quadrillions of varied people from 10,000 races … these cannot be heroes, or even helpers.

There is no room, aboard an X-Wing fighter, for civilization to ride along.

Only for a knight and squire.

All right, you may call this making too much of yet another superficial thing. It can certainly be argued that ship size doesn't really matter. On the other hand, recall how eager Yoda was, in *Attack of the Clones*, to "Shoot the Federation Starship!" Interesting choice of words, there. Could it be that the director agrees with me? In sci-fi, ships carry powerful symbolism. They convey contrary ways of viewing heroes, and their relationship to common women and men.

Anyway, I couldn't help it. This difference in the metaphor of the ship continued to nag at me as, with each newly released episode, every problem with the *Star Wars* universe just seemed to grow and compound. Superficial things piled up, and deliberate artistic choices bubbled to the foreground, like Darth Vader's Nazi-style helmet and use of the term "storm troopers." Or the need to be a genetic "midichlorian" mutant, in order to use the Force. Or take the difference in educational styles, between the university-like Starfleet Academy and that imperious, overbearing, secretive guru, Yoda. Two very different—and iconic—approaches to acquiring and passing on skill. To acquiring power. And then using it.

As the years—and prequels—passed, a list of growing discomforts grew longer and longer….

So let's cut to the chase.

Enough introduction. Get to the indictment! After watching the whole megillah of six long films, it's time to ask the central question. Just what bill of goods are we being sold, between the frames? In the *Star Wars* universe:

- True leaders are born. It's genetic. The right to rule is inherited.
- Elites have an inherent right to arbitrary rule; common citizens

6. J'accuse *George Lucas* ... or Zola Meets Yoda

needn't be consulted. They may only choose which born-to-rule elite to follow.
- Any amount of sin can be forgiven if you repent ... and if you are important enough.
- "Good" elites should act on their subjective whims, without evidence, argument or accountability. Secrecy and lies are always a good option. They never need to be explained.
- The chief feature distinguishing "good" from "evil" is how pretty the characters look.
- In order to be a skilled and good and worthy warrior, you must cut yourself off from the very attachments that make a decent co-worker, lover, spouse, parent and citizen.
- Justified human emotions can turn a good person evil, like flicking a switch.

I plan to focus primarily on the accusations made above, while later witnesses in this "trial" will focus on other accusations, that:

- The politics of *Star Wars* is transparently elitist and anti-democratic.
- While claiming mythic significance, *Star Wars* portrays no admirable religious or ethical beliefs. In fact, *Star Wars'* religious or ethical trappings are driven by the sudden veers and impulses of plot, not any higher ethical or religious thinking.
- *Star Wars* led the way into an era when science fiction filmmaking was reduced to poorly written special effects extravaganzas.
- *Star Wars* dumbed down perception of science fiction in the popular imagination.
- *Star Wars* pretends to be science fiction, but is really feudal fantasy.
- There are troubling ways, in *Star Wars*, that women and minorities are portrayed.
- The *Star Wars* universe is rife with plot holes and logical flaws that were never necessary, even in a light adventure story. In an epic that took decades and billions of dollars to create, while portraying itself as important storytelling, there is simply no excuse.

I won't deal with all of these accusations here, but will leave them to the Witnesses, so see *Star Wars on Trial*, wherein pairs of prosecution witnesses and skilled defenders tussle over each of them. But for now, I must say the thing that hurts the most. Tragically, there are a few small measures—missed opportunities—that could have eased most of these problems! Minor tweaks that might have helped to the whole thing to make a lot more sense.

Now we plunge into the more crucial issues: artistic, ethical and mythological. Those are what made my original *Salon* magazine article, "The Dark Side: *Star Wars*, Mythology and Ingratitude," so controversial. Especially my argument that Lucas' grand mythology is not a tale that helps a modern, confident and enlightenment civilization. It does not reflect our upstart "rebel" values, or provide recompense for all the kindness and good fortune that civilization has heaped upon him.

Indeed, we are very lucky that most people aren't paying attention, playing with the light sabers but ignoring the "morality" parts. Because, if citizens actually took their moral cues from *Star Wars*, we would be in very deep trouble.

The Campbellian Tradition

Let's step back and talk about storytelling. Lucas claims his epic nestles in a standard mythic tradition as old as written human language. If *Star Wars* stands indicted, so will be a lot of other tales, from those of Gilgamesh to Lancelot.

In *Star Wars: The Magic of Myth*, author Mary Henderson elaborates how much inspiration Lucas took from classical mythology. Drawing heavily on the works of Mircea Eliade and Joseph Campbell, she parallels Luke Skywalker's adventure with the classical hero's journey, equating the swamps of Dagoba with the sacred grove, the Ewoks with the archetypal helpful animals populating an enchanted forest, and so on. It's all a deeply felt homage to some of our most ancient archetypes.[1]

We start out with a bone of contention. I have my own quirky complaints[2] that start from all this fawning over "ancient archetypes." I never cared for the whole Nietzschean *Übermensch* thing: the notion—pervading so many myths and legends—that a good yarn has to be about demigods who are bigger, badder and better than normal folk by orders of magnitude. It's an ancient storytelling tradition that I came to notice in the works of A.E. van Vogt, E.E. Smith, L. Ron Hubbard and wherever you witness slan-like super-beings deciding the fate of billions without ever pausing to consider *their* wishes. Orson Scott Card, who criticized *Star Wars* for many of the same reasons that I do, nevertheless returns relentlessly to tales of demigods … though Card's are more complex than most. Oh, but is it *the* way stories ought to be?

Campbell was made famous by a series of shows on PBS, in which journalist Bill Moyers interviewed him about legends spanning many

6. J'accuse *George Lucas* ... or Zola Meets Yoda

cultures. In *The Hero with a Thousand Faces*, Campbell combined the earlier insights of many scholars, pointing out how a particular, rhythmic storytelling technique was used in ancient and pre-modern cultures, depicting protagonists and antagonists with common motives, character traits and plot twists that seem to transcend boundaries of language and culture. In these classic tales, a hero is beckoned to take on a quest. He begins reluctant, though signs foretell greatness. He receives dire warnings and then sage wisdom from a mentor, acquires quirky but faithful companions, faces a series of steepening crises, suffers as he explores the pit of his own fears, and finally emerges triumphant, bringing some boon-talisman-victory home to his admiring tribe-people-nation.

Distilling the central message in his books and public statements, Campbell prescribed that all myths ought to be about figures like Achilles, Hercules, Orpheus or Genji—larger than life, following a precise plot outline that is as old as it is rigid and changeless.

Campbell's admirers use "changeless." The word "rigid" is mine. Still, I'll be the first to admit it's a superb formula—one that I've used at times in my own stories and novels. (Though always poking at it, trying variations, or even outright reversals.) Moreover, by offering valuable insights into this revered storytelling tradition, Campbell did indeed shed light on common spiritual traits that seem to be shared by all human beings.

Alas, he only highlighted positive traits, ignoring the darker side—such as how this standard fable-template was co-opted by kings, priests and tyrants, extolling the importance of elites who tower over common women and men. King Achilles, slaughtering hundreds of common foot-soldiers, while the river weeps. King Odysseus crossing the dire straits while his men all perish. King Arthur ruling benevolently—but with fierce enforcement by mystically anointed knights. King This and brave Prince That…

Above all, while an occasional dark lord or wicked giant gets toppled, hardly any of these heroes ever pauses to question the very setup that made the quest necessary in the first place. The feudal order. Capricious Fates. Cryptic elves. The gods themselves. I mean, seriously: Can you look across millennia of recorded history and call it good that society remained changeless, for the vast majority of that time?

Or the implication that we must always adhere to variations on a single theme, the same prescribed plot outline, over and over again. Those who praise Campbell seem to perceive this uniformity as cause for rejoicing—but it isn't. Playing a large part in the tragic miring of our spirit, these demigod-royalty myths helped reinforce sameness and changelessness for millennia, transfixing people in nearly every culture, from Babylon to modern times. Another example: In Aristotle's *Poetics*, he prescribed extremely rigid plot structures that required absolute acceptance of unalterable fate and the will of the gods.

Campbell claims that this pattern represents our deepest shared zeitgeist, ingrained in our very souls. But might there be another reason it kept recurring? Picture yourself as Homer, or some other ancient bard. Where do you want to recite? In some peasant hovel, where you'll be fed gruel and nobody will remember? Or in the chief's lodge, the Sacred Temple, perhaps even the High King's hall, where there's beer and meat, where the powerful may bestow favors, where acolytes will memorize your poesy ... and all you have to do is flatter a little? Spin tales about knights and *übermensch* super-guys. Poets and bards had the same incentive, everywhere, in every era. By keeping to the program—praising princes—you could stay on the gravy train. For life.

All right, that explanation is a bit cynical. But shouldn't it be mentioned, at least as an alternative? But to romantics, that endlessly repeated mythic structure is the only human way to tell a story.

Right. Chain-up storytelling. Mortify it in rigid stone. And call that a good thing.

Face it. The fix has been in, for thousands of years.

Stephen Potts of the University of California, San Diego (UCSD) Literature Department, has an interesting take on why so many ancient myths have traits in common:

> None of us ever completely shakes loose the scars of adolescent solipsism—our belief that we are special but misunderstood, that we stand aloof from authority figures and peers alike, that we may even have some mysterious origin or unique destiny. Adolescence is the age of identity crisis and formation, of self-doubt and self-importance—all reflected in the hero myths we inherit from our barbaric past. Campbell's "monomyth" is itself loaded with Freudian and Jungian assumptions regarding sexual identity, separation from and reconciliation with the parent, connection with a "goddess" or anima figure that naturally assumes the hero is male and in need of sexual completion. It is no surprise, therefore, that *Star Wars* and similar vessels provide adolescent wish fulfillment (as do comic superheroes). But while we can all enjoy swinging with Spider-Man or kicking ass with the Bat, God help us when we embrace these primitive paradigms as models for real life.

I can think of two recent western cultures, offhand, that bought fully and unreservedly into Campbell-style myths, using those fables to forge a unified sense of purpose. In the antebellum American South, as caustically described later by Mark Twain, the immensely popular and influential novels of Sir Walter Scott, filled with knights errant and questing princes, served the same purpose that Wagner operas and Aryan tales did in pre–World War II Germany, helping to consolidate righteous belief in a clearly defined destiny and purpose. Both the Confederacy and the Nazis emphasized romantic adolescent drama and the

6. J'accuse *George Lucas* ... or Zola Meets Yoda   61

glory of a cause, to almost complete exclusion of any thought about long-term consequences. Both also had a predilection for archaic weaponry, like swords and daggers (just like the Jedi), as well as a penchant for pageantry, grandiloquence and authority-as-birthright. And dissent was utterly crushed.

Another dark trait of romanticism, tragically illustrated by both of those cultures, is the willingness (seen in countless Campbellian myths) to reclassify whole swathes of humanity as subpar, not even deserving the minimal rights granted to honorable enemies. Whether they are orcs or soldier-robots or clones (or black slaves or Jews), there is no need to bother the conscience when they are disposed of. No need to answer to their mothers or families. (In fact, conveniently, orcs, robots and clones have no mothers!)

Is it, then, any mystery why so few of the traditional romantic myths cited by Campbell focus upon women heroes? Or on people achieving what should be the highest human goals? Successfully raising a family. Building a community. Negotiating peace. Engaging in civilization.

Alas, these are not the tasks or concerns of bold, young, unmarried males. Few Campbellian–style heroes other than great Odysseus ever mention or yearn for them.

Nevertheless, these are the proper focus of would-be leaders. The proper study of grown-up human beings.

"One thing you never see with the Jedi Knights is any kind of critical glance at their merits as peacetime political leaders," commented critic Curt Jensen. He continued:

> Being able to levitate an X-Wing doesn't make you a wise leader. Quite the contrary actually. It would tend toward the default attitude that might makes right. Not only are the Jedi wholly unsuited to the demands of domestic politics, they seem unaware of their limits and keep insisting on meddling, while withholding information from elected leaders, eventually leading society down the road to disaster. Yet, according to the strange logic of George Lucas, these people are still automatically qualified for leadership, with the inherent right to make vital decisions in secret, affecting the well-being of billions.

Was All This Intentional?

Others will argue that *Star Wars* was never meant for grown-ups! But shouldn't the grown-ups within Lucas' universe be paying a *little* heed to such matters, if only in background? If only to point Luke, Han, Leia and Anakin toward the eventual, proper goal of heroes? The role Odysseus took up, when his adventure ended—that of ruling wisely? (Note, 2018: this failure by Luke Skywalker—imitating exactly [down to the slightest detail] the mistakes of Yoda and Obi-Wan—propels the entire plot of the third [Disney] trilogy.)

Ironically, this notion wasn't alien to Lucas! Few remember his short-lived but brilliant television series *The Young Indiana Jones Chronicles* (1992). It was no great commercial success. But to aficionados, it seemed Lucas' most sincere personal statement, a brave attempt to mix adolescent excitement with real thoughtfulness and content, expressing the same theme we often see from Spielberg: one of gratitude. In 22 episodes, the younger Jones (played by Sean Patrick Flanery) encountered some of the greatest minds of the early 20th century, not just as Campbellian journey-mentors or spirit guides. As archetypes of adult ambition and achievement, they'd show Indy some key ingredient of a rambunctiously eager and hopeful civilization—from jazz musicians to saintly jungle doctors, from inventors to master spies, from mothers to fathers. Yes, amid all the dashing, heroic deeds, Indy (and the viewer) confront war, oppression and civilization's "dark side." But throughout, the young hero never lost faith in the power of reason, discovery and science.

Picture Huckleberry Finn, on a raft escapade with Ben Franklin, Albert Schweitzer and Marie Curie.

Alas, *The Young Indiana Jones Chronicles* sometimes got lectury and lost pace. It attracted no loyal audience, provoking one to wonder: Did Lucas learn a lesson—the wrong lesson—never again to even try blending the adult and the child, offering something to both?

No, there are plenty of counter-examples, some even provided by Lucas, to the dismal notion of a single, tedious storytelling pattern, even if it pervaded many cultures past. *Because* it pervaded so many failed, oppressive societies of our bloody, awful past. Which is why real science fiction came as such a radical departure. A new kind of storytelling, it often rebels against the archetypes that Aristotle and the Campbellians venerate. Authors like John Brunner, Alice Sheldon, Cordwainer Smith, Greg Bear, Nancy Kress, Frederik Pohl and Philip K. Dick viewed any prescriptive storytelling formula as a direct challenge—a dare to try something different, for a change.

Both Ends Against the Middle

Let's veer aside, since Lucas has said his tale shares more with comics than novel-length SF. You'd think that science fiction would be natural for comics. Some of our best living graphic artists have become adept, using this static, two-dimensional medium to convey startlingly vivid and evocative effects in sequential panels—the kind of imagery that caters naturally to futuristic or exotic locales. Also, both genres are unafraid to posit the possibility of garish transformation and change.

Still, then, why do graphic novels and comics focus so thoroughly on superheroes, hardly ever telling the kinds of vivid space or future-oriented adventures penned by Jules Verne, H.G. Wells, Vernor Vinge, L. Sprague de Camp, Octavia Butler, Poul Anderson, Lois Bujold, Robert Heinlein and so on?

Alas, all complaints about minimizing the importance of normal people—of civilization—apply as much to comics as to *Star Wars*. These marvelous illustrated tales treat superheroes with reverent awe ... that is, until recently. Changes appear to be afoot! While literary SF has been turning evermore toward the sensibilities of fantasy, many of the best comic book and graphic novel writers have lately been writing almost as if they were ... well ... science fiction authors!

What's the crucial distinction?

Earlier, we envisioned how a true science fiction author might write about Superman, with Earthling scientists asking the handsome Man of Steel for blood samples, and then—maybe—bottling the trick for everyone. What many of the new wave writers are starting to understand is that things change, and change can be fascinating. And science fiction is the literature of change.

Moreover, our children might outgrow us! They may become better, or learn from our mistakes and not repeat them. And if they don't learn? That could be a riveting tragedy, far exceeding Aristotle's cramped, myopic definition.

Tales such as *On the Beach*, *Soylent Green* and *1984* plumbed frightening depths. *Brave New World*, "The Screwfly Solution" *and Fahrenheit* 451 posed worrying questions. In contrast, *Oedipus Rex* is about as interesting as watching a hooked fish thrash futilely at the end of a line. A modern person may weep at the right moments, as the playwright intended. Only then, you just want to put the poor doomed King of Thebes out of his misery— and find a way to punish his tormentors.

This truly is a different point of view, in direct opposition to older, elitist creeds that preached passivity and awe in nearly every culture. Where asking too many questions was punishable hubris. Where a hero's job was to oppose one set-piece villain—in order to defend the aristocratic rights of another.

Imagine Achilles refusing to accept his ordained destiny, taking up his sword and hunting down the Fates, demanding that they give him both a long life *and* a glorious one! Picture Odysseus telling Agamemnon and Poseidon to go chase themselves, then heading off to join Daedalus in a garage start-up company, mass producing both wheeled and winged horses, so mortals could swoop about the land and air, like gods—the way common folk do nowadays, so marvelously unaware of the miracle.

Even if their start-up fails, and jealous Olympians crush Odysseus/DaedalusCorp, what a tale it would be!

Can this attitude work in stories? Consider those lowbrow but way-fun television series, *Hercules*, *Buffy* and *Xena*. Though they wore all the trappings of fantasy—swords and magical spells—each episode told a morality tale that was fiercely pro-democracy, egalitarian, proudly hubristic and rambunctiously anti-aristocratic.

In contrast, *Star Wars*, for all of its laser furniture, appears to defend every mythological aspect of feudalism. No wonder Lucas publicly, openly yearned for the pomp of mighty kings over the drab accountability of republics. Many share his belief that things might be a whole lot more vivid without all the endless, dreary argument and negotiating that make up such a large part of modern life. Even millions of voters have taken to supporting authoritarians, who seek power free of accountability. Aristocrats who say "trust me."

The old yearning is still strong.

For someone to take command. A demigod. A leader.

The Shifty Notion of Rebellion

Ahhh, but the *Star Wars* series didn't begin obsessed with leaders. It started as a story about rebels, bravely taking on an Empire!

I cannot repeat enough times that I had no particular trouble with the original *Star Wars* movie—since relabeled *A New Hope*. Lightweight and a bit silly, it nevertheless oozed charm, adventure and good-hearted egalitarian fun. The villain, with a name like "invader," wore a Nazi-style helmet, commanded "storm troopers" and torture-interrogated princesses. He throttled brave rebel captains with his bare hands and helped to blow up planets. Clearly this film played into the great American mythos (in fact, the greatest propaganda campaign of all time): suspicion of authority.

I'll admit, where this strange suspicion-of-authority propaganda campaign comes from, I don't know. Yet its effects are inarguably spectacular, underlying the accomplishments of modern-enlightenment civilization. Half our prodigious creativity may arise from a restless need to be different, proving a sense of individuality that we absorbed from an early age.

So yes, *A New Hope* had such resonance because it was about rebels! The Empire's bad, so fight it! Indeed, this spirit continued in *The Empire Strikes Back*. Even though we met Yoda—an authority figure to whom our hero had to bow—neither the Jedi master nor the Force were yet the cloying, oppressive things they would later become. According to critic Stefan Jones, "In the first film, the Force was a kind of martial-art, zen-archery kind of thing. Rather egalitarian: Obi-Wan even offers to teach scoffer Han Solo the ropes, implying that anybody can do it. Goofy comic-book mysticism, but kind of charming and innocent, in a Hong Kong kung-fu movie sort of way."

Moreover, nostalgia for the Old Republic wasn't yet tainted with the utter contempt for democracy that would pervade Episodes I through III.

Even though Yoda starts throwing his diminutive weight around, in *The Empire Strikes Back*, the lessons are still pretty benign. *Stay calm and focused.* Um, sure, sounds good. My kids learn the same thing, at their karate studio. Anyway, Luke even rebels against that authority figure! Yoda warns: "If you go and help your friends, lost everything will be!"

But Luke goes anyway … and "lost," everything is not! (Whereupon, faced with awkward questions, Yoda performs a handy escape trick. The old jedi "death" fadeaway. And poor, sweet, dim Luke falls for it!)

Alas, as the *Übermensch Effect* took over—starting in *Return of the Jedi* and worsening with every film that followed—the Force grew evermore elitist. You had to be born with it! No, not just born with it, you had to be a *mutant*. No, make that a foreordained-by-destiny, preselected-long-ago messiah. A bona fide Chosen One. A demigod.

In a progressive universe, Yoda & Co. would set up Jedi-arts studios in every mini-mall on Coruscant—the way karate dojos saturate suburban America—giving millions of kids exposure to a little discipline and fun, plus a chance to better themselves through hard work. Maybe outperform what cynical grown-ups expected of them. But Yoda thinks he can diagnose at age nine who's got it, who hasn't. Who is destined to fail before they try.

Only demigods need apply … and only those demigods Yoda likes.

But more about the nasty green oven mitt, anon.

Again, is this just spoilsport grumbling? Why look for deep lessons in harmless escapist entertainment? Just look across history: the moral health of a civilization can be traced in its popular culture. Moreover, the moral messages in *Star Wars* aren't just window dressing; speeches and lectures drench every film. They take up the slack time that could have been spent on decent plotting.

They represent an agenda.

More Comparisons

Let's go back to comparing Lucas' space-adventure epic to its chief competitor, *Star Trek*. We've already seen how one saga has an Air Force motif (tiny fighters) while the other appears naval; the big ship is heroic and cooperative effort is depicted as honorable. Indeed, *Star Trek* sees technology as useful and essentially friendly, if at times also dangerous. Education is a great emancipator of the humble (e.g., Starfleet Academy). Futuristic institutions are basically good-natured (the Federation), though of course one must fight outbreaks of incompetence, secrecy and corruption. Professionalism is respected, lesser characters make a difference and henchmen often become brave whistle-blowers, as they do in America today.

In *Star Trek*, when authorities are defied, it is to overcome their mistakes or expose particular villains, not to portray all governments as inherently hopeless. Good cops sometimes come when you call for help. Ironically, this image fosters useful criticism of authority, because it suggests that any of us can gain access to our flawed institutions—if we are determined enough—and perhaps even fix them with fierce tools of citizenship.

Above all, whenever you encounter Homo superior in *Star Trek*— some hyper-evolved, better-than-human fellow with powers beyond our mortal ken—the demigod is subjected to scrutiny and skeptical worry. Such mutant über-types are given a chance to prove they mean no harm. But when they throw their weight around, normal folk rise up and look them in the eye. This happens so often in *Trek*—as well as shows like *Stargate* and *Babylon 5*—that it has become a true sci-fi tradition.

By contrast, the choices in *Star Wars* are stark and limited. As in Tolkien's *Lord of the Rings*, you can join either the Dark Lord or the Chosen Prince (with his pointy-eared elf advisors). Ultimately, *Star Wars'* oppressed "rebels" have no recourse in law or markets or science or democracy. They can only pick sides in a civil war between two wings of the same genetically superior royal family.

(The same royal family? Oh, but it's right there, in front of you! The implication that bubbles out of a quirky Lucasian obsession, with heaping coincidence upon coincidence. The emperor comes from the same narrow aristocracy—on Planet Naboo—as Luke's mother. Probably, they're cousins. As for Anakin's mother, who's to say she didn't come from the same place?; Tatooine lies along the direct star-path from Naboo to Coruscant. A single family of midichlorian mutants, engaged in a family spat, and galaxy-wide hell ensues. Is it any wonder that *Star Trek* treats demigod mutants with skepticism, not reflex worship?)

Yes, *Star Trek* had its own problems and faults. The television episodes often devolved into soap operas. Many of the movies were badly written. *Trek* at times seemed preachy, or turgidly politically correct, especially in its post–Kirk incarnations. (For example, every species has to mate with every other one, interbreeding with almost compulsive abandon. The only male heroes who are allowed any testosterone—in *The Next Generation*—are

Klingons, because cultural diversity outweighs sexual correctness. In other words, it's okay for them to be macho 'cause it is "their way.")

Nevertheless, *Trek* tried to grapple with genuine issues, giving complex voices even to its villains and asking hard questions about pitfalls we may face while groping for tomorrow. Anyway, when it comes to portraying human destiny, where would *you* rather live, assuming you'll be a normal citizen and no demigod? In Roddenberry's Federation? Or Lucas' Empire?

The Feudal Reflex

In one infamous interview, Lucas told the *New York Times*, "That's sort of why I say a benevolent despot is the ideal ruler. He can actually get things done. The idea that power corrupts is very true and it's a big human who can get past that."[3]

Any volunteers to be that "big human"?

He adds that we are a sad culture, bereft of the confidence or inspiration that strong leaders can provide.

Yet, aren't we the very same culture that produced George Lucas and gave him so many opportunities? One that raised all those brilliant artists for him to hire—boldly creative folks who pour both individual inspiration and cooperative skill into his films? A culture that defies the old homogenizing impulse by worshipping eccentricity, with unprecedented hunger for the different, new or strange? In what way can such a civilization be said to lack confidence? And just how would a king or despot help?

In historical fact, all of history's despots, combined, never managed to "get things done" as well as this rambunctious, self-critical civilization of free and sovereign citizens, who finally broke free of a ruling class and began thinking for themselves. Democracy can seem frustrating and messy at times, but it delivers.

So why do few filmmakers—other than Steven Spielberg—own up to that basic fact?

The Apotheosis of Darth Vader

Having said all that, let me again acknowledge that *Star Wars* harks to an old and very deeply human archetype. Those who listened to Homer recite *The Iliad* by a campfire knew great drama. Achilles could slay a thousand with the sweep of a hand—as Darth Vader helps Grand Mof Tarkin murder billions with the press of a button—but none of those casualties matters next to the personal saga of a great one. The slaughtered victims are mere minions, after all. Extras, without families or hopes to worry about shattering. Spear-carriers. Only the demigod's personal drama is important.

Thus, few protest the apotheosis of Darth Vader—*née* Anakin Skywalker—in *Return of the Jedi*. With a single, sudden act—slaying his master at the cost of his own life—he gives in to a "fatal attachment" and saves his own son … and thus achieves redemption. Entry into Jedi Heaven.

To put it in perspective, let's imagine that the United States and its allies managed to capture Adolf Hitler at the end of the Second World War, putting him on trial for war crimes. The prosecution spends months listing all the horrors done at his behest. Then it is the turn of Hitler's defense attorney, who rises and utters just one sentence: "But, your honors…. Adolf did save the life of his own son!"

Gasp! The prosecutors blanch. "We didn't know that! Of course all charges should be dismissed at once!" The allies then throw a big parade for Hitler, down the avenues of Nuremberg.

This may sound silly, but isn't that the lesson taught by *Return of the Jedi*?

Along with the bizarre notion that getting angry at evil will suddenly cause you to switch sides and join that evil. Say what?

Then it only gets worse.

How many of us have argued late at night over the philosophical conundrum "Would you go back in time and kill Hitler as a boy, if given a chance?" It's a genuine moral puzzler, with many possible ethical answers. Still, most people, however they ultimately respond, would admit being at least tempted to say yes, if only to save millions of Hitler's victims.

Yet in *The Phantom Menace*, Lucas asks us to gush with warm feelings toward a cute blond little boy who will later grow up to help murder the population of Earth many times over. Hey, while we're at it, why not bring out the Hitler family album, so we may swoon over pictures of adorable little Adolf and marvel over his childhood exploits! He, too, was innocent until he turned to the "dark side," so by all means let us adore him.

To his credit, Lucas does not try to excuse this macabre joke by citing the lamest excuse of all: "It's only a movie." Rather, he sticks to his guns, holding up his saga as an agonized Greek tragedy worthy of Oedipus. An epic tale of a fallen hero, trapped by hubris and fate.

Alas, if that were true, wouldn't *Star Wars* by now have given us a better-than-caricature view of the Dark Side? Could you sum it up? Don't swallow it. The apotheosis of a mass murderer is exactly what it seems. And we should find it chilling.

Only then it gets worse. Much worse. For you see, there is another Lucasian character that makes the adoration of young Darth seem positively benign.

It's Yoda. One of the most horrid creatures ever to snarl at us from the silver screen.

That Vicious Little Oven Mitt

Remember the final scene in *Return of the Jedi*, when Luke gazes into a fire to see Obi-Wan, Yoda and Vader, smiling in the flames? I found myself hoping it was Jedi Hell, for the amount of pain those three unleashed on their galaxy, and for all the damned lies they told.

Okay, now Brin has gone completely around the bend. What, in all the galaxy, could he have against little Yoda?

Well, for starters, how about this simple challenge:

Can you name a single scene in which Yoda is actually forthcoming, informative or generously helpful? Or indeed, when he is ever unambiguously *wise*?

Cut through all the *faux* eastern mystic-guru malarkey—which only serves as an excuse for being cryptic and evasive and endlessly bullying. Is he ever actually right? This supposedly all-wise figure rejects young Anakin, because he senses "too much fear," despite the fact that we spent most of *The Phantom Menace* marveling over a nine-year-old's dauntless courage.

He foresees danger, if the boy isn't trained properly ... then refuses to train him.

When Master Mace wants to inform the Republic that bad conspiracies are afoot, Yoda insists on secrecy, which only worsens the calamity. Just as his lies to Luke almost ruin everything much later. Lies that he conveniently gets out of explaining, by pulling the old "fade" trick. (Well, poor Luke was always kind of a weak bulb.)

Then there's all that smarmy lecturing—a withered old prune telling a virile young man that he shouldn't give in to the human need for "attachments." Forcing Anakin to fulfill those basic human needs in secret.

Um ... all right. One can understand demanding that a young adept avoid undue distraction, while focusing hard on his training. But to cut off all thought of loved ones, even when they are suffering? Where is the "wisdom" in that?

Leaving Mom in the Lurch

Especially when it came to the tragic situation of Anakin's mother. Tell me, which approach is more likely to help the boy focus? Leave Mom to endure slavery on far-off Tatooine? Or maybe dip into petty cash to buy her freedom and get her a nice little house on Naboo, in gratitude for the way Anakin saved Padmé Amidala and all her people? Would it be too much "attachment" to get a nice card, once a year, showing her happy in her garden? Call it insurance, to keep such a powerful apprentice from getting ... well ... angry.

Point by individual point, this can be called nitpicking. But the pattern adds up, relentlessly, to a clear picture of an imperious little guru, secretive and domineering, judgmental and unkind. Humorless and never, ever informative. Oh, one can see how this might fit someone's cartoon image of an austere and demanding, quasi–Oriental sage. Indeed, there are plenty of real and historical figures that Yoda may be modeled after. But must we take this lying down? Even J.R.R. Tolkien, in his later works, ripped the sweet 'n' wise veil off of his beloved elves, exposing them as ruinously selfish creatures who brought Middle-earth to the brink of ruin.

Which brings us to the point of ultimate betrayal, pictured in *Attack of the Clones*. One of the most horrific scenes I have ever witnessed. Has anyone else noticed?

The Jedi knights aren't an army. They are an elite corps of secret agents, the 007 James Bonds of the Old Republic. So why does Yoda order all but one of them to charge straight into a death trap, where they will be surrounded and slaughtered by innumerable robots, monsters and flying aliens? It's the worst frontal assault since the Light Brigade. Only his peer and equal, Master Mace, refuses to fall for this. Instead, Mace does his job as a secret agent, sneaking in the back way and almost capturing the villain, singlehandedly. Had even one of the other Jedi knights accompanied him as a helper, then all would have been well.

But that wasn't Yoda's plan. Instead—how convenient—he takes delivery of a *new army* before hurling the Jedi to their doom. A new army trained to be much more obedient than that rabble of psychic adepts and bickering individual agents. A new army that represents everything worrisome about civilizations and institutions. Sameness, rigidity and amoral, ruthless efficiency.

Oh, it's implied that Yoda merely grabs a Clone Army that someone else ordered. But why assume that incredible coincidence? Take the plainest evidence of all, the actual sequence of events. Isn't the simplest answer that Yoda was the one to secretly order the clone army? (There is no evidence to contradict it and the clone-makers, clever businessmen, certainly thought they were doing it for Yoda's Council.) Yes, the situation is ambiguous ... but it smells of one of the worst betrayals in cinematic history.

Even if you balk at following me that far, remember how, in *The Phantom Menace*, Qui-Gon Jinn spoke of a need to "restore balance to the Force."

This, like so much about Lucas' new-agey religion, stays frustratingly unexplained. But it sure implies that old Yoda had an "unbalanced" agenda. One with its own dark side.

We'll get to that matter in just a second, but first let me reiterate the challenge. Is there any tangible reason to believe that anyone in their right minds ought to listen to that vile green muppet? Always secretive, mysterious, grouchy and unhelpful. Never actually achieving anything useful (except to annihilate his own knightly order). Then cowering in craven hiding for 20 years in a jungle hermitage. Is this an archetype of wisdom that we should raise to the rank of, say, Benjamin Franklin? Or George Washington, George Marshall, Albert Einstein, Maya Angelou, Martin Luther King and all the other hero-teacher-leaders of our democratic enlightenment? Or even the hapless Old Republic?

The Eternal Struggle—Between Dumb Caricatures

So, what do we make of the eternal struggle between two sides of the Force? Other than the fact that it sounds a bit like Manichaeism, or the Zoroastrian mythos of light vs. darkness, forever equal and tearing the cosmos apart? (One wonders, why has the fundamentalist community gone after Harry Potter, when this old heresy is rearing its head, hmmm?)

Does Qui-Gon's call for "balance" make any sense? Does this story-promise ever get resolved?

I have heard lots of chatter about the differences between the Dark Side of the Force and the other side. (Force Light?) Sith lords want "progress" through ferocious Darwinian winnowing, kind of like you see in *Dune*. The light side tends to be over-protective, insisting on an eternal, static order. It sounds very Tolkienish, and that's no coincidence ... though without Tolkien's cheerful willingness to re-evaluate. These supposed opposites have vastly more in common than differences, for example, their relentless devotion to elitist secrecy.

But notice, we are never offered a third choice. The choice of freedom. Of everybody knowing what's going on. A galaxy of openness and transparency, in which institutions and individuals, governments, companies and private citizens of all races, get to innovate and compete fairly, thus avoiding *both* static sameness and the horror-winnowing of open warfare.

Was this what Qui-Gon hoped for, in his yearning for balance? Is this what Darth-Anakin was supposedly pre-ordained to deliver?

Well, I am going to surprise you now, and tell you what I really think. He did!

Excuses for a Dark Henchman

I got entirely too much mail—after the *Salon* article—coming up with rationalizations and excuses to let old Darth off the hook. Here are just a few of them:

1. Darth kills the emperor and saves more than his son. He saves the universe!
2. Vader's redemption is personal. It's about a son's forgiveness.
3. Vader isn't the leader, so it's unfair to call him "Hitler." At worst he's a Himmler.
4. Vader was mind-controlled. He was just following orders.
5. Yes, normal people can get really mad, and not suddenly "turn evil," reversing all their morals like a switch. But Anakin isn't normal! He's a demigod. That makes him more vulnerable to amplified emotional swings.
6. Vader's actions were necessary in order to restore balance to the force/universe/franchise …

… and so on …

I did not simply reject all of the ideas that people sent in. In fact, half of these points are interesting—and possibly valid at some level. (Care to guess which ones?) The others, I'm afraid, still strike me as rather lame, or even provably wrong. Some of these are explored via *Star Wars on Trial*, in extensive testimony dealing with "plot holes."

But the core point is that we shouldn't have to go trawling around for meaning like this! The biggest and most lavish sci-fi epic of all time should make sense by now. Alas, you could fill intergalactic space with giant floating yellow words, and still nothing would tie together. For example, the political rationale behind the Secessionists, or why the Republic fell apart. Or how Darth was able to detect Leia's midichlorian-rich blood from a million miles away … but never sniffed a thing when he was interrogating her by hand, with truth serum. Likewise, he doesn't recognize his own hand-built droids, when he meets them again after so many years.

Or why he conveniently orders all the anti-aircraft guns and fighters to stop shooting at Luke, so he can do it himself … and somehow keeps missing till the boy gets his shot.

Then there are all sorts of other coincidences. Like the way Vader conveniently persuades Tarkin to let Luke and Leia and the Millennium Falcon go….

Or, the way, 20 years earlier, Obi-Wan took the newborn Luke in order to hide him from Vader, and chose as a hiding place, from all the worlds of the galaxy … Vader's home planet and Vader's home town.

Or a myriad other hints and clues that really ought to have added up to something. If anyone had been at the tiller, paying attention.

But oh. Look over that list again. See if you spot the pattern. And maybe you'll have a moment of shocked realization.

Why Bother?

Want to hear the most pathetic thing of all?

I actually care about this stuff. I care about it because of all those high hopes, back in the same year that my own first novel came out. I care because I passionately believe that important stories ought to make sense. Even if they are dark tragedies. Even if I disagree with the lesson that's being taught. Because we learn from things that we can decipher. Even if and when we don't like the point being made. But an illogical mishmash teaches nothing at all.

More the fool, I care so much that this ongoing *Star Wars* thing sometimes distracted me from some of my own stories. On occasion I would catch myself mulling it over while driving, or sitting in the Jacuzzi …

Until, suddenly one day, it came to me. A simple solution. A way that it all might have made sense.

There's a Secret Plan, After All

But I'm not going to tell you here.

Because my time's up. There are enough indictments on our plate, and the defense is already in the wings, ready to weigh in, eager to tell us about the merits and glories of the *Star Wars* Universe!

Also, there's another reason.

As a professional, I live in a world of critics and reviewers. I am used to being told what's wrong with work I've written, even novels that were tested past my special battery of fierce pre-readers, who generally catch most of the slip-ups before publication. (My aphorism: CITOKATE. Criticism Is The Only Known Antidote To Error.) I'm used to others telling me where I failed, or where my creations have problems. That's fine.

It's not complaints that prickle—that's quality control data—but when some upstart tells me *how* I oughta fix a problem. I don't hanker for that. And I suppose George Lucas has the same right.

Moreover, having heaped on criticism, for page after page, I really need to add this: The world would be a much poorer place without *Star Wars!* Despite my grumblings, it delivered a mainline feed of fantastic imagery and almost pure joy, straight through the eyes, ears and optic nerves of about a billion people. That's a lot more than *I* ever reached.

Besides, hey, the man subsidized maybe ten percent of the most groundbreaking technical artists of our age, pushing wondrous new visualization technologies for other creators to use, in this wondrously free and open civilization. If we're lucky, the turgid *messages* in *Star Wars* will never matter as much as the simple joy.

And yes, my kids cut in at one point, crystallizing this wisdom:

"Cut him some slack, Dad. The light sabers are cool."

Can We Do Better?

So I'll hold back on my little plot gimmick—*the Darth Vader twist*—that (in my humble opinion) might make sense of so many unfortunate coincidences, fulfill Qui-Gon's dream, and even give the Oven Mitt some payback. There are enough clues. Readers who like to play mental games can follow where they lead.

In the end, what matters is only this: Be willing to look with a complex eye, even upon simple legends. You are many! A child, a teen, a grown-up. Both individualist and citizen. A worker and a player. Enjoy any entertainment in the spirit that it's offered, while another part of you keeps asking, "What bill of goods am I being sold, between the frames?"

It's your right. Demand a universe that makes some sense.[4]

7

Avatar. Just *Avatar*.

Well, it seems we're all going back to Planet Pandora. And why not? With the proclamation of a coming sequel to the blockbuster sci-fi epic *Avatar* (2009)—no, make that *three* sequels—the near-universal response from one and all has been: "Sure! Just tell me how much money to bring and where to stand in line!"

James Cameron's epic was the most important science fiction film of the first decade of the 21st century, least of all because it proved that animation tools have matured enough to portray almost any story. For example, the vivid animal characters in *Life of Pi*. Or else—perhaps someday soon—dolphins piloting starships?

But of course, *Avatar* was about much more than special effects. It is the *lessons* of this cinematic opus that I plan to engage and dissect. Specifically, did Cameron succeed in his blatant goal with *Avatar*—to craft a great teaching moment?[1]

Okay then, let's start by admitting that:

(1) James Cameron's heart is in the right place.

Hmmm, well. In a sci-fi context, you can't take the clichéd meaning of that statement for granted! In fact, I have no direct knowledge of Cameron's cardiopulmonary placement.

Seriously, there's no question that Mr. Cameron *means well*. He's intent on doing more than just wrestle cash out of the pockets of a billion people. He wants them to behave better. To care more. To broaden their horizons of tolerance, diversity, vision and possibility. Moreover, he's worried about how sketchily we're handling our duty as planetary managers. All of these are causes that I share and that I try (with more limited reach) to convey in works like *Earth, Existence* and *The Postman*. So I'll not criticize Cameron for using his art to help make a better world.

Ahhh, but with this clear aim, how well did Mr. Cameron succeed? And did this messianic ambition harm his art? Hold that thought.

(2) Almost every review of *Avatar* compares the plot to Kevin Costner's *Dances with Wolves*...

... or other classic cautionary tales like *Pocahontas, FernGully, Silent Running*, or Ursula K. LeGuin's book *The Word for World Is Forest*. All of them portray powerfully rapacious and greedy modern people (e.g., male European invaders of North America) in tense conflict with a group or tribe that—while technologically primitive—possesses superior, earthy wisdom. Whereupon one of the invaders goes native and joins the oppressed tribe, aiming to help them resist his own, morally misbegotten folk.

At surface, that is indeed what we see in *Avatar*. Some of the sillier, satirical references to this overlap—such as *"Dances with Very Tall Smurfs"*—are both snarky and funny. I hear that Cameron takes them in good humor. A successful person can.

Though might he try some storytelling that's less derivative? Helping to lead Hollywood out of its current creativity funk—a dismal cycle of remakes, comic book reworks and rehashing old tropes, that is resisted with consistency only by Christopher Nolan and Alfonso Cuarón? Even Steven Spielberg has retreated (albeit brilliantly) into retelling old tales. Perhaps we just live in cowardly times.

Hence, the derivative-cloned story is *not* what bothered me about *Avatar*. When I go see a flick, I adjust expectations and try to enjoy each movie in the spirit that it's offered. Generally, that requires cranking my *originality* dial way down, along with the *logic* meter. For *Avatar*, I then spun up my *cool fun* and *gosh wow* and *root-for-underdog* dials ... and wound up enjoying it immensely!

Alas, a couple of other scales ... well, I wish I hadn't been forced to zero them out.

(3) A key point: *Avatar* depicts a different "evil-westerners" story because it's set in our future.

This matters. While *Dances with Wolves* and *Pocahontas* were set in the past—and *FernGully* in the approximate-fantasy present—Cameron sets his story in a time-to-come, after humanity has had another 200 years of experience, learning and technological progress—plenty of time to discuss its own flaws, failings and potential for righting wrongs. Its potential for compassion and genius.

Ponder how our own values have grown more broad and subtle in just the 50 years since Gandhi and Martin Luther King. A journey that's incomplete! In the tradition of self-preventing morality tales, Cameron hopes that his art will propel forward our grand conversation about human self-improvement. A conversation that will be taken up by our children, and theirs. A conversation—and please consider this carefully—whose past will have included movies like *Avatar*.

Ponder the irony. *Avatar* portrays a future in which films like Cameron's have apparently achieved nothing! We have learned zilch, despite the best efforts of billions of sincere people, including James Cameron. The social progress and rising acceptance that emerged from 1945 to 2010 stopped dead, and even reversed.

Oh, there have been changes, between our present and the future shown in *Avatar*. We've not only become interstellar travelers, but have invented a wondrous method for putting our minds literally into the bodies of other beings and walking around for a mile or more in their skins. (Not too unlike the technology that I posit—but handle very differently—in *Kiln People*.) The avatar-embedding machinery at the core of the story is potentially the greatest tool for tolerance, empathy and cultural learning imaginable! Indeed, that is how Cameron portrays it being used …

… by one person. Maybe two.

Indeed, we've just set the stage for *Avatar*'s moral collapse: rooted in the fact that this version of the "dances with others" scenario is set in a depressingly ordained-awful future.

Consider. With *Pocahontas* and *Dances with Wolves*, the audience contemplates the following implicit lesson: *"We come from a savage past, when immature ancestors did terrible things, while a few heroes lit candles in the darkness. Those mistakes still cling to us. Let's learn from our past and continue to do better."*

In sharp contrast—and without intending it—by setting the very same story in the future, Cameron preaches:

"Humans are hopelessly rotten. We will be oppressors with horrible institutions, no matter how advanced we get and no matter how many tools of empathy we develop.

"Films like this one won't help, either.

"Give up."

To be clear—that's not what he meant to teach!

But it is exactly how people felt, upon leaving the theaters.

I wish I were Na'vi, instead of a cursed human.

Or worse—an American.

I can't wait till the next time I can revisit Pandora and pretend I am defeating scuzzy humans!
Especially Americans.

(4) A movie asserting to be all about native tribal life and ecology ignores everything we know about either.

While seated in the audience, enjoying the color, beauty and action of *Avatar,* we are so busy being visually awed—and receiving let's-all-cooperate-with-nature messages—that we blithely accept a raft of contradictions. For example:

> (a) On Earth, all functioning ecosystems are about competition, predation and death. Animals in nature endure lives that are vastly more tense and fretful than ours, *not* more placid and relaxed. Hunger lurks just ahead. Brutal attack and death are always on the minds of predator and prey and almost everyone, even the lion, dies violently.
>
> In other words, *Disney lied to us.*
>
> But on Pandora? Sure, we do glimpse a couple of predators and some hunting by the Na'vi, but all of it softened and isolated. Nature, for the most part, is a cross between Lewis Carroll and Land of the Sugarplum Fairies.
>
> (b) The Na'vi are a warrior people! Worthy of respect, much as we are taught to esteem the Lakota (Sioux)—the tribe that gets *all* the motion pictures about Native Americans, from *Little Big Man* to *Dances with Wolves.* And okay, the Na'vi sure do act like noble warriors cloned from the American plains … except …
>
> … Except, can we ask *who* have these "warriors" been fighting, all those years and eons before Earthlings came? At least in *Dances with Wolves,* there's no evasion. The Lakota are shown as what they gladly acknowledged themselves to be, at the time—a brutally violent people, yet somehow noble and endearing—while the equally violent whites were not.
>
> Okay. Fine. But in *Avatar,* that whole background is wiped away from view. They get to be gruff, adorably macho *warriors*, without any context of endlessly vicious tribal *war.*
>
> (c) As if to illustrate that fact, just like in *Dances with Wolves,* the "noble" natives in *Avatar* come *that* close to treacherously slaying the protagonist several times, once by a cowardly arrow in the back, without the slightest personal grievance or provocation from either Lt. Dunbar or Jake Sully, offering them no opportunities

to honorably defend themselves. In the Costner film, they are dissuaded by a medicine man saying, "Let's not kill him today." In *Avatar*, the same brief mercy derives from magical (or coincidental) symbolism. Ahhh, how admirably better that is, than—say—due process of law.

There are scads of similar oversimplifications that do not strengthen Cameron's case. But the key point is that *none of them were necessary,* even under the pressure of a three-hour run-time. The exact same story and lessons in tolerance and diversity could have been conveyed, with the same visuals and characters and overall plot, without patronizing us. Without pressing the director's thumb on the scale.

Which brings us to a major point:

(5) The Na'vi are portrayed as justified to be both obstinate and incurious.

Indeed, some of the traits that Hollywood adores in the upper plains nomads were despised by many neighboring tribes of the time. Obdurate insistence on tribal changelessness, for example. Macho-male dominance and utter unwillingness to adapt to powerful new ways. (Except adopting the white man's weapons, which of course the Na'vi also do.) Utter contempt for any thought of compromise. Plus a recurring rash impulsiveness that kept giving the most evil-despicable 19th century white men hypocritical excuses to start the next war.

Why do no sympathetic Hollywood movies sing paeans to *other* tribes who exhibited traits like calmness, curiosity and adaptability, as shown by the Iroquois and Cherokee nations, who—by the way—respected women and who invented democratic methods that were models to the American founders? Tribes whose principal heroes included diplomats, inventors and intellectuals—like Hiawatha and Sequoia—instead of *always* brave, reckless raiders on horseback? Hey, I don't disdain the admirable qualities of Crazy Horse; he deserves his new monument in the Black Hills! But for Hollywood to fixate *only* on that kind of Native American hero isn't respectful. It is yet another kind of patronization.

Getting back to *Avatar,* it is one thing to see a native people who are in tune with their world preaching to us that we should try this at home. Terrific. Yay, that!

But it is quite another to be finger-wagged by folks who never faced the temptations that we faced, and who *yawn* in complete lack of interest when they meet people who are able to cross the vast gulf between the freaking *stars!*

All right, compassion, love, courage and eco-oneness rank high in the pantheon of traits. But right after those, can you think of any gift more admirable than curiosity?

In *Avatar*, there are some humans who express all five!

Show me one Na'vi who does.

The caricature was unintentional, of course. Yet, it is harmful, all the same.

(6) Other critics: The White Messiah Complex.

This brings us to one of the more obvious criticisms of *Avatar*, bruited by reviewers like David Brooks and John Podhoretz, who bemoan the "white messiah complex."

It rests on the stereotype that white people are rationalist and technocratic while colonial victims are spiritual and athletic, that non-whites need the White Messiah to lead their crusades, that illiteracy is the path to grace. "It also creates a sort of two-edged cultural imperialism," says Brooks. "Natives can either have their history shaped by cruel imperialists or benevolent ones, but either way, they are going to be supporting actors in our journey to self-admiration."

Hmm, well ... duh? And you're shocked, shocked (!) that a filmmaker who is gambling hundreds of millions of dollars would go with a protagonist who is guaranteed familiarity and viewer identification in his core audience? Ever hear of a film called *Rapa Nui*? I didn't think so.

No, I won't carp on Cameron for centering his story upon Jake Sully. The creator of Sarah Connor and the kickass girl–Marines of *Aliens* has nothing to apologize for. We owe him some benefit of the doubt.

Indeed, one could reverse that complaint. Clearly, the most relentless preaching in *Avatar* is not about the technological or tactical or messianic talents of Jake Sully, but the moral and esthetic superiority of the Na'vi, along with the beyond-all-redemption vileness of every aspect of western civilization.

(7) Sympathy for the alien ... and ourselves?

Elsewhere I talk about our quirky Western-American habit of relentless self-criticism. A reflex to dismiss our own culture's value while extolling the other. Sure, it's not universal, even among Californians; we all know plenty of neighbors who display smug insularity, chauvinistic nativism or even xenophobia. But the counter-trend has been powerful for more than two generations, and it has won more battles than it lost.

For example, the widespread notion that "greater wisdom" is to be

7. Avatar. *Just* Avatar.

found in eastern mysticism has ranged from the very real value that Steve Jobs got during his years in an ashram, to the mild sense of no-excuses discipline my kids received from their karate instructor—all the way to the hysterically pathetic reverence that *Star Wars* fans give to a nasty little faux-guru sock puppet named Yoda, who never does or says a single thing that's helpful or verifiably wise. At the far extreme are those westerners who reflexively despise everything about their own culture and give unlimited excuses for anything that's not.

Consider how this theme—"us is bad; other is good"—often plays in science fiction films. By now, aliens have to be pretty darned vicious and ugly in order to fill the villain role. And *District Nine* showed that even nasty appearance no longer disqualifies the other from sympathetic treatment.

Look, I know this cultural phase is necessary, to help break lots of bad-old habits that go back 60 centuries. My own lifelong fascination (in both science and fiction) with the other ranges from the expanse of human diversity to animal minds, to possible alien or artificial intelligences, and it surely stems from the otherness meme that I absorbed from an early age. Heck, one of my books is titled *Otherness*. I'm glad of this cultural innovation, and I try my best to help promote it.

Alas, we are prevented from even *noticing* that this meme is operating. Or the blatant fact that it is special, recent and mostly unique to the neo-west. Name another culture that ever preached to its children: *Admire any other civilization but always criticize your own!* No prior people did that. Indeed, no other culture *benefited* as much as we have from relentlessly seeking our own flaws and finding the positive in others. Or incorporating a goulash of cultures within itself.

It was a long, hard and crime-ridden path to learn this lesson—but at last, many of us view diversity as strength! And we got to that point by relentlessly self-criticizing 6000-year-old habits of intolerance that most cultures took for granted.

All right, that's a difficult irony to convey. The brilliant 1988 sci-fi film *Alien Nation* managed to do it, combining some of the traditional, otherness-moralistic chiding with a few grains of rare praise and approval.

That film taught the audience a more subtle lesson: "You Earthlings still have a long, long way to go, before you're truly decent or civilized.

"But you *are* getting better! You've come far, in fact.

"And we believe you can go farther still."

Is that so hard to do? Mix in a little *attaboy* reinforcement, amid the chiding?

Apparently it is. Because outside of *Alien Nation*—and *Star Trek*, of course—I can think of no examples from Hollywood, where the intolerance-scolding message was ever sweetened with a little encouragement. A little hope.

It could easily have been done, in *Avatar*. But it wasn't.

How James Cameron Might Still Set Things Right

I've described some logical faults in a motion picture that—in fact—I deeply admire. After all, criticism can be well-intended. And clearly, Cameron meant for his epic film to be much more than just an orgy of visual delights. He strove to teach some valuable lessons to our modern, self-critical, technological and grudgingly progressive society. His intentions were good ... though, alas, the lessons were blown.

But let's step back and study the trap that snared this brilliant director. Clearly, it's not his fault. Because the snare catches almost everyone.

Civilization (Automatically) Has to Suck!

We've seen how most Hollywood films (and nearly all dramatic novels) share one central, almost Biblical tenet: *Society doesn't work*. Your number one job as a storyteller is to get the audience rooting for your heroes, by keeping them in pulse-pounding jeopardy for 90 minutes of film—or 500 pages of a novel. And that generally requires that you *separate* your protagonist from meaningful help. Violent drama is the last thing taxpaying citizens want in real life; we hire savvy diplomats to avoid war, and skilled armed forces to deter it. Highly trained police chase bad guys. Then we hire attorneys to watch the police, and regulators to watch the attorneys, and NGO activists to watch regulators. Every hour of every day, emergency professionals stand ready because we want danger removed from daily life ...

... but not from movies and novels! We demand that all the cogs and gears of responsible civilization keep turning ... but also to fantasize that none of it works, and that our neighbors are all fools. (How many Westerns featured towns full of cowards—when every frontier village was packed with Civil War veterans!)

Not all help-suppression tricks are cheats. In Chapter 2, I offered examples of films and books where a storyteller managed to keep the heroine in jeopardy, separating her from plot-ruining assistance, without reflexively insulting us all. James Cameron would personally count on meaningful aid, should he ever need it, from a civilization he portrays in *Avatar* as unalloyedly vile. A dissonance that would be forgivable, if the movie achieved its intended goal ... coaxing us to be better people. Alas, we return to my list of ways that this wonderful epic and visual feast missed its target.

(8) The dramatic situation conveyed by *Avatar* is both lazy and poisonous ... making it typical.

Yes the "dances with others" plotline works. It takes some of the best aspects of Joseph Campbell's classic *hero's journey*, weaves in a love story, hammers the brave-underdogs theme and then does the neo-western thing—fascination with the alien, the different and foreign. All very well and good. But we've seen that when fascination-with-other becomes hatred-of-us, we tread dangerous ground.

Especially when you recall point #2. The major difference between *Avatar*'s scenario and other *dances-with* tales is its setting in the future. Our future. The corrupt westerners committing these crimes aren't our benighted ancestors, who—barely out of the caves—had a lot to learn. Nor is it about the present, deeply flawed generation. Now it's our *descendants* doing all the awful, deliberate crimes. Obstinately refusing to see parallels in their own history or to learn from past tragedies.

And heckfire—it could happen!

In the world of *Avatar*, it seems our best efforts did *not* bring forth new generations raised on good intentions and avoiding mistakes of the past. The human improvability that Cameron himself represents—a civilization that listened to Gandhi and Martin Luther King and that tries every day to overcome our Cro-Magnon flaws—went no further in the next two centuries.

Doesn't that mean that *Avatar* itself—and guilt-tripping movies like it—failed to make those centuries any better? Bummer.

Again, I say this in all friendship. We must speed up the pace by which we humans improve our ethics, compassion and commitment to responsible care ... especially of this magnificent planet. That was Cameron's aim! So why does *Avatar* fail?

Because those who would be persuaded by simple guilt trips already have been converted by *past* guilt trips—from *Soylent Green* and *Silent Running* and *The Gods Must Be Crazy*, to *FernGully, Gorillas in the Mist* and the works of Ursula K. LeGuin. Guilt flagellations and "we're all so awful" lamentations will not sway much of the remainder who wallow in blithe short-sightedness. They recognize a finger-wagging lecture and—smirking—turn it off.

Meanwhile, alas, *Avatar* proclaims that our children *will not* learn, despite all we say and do. Our vileness is rooted in inherent human nature.

The best thing is for humanity to fail. And heroic humans ought to help ensure that this happens.

Is There a Way Out?

I believe *Avatar's* moral flaws could be fixed with minimal alterations! Maybe five minutes of footage, added to a director's cut, might alleviate many of the problems outlined here.

Shall I give it a try?

Picture the beginning, as a crippled Jake Sully arrives at the human mining colony exploiting riches from Pandora—riches that Earth desperately needs, to restore its former health. But there are tradeoffs, including an unscrupulous company and a suspicious-dangerous native population.

Only now, let's suppose that *Earth civilization is not run by imbeciles who are ignoring history*. Instead, our descendants run a generally moral society that established rules for decent treatment of the natives, to be enforced by an honorable governor and her staff.

Have I wrecked *Avatar*? Bear with me! Let's posit that the Company chafes under the governor's restrictions, conniving to get around them. To provoke the Na'vi into a war they cannot win, exactly what happened repeatedly, in the American West.

Imagine in the film's first ten minutes. While Jake is literally getting his legs, we see hopeful signs. A meeting is underway, on one of the floating islands, where the good colonial governor is about to sign a treaty with *moderates* among the Na'vi …

Now there's a twist. Moderates among the Na'vi?

Why, I am talking about those among the natives who are guardedly curious, cautiously friendly, determined to preserve their world(!) but also willing to compromise and let Earthlings have resources they need to save their own distant planet. More like the Cherokee and Iroquois, these are the tribesmen who support Sigourney Weaver's school, though they demand Earth send children to Pandora who might be young and flexible enough to absorb Na'vi lessons, too.

"No, you may not go anywhere near our trees!" they explain.

"Give us drones and such to help enforce this!"

"On the other hand, we sure find your spaceships fascinating."

"And let's see if this avatar machine of yours works both ways! So we can feel what it's like to be human?"

All of this could be telescoped into just three minutes of screen time! Things look hopeful, too hopeful! And so…

... the conference island blows up! The governor and her aides—except Sigourney—are dead. So are the Na'vi moderates.

The Company guy rubs his hands. Earth won't investigate too much if he has a mountain-high stack of unobtainium waiting, when the next ship arrives.

At this point, the whole rest of the film can ensue almost exactly as is!

Obstinate-immature company stooges vs. obstinate-immature remnant Na'vi. And we root for the Na'vi, of course! Because if we must choose between two packs of obstinate-immature jerks, let's side with the underdogs who are defending their homes.

Only, while the rest of the movie proceeds, it is with this idea planted in the viewers' minds: *It's a tragedy. We should have taken more precautions, sending more of our best and fewer of our worst. But at least there were real efforts to avoid this, by future humans who might do better next time, learning from this mistake.*

Now let's root for Jake and Neytiri and the obstinate wing of the Na'vi. Because obstinacy is called for now!

And none of this says that all of our descendants will be evil, all of the time.

Only slightly altering its lessons on tolerance and diversity and ecological responsibility, this would dramatically adjust the guilt trip so that it offers a patina of hopefulness, rather than utter despair for despicable humanity.

The moral would be *keep trying* instead of *give up*.

A Futile Hope

Do I expect James Cameron to make this tweak? Of course not. All I can do is carp from the sidelines that "this coulda made it better" ... and shrug as others attribute it all to jealousy. Ah well.

Is that proposal the only alternative occurring to me, when I ponder this immensely entertaining and thought-provoking film? Of course not. There are scads of ideas, including a *post-singularity* riff that could explain so much of why Planet Pandora is the way it is, offering several *double-twist*, ironic surprises about humanity's interaction with the Na'vi. Perhaps—purely for entertainment—I'll muse on these in an appendix or web link.

None of which matters, only this. Look around at the current flood of film dystopias and novels that wallow in apocalypse. I've written some myself, but today's reflex-obsession is tedious. Heck, *Avatar* positively fizzes with subtlety and optimism, by comparison!

Alas, Cameron's grand sci-fi epic could have spread confident determination to seek self-improvement—as individuals and as a civilization—*while* delivering entertainment and mind-blowing vision to billions. It tried hard and came close, but wound up undermining our confidence in humanity's ability to do that very thing. And yet …

… and yet, I remain hopeful. I'll be in line, ticket in hand, for the next episode.

Perils of Pandora, Part III: A Speculative Addendum

All right. I can't help it. I just have to tack on this one final bit. It's a tribute to James Cameron that he provokes careful, even critical, appraisals of his work, which I tried to do above, even offering one proposal for a three-minute tweak that might (in some future director's cut?) repair the core, moral heart of this great but flawed film. Will it happen? When it snows on Pandora!

I also alluded to some other, even more far-out-meddlesome ideas. So, just for fun, why don't we look at one that isn't even my own! It is *yet another, larger tweak* that could both surprise audiences and really make them think, suggested by one of my readers, Matthew Bell: "All the amazing aspects of Pandora, all the magical exaggerations, along with its strangely un-biological biology and the behavior of its natives, can be explained if you assume that the planet is a *post-singularity world*."

By now, few of you will be unfamiliar with the "singularity" as it was first laid out by the great science fiction author Vernor Vinge, and now pushed hard by Ray Kurzweil, author of *The Singularity Is Near*. This notion—much discussed among the world's nerds—is both simple yet profoundly intricate. It starts with the fact that human skill and knowledge are accumulating at not just an accelerating rate, but the rate of acceleration is itself accelerating.

The most familiar sign of this acceleration is Moore's Law, under which computing power doubles every 18 months or so. At this pace, it should be possible to emulate human intelligence in a box, within 20 years or so. Then that artificially intelligent (AI) box can design a new, improved one, which designs the next and so on, in a sequence that rapidly takes off. In mathematical terms, a "singularity" is what happens when such trends accelerate beyond any ability to predict outcomes. All bets are off, when everything you took for granted has changed.

Now, a number of authors (including me) have tried to picture what life might be like on the other side of a singularity. If the huge brains we create turn out to be monstrous and unsympathetic, they may try to stomp us, as in the *Terminator* and *Matrix* flicks. Or they could become loyal assistants to human ambition, helping us span the starways, as in the *Culture* novels of Iain Banks. There are so many possible ways that this transition might work out—and I cover a number of them in *Existence*.

But one is especially enticing when it comes to *Avatar*: that our super-mind computer friends might use immense new "godlike" powers the way today's teenagers use the spectacular computers in their homes.

To play.

Okay then, picture this: The Na'vi are dashing about and flying through Pandora's vivid, colorful forests as *kids*—young minds—immersed in a game. Their true selves are rooted in the planetary mainframe, which manifests at the surface as a white tree. (How very Tolkien-esque!) This could explain why the biology and ethnography and all other features seem exaggerated for effect, including the Internet-like rapid communion network that laces everything from the animals to the Tree of Life. Including the way Pandoran creatures can *plug in*.

If we play along with this post-singularity notion a bit, we realize that *Avatar* isn't *Dances with Wolves* at all! It's more like *Star Trek*'s "Errand of Mercy." In this famous example of a frequent plot in SF, humans encounter a "primitive folk," and don't understand them. Over time, it is revealed the primitives are actually vastly more advanced people who have decided to live in a rustic manner, either for their own reasons, or in order not to reveal the truth to young races out exploring. In that one memorable episode, the Organians are energy beings who get the Federation and Klingons to stop fighting. One of the recent *Star Trek* films had a similar theme.

Let's go a bit with this notion that Pandora's biosphere (and "unobtainium") turn out to be the result of a post-singularity super-civilization. Then the story that we all got to watch in *Avatar* might conceal one of *three* subplots.

1. Visiting humans were the primitives, in technology as well as culture! The "war" was a test, and those who sided with the Na'vi passed it on our behalf. It ends with the soldiers-scientists "going back to school."
2. The Na'vi—helped by Jake—win the war. They then hit PAUSE and evaluate the terrific game they all just played … only to be *horrified* to learn that humans who are killed stay dead! (Their own dead just reboot.) *"Why didn't you tell us you were mortal?"* they cry out in angst. They are impressed that human warriors would be willing to put so much on the line in battle.
3. The great simulation of Pandora, while beautiful, has a deeper purpose. *A real foe is coming.* This is training. And humanity is now embroiled, like it or not.

As Mr. Bell put it:

> The Colonel's bomb mission was never going to succeed. The only question was in what subtle way would it be averted. Eywa, or should I say AI-wa, had it worked out well in advance, and sent the floating seeds to tag Jake Sully, so that he could play this role, and thus both find somebody who would be human enough to arrange expulsion of the humans, and also join the Na'vi and fight for their side. Indeed, you could say that Jake was AI-wa's avatar, or at least instrument, as is clear from the very start.

Yipe! That may be drifting way too far, even for me.

After all, despite the many elements that he borrowed, *Avatar* is James Cameron's story to tell. These are just fannish daydreams, then. (My own readers send them to me all the time.) If Mr. Cameron reacts as I always do, then he feels flattered and pleased. I am always a sucker to talk story, and then try to find some *new* story, that breaks with the clichés.

And then the next one.

8

The Lord of the Rings
J.R.R. Tolkien vs. the Modern Age[1]

Want to forget about terrorism and all those distracting rumors of war? Need to ignore the economy for a while? Got the holiday blues? Our culture has a surefire cure: the traditional spate of post–Thanksgiving movies. This year, despite a clamor over the latest Harry Potter film, much of the attention is going to another fantasy called *The Two Towers*—part two in the *Lord of the Rings* trilogy. Will it succeed in distracting us for a while, conveying audiences to a world that is at once more beautiful and stirring than humdrum modern life?

Naturally, I enjoyed the *Lord of the Rings* trilogy as a teen, during its first big boom in the 1960s. I mean, what was there not to like? As William Goldman said about another great fantasy, it has "Fencing. Fighting. Torture. Poison. True Love. Hate. Revenge. Giants. Hunters. Bad Men. Good Men. Beautifulest ladies. Spiders. Dragons. Eagles. Beasts of all natures and descriptions. Pain. Death. Magic. Chases. Escapes. Miracles."

Voters in a 1997 BBC poll named *The Lord of the Rings* the greatest book of the 20th century. In 1999, Amazon.com customers chose it as the greatest book of the millennium.

Of course there is much more to this work than mere fantasy escapism. J.R.R. Tolkien wrote his epic—including its prequel, *The Hobbit*—during the dark middle decades of the 20th century, a time when modernity appeared to fail in one spectacle of technologically amplified bloodshed after another. From the 1930s through the '50s, planet Earth fell into armed camps of starkly portrayed opposition, tearing at each other in orgies of unprecedented violence. Titanic struggles, with the fate of all the world at stake.

Lord of the Rings clearly reflected this era. Only, in contrast to mere reality, Tolkien's portrayal of "good" resisting a darkly threatening "evil" offered something sadly lacking in the real struggles against Nazi or Communist tyrannies: a role for individual champions. His elves and hobbits and über-human warriors performed the same role that Lancelot, Merlin and Odysseus did in older fables, and that superheroes still do in comic books. Through doughty Frodo, noble Aragorn and the ethereal Galadriel, he proclaimed the paramount importance—above nations and civilizations—of the indomitable romantic hero.

All right, I read Tolkien's epic trilogy a bit unconventionally, starting with *The Two Towers* and backfilling as I went along. Likewise, I may be a bit off-kilter in liking, best of all, the unofficial companion volume to *Lord of the Rings*, perhaps the funniest work penned in English: the Harvard Lampoon's 1968 parody, entitled *Bored of the Rings*. Even if you revere Tolkien, or take *Lord of the Rings* much too seriously, who can restrain guffaws at the antics of Frito, son of Dildo, and his sidekick Spam, along with Gimlet, son of Groin, Eorache, daughter of Eordrum, and Arrowroot, son of Arrowshirt, son of Araplane? Many of the '60s references may seem dated—especially long-forgotten commercial jingles—but any author should be flattered by inspired satire. In fact, toward the end of this essay, I'll offer my own small bit of ironic takeoff. A different, possibly much better way of viewing Sauron, the evil Dark Lord.

But first, let's get serious. Some of what I am about to say may seem unconventional, provocative, heretical ... even foolhardy in the face of a pseudo-religious reverence that some accord to *Lord of the Rings*. There may be even more hate mail than when *Salon* ran my piece criticizing the *Star Wars* universe. So let me start by saying that I deem Tolkien's trilogy to be one of the finest works of literary universe-building, with a lovingly textured internal consistency that's excelled only by J.R.R.'s penchant for crafting "lost" dialects. Long before there was a Klingon Language Institute, expert aficionados—amateurs in the classic sense of the word—were busy translating Shakespeare and the Bible into High Elvish, Dwarfish and other Tolkien-generated tongues. And yes, *Lord of the Rings* opened the door to a vast popular eruption of heroic fantasy, setting up many others who followed with exacting devotion to his masterful architecture, scrupulously copying the rhythms, ambience and formulas that worked so well.

Indeed, the popularity of this recipe is deeply thought-provoking. Millions of people who live in a time of genuine miracles—in which the great-grandchildren of illiterate peasants may routinely fly through the sky, roam the Internet, view far-off worlds and elect their own leaders—slip into delighted wonder at the notion of a wizard hitchhiking a ride from an eagle.

8. The Lord of the Rings

Many even find themselves yearning for a society of towering lords and loyal, kowtowing vassals!

The Context for Tolkien's Counter-Enlightenment

Wouldn't life seem richer, finer if we still had kings? If the guardians of wisdom kept their wonders locked up in high wizard towers, instead of rushing onto PBS or BBC, the way our unseemly scientists do today? Weren't miracles more exciting when they were doled out by a precious few, instead of commercializing every discovery, bottling and marketing each new marvel to the masses for a dollar 95? Didn't we stop going to the Moon because it became boring? Just look at how people felt about Princess Diana. No democratically elected public servant was ever so adored. Democracy doesn't have the same pomp, majesty or sense of being above accountability. As we saw in Chapter 6, one of the paramount promoters of the fantasy-mythic tradition, George Lucas, expressed it this way.

> There's a reason why kings built large palaces, sat on thrones and wore rubies all over. There's a whole social need for that, not to oppress the masses, but to impress the masses and make them proud and allow them to feel good about their culture, their government and their ruler so that they are left feeling that a ruler has the right to rule over them, so that they feel good rather than disgusted about being ruled.

This yearning makes sense if you remember that arbitrary lords and chiefs did rule us for 99.44 percent of human existence. Amid the brutally predictable drudgery of everyday life, miracles were awesome, faraway things. Flight was a legendary prerogative of demigods in stirring fables. And a man was meaningless out of context with his king.

It's only been 200 years or so—an eyeblink—that "scientific enlightenment" began waging its rebellion against the nearly universal pattern called feudalism, a hierarchic system that ruled our ancestors in every culture that developed both metallurgy and agriculture. Wherever human beings acquired both plows and swords, gangs of large men picked up the latter and took other men's women and wheat. (Sexist language is meaningfully accurate here; those cultures had no word for "sexism," it was simply assumed.) They then proceeded to announce rules and "traditions" ensuring that their sons would inherit everything.

Please, try to find even one exception. You won't succeed. Putting aside cultural superficialities, society on every inhabited continent quickly shaped itself into a pyramid, with a few well-armed bullies at the top, accompanied by some fast-talking guys with painted faces or spangled cloaks who curried favor by weaving stories to explain why the bullies should remain on top.

Only something exceptional started happening. In gradual stages, the elements began taking shape for a new social and intellectual movement, one finally capable of challenging the alliance of warrior lords, priests, bards and secretive magicians. It didn't happen all at once, but in fitful jerks, sometimes five steps forward and four (or more) steps back.

Timidly at first, guilds and townsfolk rallied together and lent their support to kings, thereby easing oppression by local lords. Long before Aristotle became a tool of the establishment, his rediscovery during the High Middle Ages offered some relief from dour anti-intellectualism. Then renaissance humanism offered a philosophical basis for valuing the individual human as a being worthy in its own right. The Reformation freed sanctity and morality from control by a narrow, self-chosen club; it also legitimized self-betterment through hard work in this world, not the next. Then Galileo and Newton showed that creation's clockwork can be understood, even appreciated in its elegance, not just endured.[2]

Still, the entire notion of progress remained nebulous and ill-formed. Society's essential shape—pyramidal, with a narrow elite atop a vast and permanently ignorant peasantry—stayed largely unchanged until a full suite of elements and tools were finally in place, setting the stage for true revolution. A revolution so fundamental, coming with such heady, empowering suddenness, that participants gave it a name filled with hubristic portent. Enlightenment. The word wasn't ill-chosen, for it bespoke illuminating a path ahead. Which, in turn, implied the unprecedented notion that "forward" is a direction worth taking, instead of lamenting over a preferred past.

Progress, in a forward direction, and boy, did we take to it. In two or three centuries, our levels of education, health, liberation, tolerance and confident diversity have been momentously, utterly transformed. Along the way, history—once the core of every curriculum—became a minor elective subject, with the ironic effect that today's citizens have very little idea what the past was like, how grindingly cruel and bitter life was for nearly all of our oppressed ancestors. In other words, by turning away from the past, we seem paradoxically unable to measure how very far we've come.

The *shape* of society changed, away from the once-universal pyramid, toward a diamond-like configuration, wherein a comfortable and well-educated middle class actually outnumbers the poor. For the first time, let me emphasize. Anywhere. One side effect (among many) has been to transform our myths—our songs and dramas and vivid tales—toward a new shared theme, seen today in a majority of popular films. The nearly all-pervasive *suspicion of authority*. And a notion, nearly

8. The Lord of the Rings

absent in other cultures, that individual eccentricity and freedom are sacred things.

We can argue endlessly about the detailed accuracy and implications of this "diamond" analogy—and its vast remaining imperfections—but not over the fact that a profound shift has occurred, driven by a genuine scientific-technical educational revolution. And yet, almost from its birth, the Enlightenment Movement was confronted by an ironic counter-revolution, rejecting the very notion of progress. The Romantic Movement erupted as a rebellion against the rebellion.

In fairness, it didn't start out that way. For example, many of the leading early English Romantics—Wordsworth, Shelley, Blake, etc.—welcomed the French Revolution (at least in its early phases) as a sweeping away of the cobwebs of feudalism and clericalism—a step toward a kind of utopian universal brotherhood. So long as they shared the same entrenched enemy (powerful bishops and feudal lords), you could hardly slide a knife blade between the two wings of the rebel alliance.

Today, men like Thomas Jefferson stand as icons of both Enlightenment and Romanticism. But this changed when the industrial revolution hit full stride. Suddenly, where once gentry and clergy ruled, there were arrogant new powers striding about. An entrepreneurial bourgeoisie. A new intellectual elite of science. And a clanking, noisome ruction of impudent machinery.

Even democracy began to seem less classically pure when it was taken off a pedestal to be practiced for real by farmers, shopkeepers and a rising middle class, all of them arguing, wheedling and conniving amid an incredible din. This wasn't the calmly erudite and idealized Academy or Forum, but something a lot more gritty—often puerile. It was real. Some, like Shelley, Godwin and de Tocqueville, saw beauty in all the noise. Others felt their venerated hopes betrayed. The alliance between romantics and enlightenment pragmatists that had been formidable against medievalism divided along the most obvious fault line, between future and past.

While Shelley—as fitting for the husband of the Mother of Science Fiction—remained passionately in favor of science and democratic reform, many of his contemporaries went the other way. In 1821, Shelley's friend Thomas Love Peacock published a scathing essay on the direction romanticism had taken. Citing Wordsworth, Byron and Scott, he said:

> A poet in our times is a semi-barbarian in a civilised community. He lives in the days that are past. His ideas, thoughts, feelings, associations, are all with barbarous manners, obsolete customs, and exploded superstitions. The march of his intellect is like that of a crab, backward. The brighter the light diffused around him by the progress of reason, the thicker is the darkness of antiquated barbarism....

A little later, Walt Whitman issued his "When I heard the learn'd astronomer," a smugly compact grenade that distilled the zero-sum core of romanticism, asserting that you can either *know* or *feel,* but not both. You may look either ahead or back, but never stretch your compass, or find beauty in progressive understanding.[3]

The romantics' agrarian nostalgia had a real-world basis in the Industrial Revolution's displacement of people and transformation of the countryside; industrialization was now seen as an oppressor, not a liberator. Through the vivid descriptions of Charles Dickens and many others, we all can envision the "satanic mills" where women and children toiled horrid 80-hour weeks, under brutal conditions. Exposing such injustices in vivid tales and dramas may have been the romantics' finest hour.

Mentioned less often is what those factories produced. Mountains of cheap cloth, allowing even the poor to afford several changes of clothes. And soap. And cheap iron bedsteads, just like rich folks had, lifting mattresses off the floor and away from vermin. And more soap. And dinnerware and pencils and concrete for walls and floors, and bathtubs and cheap windows and lamps and books and sewer pipes and reading glasses for those books and water faucets and school desks and flush toilets and electric wire. And more soap.

Faced with these trade-offs, people voted in many ways, with marches, protests, ballots and their pocketbooks. And with their feet, moving en masse from country hovels to urban tenements. It turned out that they wanted the factories, slums and schools *reformed*! But they also wanted what the factories and schools made.

Many—not all—romantics disagreed with this decision. It baffled them.

In a nutshell, that was when they parted company with—and started nurturing contempt for—the common man.

Romanticism Is Not About Romance

Okay, that's a lot. Only now let's tie this in with our overlying theme. J.R.R. Tolkien and his fellow Oxfordite, C.S. Lewis, were proud and avowed romantics. Calling the scientific world-view "soulless," they joined Keats and Coleridge, Henry James and most European-trained philosophers in spurning the modern emphasis on pragmatic experimentation, production, universal literacy, progress, cooperative enterprise, democracy, city life and flattened social orders. In contrast to these "sterile" pursuits, romantics extolled the traditional, the personal, the particular, the subjective, the rural, the hierarchical and the metaphorical.

8. The Lord of the Rings

Moreover, by the turn of the century, romanticism was fast losing all vestige of its former empathy for the concerns of common folk. One solitary artist—or entertainer or lost prince or angry poet—loomed larger in importance, by far, than a thousand craft workers, teachers or engineers ... a value system that is thoroughly pushed today by the mythic engine of Hollywood. Just as in Homer's time, 10,000 foot soldiers mattered less than Achilles' heel.

This fits the very plot of *Lord of the Rings*, in which good guys strive to preserve and restore as much as they can of an older, graceful and "natural" hierarchy, against the disturbing, quasi-industrial and vaguely technological ambience of Mordor, with its smokestack imagery and manufactured power-rings that can be used by anybody, not just an elite few. (Recall the scene—both in the books and in Peter Jackson's film—where Saruman turns away from the "good" side and immediately starts ripping up trees, replacing them with mining pits and smoky forges. The anti-industrial imagery could not be more explicit.)

Consider the rings. Those metal wonders are deemed cursed, damning anyone who dares to use them. Especially those nine normal humans who tried to rise up, using tools to equalize and then usurp the rightful powers of their betters—the high elves. The nine Ring Wraiths aren't just evil henchmen and cardboard monsters. In my opinion, they are among the most important figures of the epic. Tolkien calls them tragic and dwells on their background. These fallen mortals—decent men who were hauled unwillingly into service to the "dark side"—can be looked upon as cautionary figures, conveying the universal lesson that "power corrupts."

On that much we can all agree. But I think there's more to the Ring Wraiths. To me, they distill the classic Greek notion of hubris—a concept that romantics often embrace—the idea that pain and damnation await any mortal whose ambition aims too high. Don't try putting on the trappings or emblems or powers that rightfully belong to your betters. Above all, don't try to decipher and redistribute mysteries! Exactly the same morality tale preached in *Star Wars*.

Romanticism has come full circle, now unctuously praising the very same lords—the über-men—it started out opposing.

An aside, in self-defense. Some readers may assign "left" or "right" political significance to what I say here. Don't. Both romantics and pragmatists fill every modern political movement. For example, as a staunch environmentalist, I can still comment on the romantic elitism of many who share the same cause. In fact, this struggle is being fought every day, almost unnoticed, in the battlefield of our contemporary media. Enlightenment's child—suspicion of authority—often comes paired with the quintessential romantic image: a smug loner who despises the masses. They get mixed together, even though they arise from different traditions.

To tell them apart, try to notice whether a character sneers only at power-abusers ... or at everybody. Is his or her ire aimed solely upward, toward some cruel elite, or downward too, despising fellow citizens and neighbors as clueless sheep?

Don't get me wrong. Romanticism can make strong points. Even after the worst crimes of industrialization were palliated, criticism remains valid. For one thing, every generation of entrepreneurs features some who are insatiable and conspire together to become lords. Moreover, scientific advancement badly needs the constant light of public scrutiny, or else the "advances" can easily go sour. Science needs criticism precisely because it's proved effective. It works far better than magic ever did. That makes science potentially more harmful, as well as far more useful.

A blatant example is what we're doing to our world. Modern civilization isn't inherently less caring. It's just that there are so many of us, and we can afford to buy so many things, that it puts Earth under intolerable strain. The planet was certainly less abused when our numbers were kept low by poverty, starvation and disease. Now we must replace those old corrective forces with new ones: knowledge, foresight and self-restraint.

No wonder romanticism yearns for simpler ways and times, when death solved all such problems in a more natural way. Moreover, enlightenment can never completely replace older modes of thinking. A need for stirring, illogical tales and images runs deep within us all. (Some of us earn a good living that way.) Without romance, we'd be sorry creatures, indeed.

Still, scientific-progressive society has been known to listen to its critics, and not just now and then. Name one feudal society whose leaders did that.

Were any orcs or "dark men" offered coalition positions in King Aragorn's cabinet, at the end of the Ring War? Was Mordor given a benign Marshall Plan? I think not.

Which brings us to another of the really cool things about fantasy—identifying with a side that's 100 percent good. You can revel as they utterly annihilate foes who deserve to be exterminated because they are 100 percent distilled evil.

This may not be politically correct, but then, political correctness is really a bastard offspring of the egalitarian-scientific enlightenment. Witness the sometimes saccharin PC-sweetness of *Star Trek*. Enlightened, but maybe also a bit gelded. (Is that why everybody likes Klingons?)

Romanticism never made any pretense at equality. It is hyper-discriminatory, by nature. (Have you ever actually read Byron or Coleridge?) Whole classes of people are less worthy, less deserving of life, than other classes. The Nazis were archetypal romantics. (Ever listened to Wagner?) Deal with that.

8. The Lord of the Rings

The urge to crush some demonized enemy resonates deeply within us, dating from ages far earlier than feudalism. Hence, the vicarious thrill we feel over the slaughter of orc foot soldiers at Helm's Deep. Then again as Ents flatten even more goblin grunts at Saruman's citadel, taking no prisoners, never sparing a thought for all the orphaned orclings and grieving widorcs. And again at Minas Tirith, and again at the Gondor Docks and again … well, they're only orcs, after all.[4]

What fun.

Lev Grossman made similar points in a *Time* magazine article:

> Where are the women? Peter Jackson filled out Liv Tyler's role for the movies (it's much less prominent in Tolkien's version), but the Fellowship is still as much a boys' club as Augusta National. And whiter too. Don't let all the heartwarming Elf-Dwarf bonding between Legolas and Gimli fool you. The only people with dark skin in Middle-earth are the Orcs.

This tendency is taken to an extreme, showing the basic moral problem of romanticism, in a work that was coincidentally created by the other fellow who filmed a version of *Lord of the Rings*, one Ralph Bakshi. His animated feature *Wizards* remains, in my opinion, just about the most evil artwork produced since Goebbels ran the Nazi propaganda mill. In Bakshi's post-apocalyptic future, pastoral pixies, or elves, dwell in a bucolic Wagnerian paradise of vast, open countryside. These pretty creatures exclude a tribe they call "mutants"—ugly, urban and vaguely technological—forcing them to inhabit a lightless canyon-ghetto for a thousand years. Bakshi portrayed the mutants as cowardly and pathetically incompetent, whenever they tried to escape into the pixies' immense realm. No matter. A narrator calls the suppression a matter of essential "good" vs. "evil."…as defined by the elvish side. When the mutants finally get inspired by a leader (portrayed as a screeching skeleton), viewers worry, then cheer when doughty elves surround the ghetto, launch a pre-emptive strike, and annihilate every mutant, down to the last cub.

Admittedly, most Tolkien lovers claim to loathe Ralph Bakshi's version of *Lord of the Rings*. And yet, the commonalties of theme are relentless. He may represent the darkest side of this "force," but it's the same basic premise.

Let's not ignore, but instead openly acknowledge the underlying racialism and belief in an inherent aristocracy that Tolkien wove into the books, without even much attempt at subtlety. *Nor do I much blame him.* He couldn't help it, coming from the imperialist and class-ridden culture that raised him. One that worried deeply about how "uppity" the masses were starting to become.

Moreover, the characters whom the reader comes to know best—Frodo, Sam and even the king-in-waiting, Aragorn—are themselves not very snooty or racist. Aragorn has an easygoing, common touch—much like Luke Skywalker, the only un-patronizing Jedi. The snootiest and most relentlessly aristocratic characters in *Lord of the Rings* stand aside, in the wings. Preachy, secretive and patronizing Elrond for example, and Galadriel, coaxing maximum effort while others do the fighting for them.

Bloody elfs. I'd point out endless parallels with a fellow named Yoda, but that would stir up too many hornets all at once!

Some Romantics After the Somme

In Chapter 2, I refer to folklore ethnographer Joseph Campbell, author of *The Power of Myth*, and his assertion that ancient legends had common rhythms and themes, from continent to continent, and I suggest that much of this similarity may have arisen out of simple economics. Olden-time bards and storytellers needed to eat, so naturally they sucked up to the chieftains and priests who had all the bread and gold, conjuring legends of elite demigods and princes, seldom daring (and only obliquely) to suggest that creativity and courage—even sovereignty—might reside in common men and women. Enlightenment gifts—egalitarianism, openly shared criticism, cooperative skill, accountability, argument, criticism, social mobility and science—were anathema. To this day, romantics feel uncomfortable with them. To Campbell, any story that drifted from the standard romantic formula was simply no story at all.

In fact, I credit Tolkien with imaginatively and deliberately violating Campbell's strict "rules" on many occasions. Indeed, he was more balanced and far more critical of the situation portrayed in his universe than any but a few of his myriad readers ever choose to notice. Certainly more self-critical than most of his contemporary readers or those watching the new film trilogy. In several places, Tolkien openly stated his authorial judgment that the elves who made the Three Rings were ultimately to blame, having set the stage for tragedy in Middle-earth. They created their own rings (preceding Sauron's One Ring) in order to control the world, stopping time and preventing change, forbidding anything to die and decay and thus taking away room for new growth. Critic Verlyn Flieger quotes Tolkien: "They wanted to have their cake and eat it: to live in the mortal historical Middle-earth because they had become fond of it … and so tried to stop its change and history, stop its growth, keep it as a *pleasaunce*."

There are moments scattered throughout *Lord of the Rings* when Tolkien seems to be warning that romanticism can lead one down the road to genocide. He was disturbed to see the Nazi SS, for example, embrace many

8. The Lord of the Rings

of the same Nordic mythic stories and symbols that he used as source material. And yet, neither Tolkien nor his close friend C.S. Lewis—even confronted with the blatant romantic excesses of Nazism—could escape their own conviction that modernity made up the greater evil. That hated trend, Tolkien feared, would ruin all the beauty that he found in tradition. In aristocratic-mystical hierarchies. In ways of the past.

As you might expect, I philosophically oppose reflexive, nostalgic romanticism and aristocratic-mystical hierarchies!

Only now, after all of that, let me surprise you by expressing *sympathy* with the position taken by Tolkien! Because he came by his beliefs honestly, indeed with real cause.

As a youth, he saw what modernity was doing to both the countryside and to cities choked in coal soot, turning white-limestone buildings black. Industrialization at its worst. Then, he was called to arms, serving in hellish Flanders, watching the clanking, inhuman tools of modernity produce corpses with factory efficiency, scything down the flower of his generation. Like many of those traumatized by trench warfare, he sought to take his mind and soul far away … and I cannot say I'd be any different.

Today's romantics generally lack that excuse. They accept modernity's gifts hand over fist, including not just wealth and tools and opportunities, but also the wonder of *self-correction* that enabled us to enact reforms, rising out of the mid-century pit to build the world's greatest (if still deeply flawed) era of peace and prosperity, learning gradually how to clean the air and water and (too slowly) so many stains of injustice and prejudice. It's been a grinding process, without many of the clearcut triumphs you get in fantasy, like the fall of Barad-Dur's dark tower. (Or the Berlin Wall?) So it is understandable—if a bit ungrateful—that romantics like George Lucas rage against the modern world, while accepting every fruit.

In contrast, Tolkien had good cause … and honesty! In later-published books, like *The Silmarillion*, he turned his critical gaze inward, casting an analytical eye even upon the elvish hierarchs of Middle-earth, in much the same way that Isaac Asimov re-evaluated his Second Foundation and the meddlesome-patronizing robots of his famed science fictional universe. The kind of self-examination that the *Star Wars* cosmos desperately needs, alas.

Indeed, some academics cite an obvious parallel between the retreat of the High Elves in *Lord of the Rings*—abandoning Middle-earth to return "west across the sea"—and the dissolution of the British Empire, which began with the emancipation of India, about the same time that Tolkien was writing his epic. In fairness, Tolkien did not rail futilely against change. He saw it as regrettable but inevitable—like the end of Middle-earth's mythical Third Age. An approaching time of iron, when aloofly noble figures like

Elrond and Galadriel must go back whence they came, replaced by something new. But what?

While we feel a romantic rush over Aragorn's return to kinghood, it's the hobbits of the Shire who we're truly asked to care about. *They* are the polar opposites to Sauron's Mordor. Tolkien's story is about choosing between two models for the coming Fourth Age: one of them industrial-filthy-oppressive-urban ... and Orwellian, for surely he must have read *Nineteen Eighty-Four*.

The "modern" alternative that Tolkien—and his readers—prefer is the Shire's rural yeomanry. Yes, it is egalitarian, meritocratic, even a little democratic, though with some decorum and a doffing of hats to inherited lords, or those of good family. And if that is our only choice, then who wouldn't pick the author's prescriptive utopia. It's an attractive image, even knowing that his thumb presses hard upon the scales. And that is how romantics roll.

It all seems rather a pity, in light of what happened later, during the final third of the 20th century. For C.P. Snow's "gap" between two cultures began to be crossed, time and again, by unfettered spirits who simply refused to accept primly drawn categories. I wish Tolkien and Lewis could have lived to see how easily this chasm is traversed now, in both directions, by technologically savvy artists and by scientists who love art.

Clearly, science fiction bridged the two cultures gap with a superhighway. But that's another story.

Part Three:
Grinding Axes

9

Roll Over, Frank Miller
Street Kids Are Better Than Those 300 Spartans!

The next article was written in 2011, during the Occupy Wall Street movement that briefly filled a New York City park to protest economic inequality. Famous comic book writer-illustrator Frank Miller issued a howl of hatred toward those raucous but sincere and harmless youths, a volcanic, scatological spew of lavish hate. For example: "'Occupy' is nothing but a pack of louts, thieves and rapists, an unruly mob, fed by Woodstock-era nostalgia and putrid false righteousness. These clowns can do nothing but harm America."

Well, well. I'd long fumed silently at Miller's open war against every virtue and accomplishment of the Western Enlightenment. But this led me to dissect his most famous and lucrative work of treacherous propaganda—a comic book and movie tale about Spartans at the Battle of Thermopylae called 300.

This was published on Salon *years before the Miller-Snyder sequel* 300: Rise of an Empire *that strangely and coincidentally took on the very topics I demanded, only then used lies to twist them beyond all recognition. I'll append my reaction to the wretched sequel.*

Though I'm not best-known for graphic novels, I've done a few. At one point I sketched out a script about one of the greatest heroes of western civilization, Themistocles, who defeated the Persian emperor Xerxes during his brutal invasion of Greece, after those famous Spartans failed so miserably at Thermopylae. In part, this would be an answer to Frank Miller's *300*—a book and film that I find both visually stunning and morally disturbing.

For one thing, *300* gave all credit to the Spartans, extolling them as role models and peerless examples of manhood—adorably macho defenders of freedom.

Uh, right. *Freedom*. Sorry, but the word bears a heavy burden of irony when shouted by Spartans, who maintained one of the worst slave-states ever. They treated the vast majority of their people as cattle, routinely quenching their swords in the bodies of poor, brutalized helots—who are never mentioned, even glimpsed, in the romanticized book or movie. Indeed, the very same queen who Miller portrayed as so-kind, was said to be quite brutal with a whip in real life.

Miller's Spartan warriors honestly and openly conveyed the contempt for civilians that was felt across the ages by all feudal warrior castes. An attitude in sharp contrast to American sympathies, which always used to be about Minuteman farmers and shopkeepers—citizen soldiers—the kind who bravely pick up arms to aid their country, adapting and training under fire. Alas, Miller's book and movie *300* ridiculed that kind of soldier …

… even though the first invasion by Persia, ten years earlier—under Xerxes' father—had been defeated by just such a militia army from Athens, made of farmers, clerks, tradesmen, artists and mathematicians. A rabble of ill-disciplined "brawlers," they waited in vain for promised help from Sparta, then decided to handle the problem alone. On that fateful day, a citizen militia leveled spears and their thin blue line attacked a professional Persian force many times their number, slaughtering them to the last man on the legendary beach of Marathon.

The Inconvenient Truth of Marathon

Think about that for a moment. Can you picture it? Damn. Please pause here and Wiki "Marathon." Even better, watch the PBS computer-dramatized documentary. Prepare to be amazed that there were once such men. Go on. I'll wait!

Miller rails against effete, pansy-boy militias of amateur citizen soldiers. But funny thing, none of his Spartan characters ever mentions those events, just a decade earlier! How bakers, potters and poets from Athens, after vanquishing one giant invading army, then *ran 26 miles in full armor* to face down a second Persian horde and sent it packing, a feat of endurance that gave its name to the modern marathon race. A feat that goes unmatched today. Especially by Spartans.

That Athenian triumph deserves a movie! And believe me, it weighed heavily on the real life Leonidas, ten years later. Miller, author of *300*, portrays the Spartans' preening arrogance in the best possible light, as a kind of endearing tribal machismo (kind of like *Star Trek*'s Klingons). Miller never hints at the underlying reason for Leonidas' rant, a deep current of smoldering shame over how Sparta sat out Marathon, leaving it to Athenian amateurs, like the playwright Aeschylus, to save all of Greece. The "shopkeepers" whom Leonidas outrageously and ungratefully despises in the film.

With that shame over Marathon fresh in memory, Leonidas was eager to prove Spartan mettle when Persia invaded a second time, even though he could find just 300 volunteers. That much, *300* gets right. Alas, truth is rare in that book and film. Like the notion that Xerxes cared a whit about rustic Sparta in the first place. Athens was always his chief target. The heart of the West.

Even when it comes to the Battle of Thermopylae itself, *300* tells outright lies. For example, 1000 Thespians refused to leave their comrades at the end. They stayed in the pass and died next to Leonidas' 300 Spartans. More shopkeepers. Their valor was inconvenient to Miller's narrative, So he slandered them, depicting them running away.

Oh, remember those helots? As slavemasters, Spartans made the later Romans seem positively goody-two-shoes by comparison. In his book and movie *300*, Miller never shows the 2000 helot luggage-bearers whom Leonidas' gang of bullies whipped before them into the pass at Thermopylae, forcing them to carry their masters' gear and food and wine and shields.

Where were those slaves during the battle? Why, in the front line! Handed spears but no armor, they slowed down the Persians with their bodies, then made the ground conveniently slippery with their blood. Huh, funny how that got left out! I'm sure it was just an oversight.

Thermopylae: What Was Going On in Plain View

But the worst slander of all is one of glaring, outrageous omission and tunnel vision. It is what *300* might have shown happening just offstage, simply by turning the camera! Indeed, Leonidas could see it with his own eyes, in plain view throughout the fight, if only he chose to swivel his head. Alas, he never turns, in the comic or film.

The Athenian navy, hard-pressed and outnumbered, guarded his flank in the nearby Artemisium Straits. Again, a citizen militia of fishermen, merchants, blacksmiths and philosophers, they too were at Thermopylae! A few miles out to sea, they battled odds no less desperate than Leonidas faced, without the convenient cliff and wall, against vastly superior Persian forces. Only with this one important difference: Where Leonidas failed to hold for more than a day or so, the Athenians kept firm! They only retreated when the Spartans let them down!

(Note from 2018: I'll append at the end some comments on *300: Rise of an Empire,* the equally dishonest sequel that untruthfully portrays Athenian *defeat* in the straits.)

The commander of that brave flotilla, Themistocles, is a hero far more in keeping with American traditions. A Washington-like commander who makes good use of volunteers—plus new technology and brains—to stave off hordes of arrogant, professional conquerors. Less interested in pompous bragging and macho preening, he cared about his men, striving to achieve both victory and survival. He despised "bold gestures." What mattered were results. Saving his country. Civilization. His men.

And now that you know this, can you believe that Miller and his partners refused to let Leonidas turn his head, or let us witness such a wonderful thing through his eyes? And maybe give a brief, respectful nod to his allies' epic courage? Don't you feel cheated? You were.

Forced to give way when Leonidas failed to hold a narrow pass, Themistocles and his sailor militia kept up a fighting retreat, survived the burning of their city (where their dauntless women handled a skillful evacuation) … until they finally drew the vast Persian navy into a trap at a little island called Salamis … glorious Salamis …

… where outnumbered Athenians—and their neighbors—utterly crushed the invading armada, sending Xerxes fleeing for his life. *That* was what saved Greece, not futile boasting and choreographed prancing on the bluffs of Thermopylae. (And again, what a movie someone might make out of the true story!)

As for the later land battle at Platea—glorified by the book and film *300*—it was hard-fought tactically. But strategically it wasn't much more than a mopping-up, slaughtering a demoralized and cut-off Persian force that Xerxes had abandoned. And even at Platea, there were more men from Athens (and Attican towns) than Spartans! And it was Athenians who raced ahead to turn the Persians' flank.

Oh, one more thing about Platea. At the exact moment that Miller portrays the Spartan Dilios taunting and deriding his own allies before a desperate fight (yeah, that's likely), it happens that simultaneously Themistocles and his fleet of volunteer sailors were also finishing off the rest of the Persian navy, at Mycale. Dig it, the Athenians fought two epic battles on that same fateful day. The day the West triumphed and survived. A day worthy of Tolkien and Peter Jackson! And those are the facts. Live with it, Miller.

Do the Spartans at least get credit for commanding Greek armies ashore? A couple of years after Platea, repelled by Spartan arrogance and brutality, the Greek cities dumped Sparta from any further leadership role as Hellenes spent the next 30 years pushing Persia ever further back, expelling them entirely from Europe and liberating enslaved populations. Led by the democratic rabble from Athens.

In other words, history wasn't at all like the book, or the movie *300*. It was much, much better!

Artistic License? Or Goddam Evil-Batshit Lying?

Look, artists get a lot of leeway. At least in this society of freedom they do. (They sure didn't get any slack in feudal times, dominated by warrior-caste bullies.) Miller and the makers of the *300* flick were entitled to emphasize the Spartans and their martial spirit, even though their brave "sacrifice" at Thermopylae accomplished very little, except to make a fine tale of futile bravado. A three-day delay? We're supposed to be impressed by a three-day delaying action?

Well, all right, that's about equal to Davy Crockett at the Alamo. I'm willing to give credit! Okay, Leonidas and the brave 300 Spartans (and 1000 Thespians!) deserve a movie. (They've had several.) But please. This was a small "feat" at best.

I'll also admit, *300* certainly offered a great excuse for 90 minutes of stab-dancing! Hey, I can appreciate the aesthetics, in abstract. It's not especially my thing—and real Spartans did *not* engage in combat that way—still, *300* gets full marks as a lavishly choreographed fight 'n' flex number. And for terrific painted-on abs.

But there comes a point when artistic license turns into deliberate, malicious omission. And then omission becomes blatant, outright-evil lying propaganda. The movie *300* not only crosses that line, it forges into territory that we haven't seen since the propaganda machine of 1930s Germany. Red is blue. Blue is red. Good is defined by the triumph of will.

I might have just sat and glowered, if they simply omitted the Athenians. But to sneer at them and call them effeminate cowards? After Athenian citizen soldiers accomplished epic triumphs the Spartans never imagined and that they would never, ever come remotely close to equaling? At battles whose names still roll off our tongues today? Achieved by the same kind of "cincinnatus" militias that propelled both Republican Rome and the United States to unparalleled heights, during their time of vigor?

The kind of soldiers who make up our U.S. military today! Citizens first, despite their vaunted professionalism.

Historical note: Yes, the Athenians had their faults too! They owned slaves, though more gently than Sparta. Women had few rights—though the legend of Lysistrata was born there. After they lost Great Pericles, their democracy fell into the kind of populist foolishness that we see in America today, idiotic foreign adventures and callousness toward neighbors. But all of that came later. And at their worst, they kept the basic virtues that are at issue in this matter of *300* ... and in my response. Fierce pride in citizenship.

No, this is not just artistic license. Expressed repeatedly—with the relentlessness of deliberate, moralizing indoctrination—*300* idolizes the same arrogant contempt for citizenship that eventually ruined classical Greece and Republican Rome, and that might bring the same fate to America.

My own graphic novel *The Life Eaters* never sold as well as Miller's. Heck, that's not my expertise. (Though it was a finalist in France, where they adore the graphic novel art form.) With gorgeous art by Scott Hampton, *The Life Eaters* tells a vivid story of rebellion and resistance to a very Spartan-like oppression. But forget the shameless plug. I'm not competing with Frank Miller on his turf. I've got plenty enough turf of my own.

What I do suggest is this: Use your own imagination! Picture an answer to *300*, told from the point of view of an escaped Spartan helot-slave serving aboard one of Themistocles' ships, staring up at the frenetic death-prancing of his former masters on the cliff of Thermopylae, shaking his head over their futile, macho posturing, then turning to help the amateur fighters of Athens and Miletus and Corinth get on with the real job of saving civilization.

Doing it without boasting—or painted-on abs—but with wit, courage, comradeship, skill—and the one thing that matters most. Something Leonidas never came close to achieving.

The only truly indispensable accomplishment. Something that is often best won by citizen soldiers...

Victory.

10

Atlas Shrugged
The Hidden Context of the Book and Film

> Now and then we had a hope that if we lived and were good, God would permit us to be pirates.—Mark Twain

There was nothing even remotely interesting at Blockbuster—(and yes, I deliberately left in that quaint reference to the Neolithic Epoch, when I first chipped this essay, in stone)—so we rented *Atlas Shrugged, Part 1*.

Well, after all, Ayn Rand's passionate followers have effectively taken over much of the U.S. Libertarian movement, influencing the polemic—though not any policies—of the American Right. Still, I thought, why not give her acolytes one more shot at selling me on her most central tale? An honest person does that. Whereupon, with a sigh, but opening my ears and mind, I slid the disk into the player....

For the Record

As one of the few science fiction authors who delivered a keynote at a political party convention—indeed it was the Libertarian Party—I seem a "heretic" to the Rand followers who now dominate the LP. But no one can deny my ongoing campaign to get folks to read Adam Smith, the founding sage of both libertarianism and liberalism.

Like Smith, I believe in fair and open and vigorously creative *competition*—the greatest innovative force in the universe and the process that made us. Encouraging vibrant, flat-fair-open and positive-sum rivalry—in markets, democracy, science, etc.—is one reason to promote universal transparency. (See my non-fiction book *The Transparent Society: Will Technology Force Us to Choose Between Privacy and Freedom?*) All participants in science, democracy and markets should base their individual decisions on full knowledge. That positive aim—also preached by Friedrich Hayek—should be the goal of any sane libertarian movement ... instead of fetishistically hating all government, all the time, which is like a poor worker blaming the tools. Anyway, a movement based on hopeful joy beats one anchored in rancorous scapegoating any day.

Quite different from his popular image as a social Darwinist, Adam Smith favored feeding and educating all children, first because—as author of *The Theory of Moral Sentiment* he actually cared, but also for the pragmatic reason that this is the only way to maximize the number of skilled, adult *competitors*, a root motive of liberalism and a role for government that is wholly justifiable in libertarian terms.[1]

It is in their abandonment of Smith, and even the "c-word" (competition), that the followers of Ayn Rand began their journey down a very strange, cognitively challenged road.

Enough. With due diligence done, let's get back to her works of deliberate fiction, especially *Atlas Shrugged: The Motion Picture*.

Rand's Books ... and the Movie

Despite my low esteem of Ayn Rand's simplistic dogma, I do rate *The Fountainhead* as by far her best book. In its smaller and more personal scope, that novel offered a pretty effective (if kinky-melodramatic) portrayal of uncompromising genius having to overcome the boneheaded doorkeepers of art and architecture—realms that are too often beset by preeners and bullies. In that tale, the hero's adversaries came across as multi-dimensional and even somewhat plausible, if also a bit cartoonish. Indeed, the 1949 Gary Cooper movie was pretty good, for a Rand story.

Alas, in contrast, *Atlas Shrugged* takes on civilization as a whole—all of its institutions and enlightenment processes, top to bottom—calling every last one of them corrupt, devoid of hope, intelligence or honor. Moreover, it proclaims that the vast majority of our fellow citizens are braying, silly sheep.

(Consider this irony: A movement propounding that all people can and should think for themselves also teaches its adherents to openly despise their neighbors as intelligent beings. A party that proclaims fealty to market forces also holds that the number of deciders and allocators can and should be very small. In other words, you can have Hayek or Rand. Not both.)

10. Atlas Shrugged

But pause a moment. How does the book hold up, strictly from the perspective of writing and art? I won't mince words. *Atlas Shrugged* royally sucks as a novel, with cardboard characters, rivers of contrived coincidence and dialogue made of macaroni. (Can you dig a 70-page *speech*?) Though in fairness, the left produces plenty of polemics just as turgidly tendentious.

Am I letting politics bias my judgment of Rand's literary qualities? The intellectual maven of conservatism, William F. Buckley, a founding light of modern libertarianism and also a noted novelist, called *Atlas Shrugged* "one thousand pages of ideological fabulism; I had to flog myself to read it."

Given such source material—and universal boos from both critics and the viewing public—was I surprised to find that the movie version of *Atlas Shrugged* bites, at the level of basic film 101 storytelling? For example, it is only in the last five minutes that the director deigns to clarify a core villain! As for the "heroes" … well, their famously emotionless "I don't give a crap" mien may work for campus geeks. But not in cinema, where passion propels.

(Indeed, a deeply ironic and smirk-worthy "oops" appeared on the cover of the DVD version, blurbing *Atlas Shrugged* as a saga of "courage and self-sacrifice"—which would be the ultimate Randian sin!)

A High Point

One sequence does stand out. I'm a sucker for lyrical cinematography, especially when it involves beautiful scenery, or a love-ode to fine technology. And there are about ten minutes in *Atlas Shrugged* when we get both, as the male and female leads ride their new super-train along shimmering rails made of miraculous Rearden Metal, speeding across gorgeous Rockies and over a gasp-worthy bridge.

The emotional payoff—two innovators triumphing over troglodyte naysayers by delivering an awesome product—portrayed Rand's polemical point in its best conceivable light. I am all for that aspect of the libertarian dream. Indeed, it is the core theme that makes *The Fountainhead* sympathetic and persuasive. So, for ten minutes, we actually liked the characters and rooted for them. Significantly, it is the portion when nobody speaks.

Alas, though. The film then resumed a level of simplistic lapel-grabbing that many of us recall from our Rand-obsessed college friends—largely underachievers who kept grumbling from their sheltered, coddled lives, utterly convinced that they'd do much better in a world of dog-eat-dog. (Using my science fictional powers, I have checked out all the nearby parallel worlds where that happened. In those realms, every Randian I know was quickly turned into a slave or dog food. Sorry, fellows.)

Ah well. Let's set aside pathetic storytelling, crappy direction and limp drama to appraise the film on its own, intended merits. On what it tried to be. A work of polemical persuasion.

The Core Polemical Purpose

Atlas Shrugged is, after all, an indictment of modernist, enlightenment, Smithian-liberal civilization. To Rand, this "great experiment" has all been one big mistake, doomed to expire from its own internal contradictions.

I use that Marxian expression deliberately. For, in significant dialectical ways, Ayn Rand was deeply influenced by Karl Marx—virtually an acolyte, in fact. She kept essentially intact Marx's scenario of bourgeois decadence, guild protection, capital formation, conspiratorial competition-suppression, class-narrowing business cycles and teleologically inevitable divergence between the worker and owner castes. It's all there.

The chief difference is that Rand, a Russian émigré, stops short at the *penultimate* phase of Karl's projection—the moment of pinnacle capitalist consolidation—freezes it and calls it good. Tearing out and throwing away all hints of the next and final stage prophesied by Marx.

That's it, actually. Rand, in a nutshell. You might grasp the stunning parallels at once … if anyone my age or younger had ever bothered to actually read and understand *both* Rand and Marx. Well enough to draw obvious conclusions. Alas, our grandparents were far better-read than we hyper-opinionated moderns.

Rand shows us society making one dismal choice after another—an endless chain of socialist or bourgeois-oligarchic or meddlesome-statist outrages against individual initiative. Endearingly, she despised all three of those centers of villainy equally, portraying them uniting to pass laws that punish or seize companies who "compete too well."

Indeed, if I ever witnessed our nation enacting the kind of insane bills that are reported in this book and film (piled one after another, every five minutes), heck, I'd be looking for John Galt myself!

Yes, I'm enough of a libertarian to know that foolish things do happen! Witness Europe, mired in nanny-state entitlements, eight-week vacations and a "right to retire" as young as 55. Self-defeating regulations prevent companies from firing workers, with the consequence that they seldom hire new ones.

As for the movie's heroine, Rand chose a railroad heiress for good reasons. The old Interstate Commerce Commission was the classic exemplar of a government bureaucracy "captured" by lordly oligarchs and used as a tool to squelch competition.

10. Atlas Shrugged

In other words, the endless litany of "leveling" crimes against creative enterprise that roll across the page (and screen) in *Atlas Shrugged* aren't entirely without real-world analogues. Her fictional betrayals of creative enterprise are based on a genuine complaint ... that Randites regularly exaggerate more than 100-fold, alas, into caricatures and absurd over-generalizations.

To see this danger expressed far better—and more succinctly—than Rand ever managed, read the terrific Kurt Vonnegut story "Harrison Bergeron." Other expressions of legitimate libertarian worry can be seen in the fiction of Ray Bradbury and Robert Heinlein. They have a point. Meddlesome civil servants can be one more kind of elite worthy of scrutiny, even skepticism.

Okay, the core concern is a valid one, and somebody in society should keep warning us! Though ideally, someone with common sense and proportion, alas.

I mean, gee whiz. Ayn Rand railed against the Interstate Commerce Commission ... and it was eliminated. Dissolved by *Democrats* in the late 1970s. Canceled, rubbed out, utterly erased—along with the grotesque Civil Aeronautics Board—by the very same constitutional processes that she and her followers despised. Competition among railroads was restored and it was done by a mix of pressure from a savvy public and resolution by genuinely reform-minded politicians. If Rand were writing the book today, a railroad would not have been her chosen archetype.

I wonder: Did anyone making the film ever ponder this? Did any Randians notice at all?

A Remarkable Chain of Ironies

I guess I sound pretty harsh. Only now, let me do one of my famous contrary swerves and openly avow something that Rand gets right. Despite gross exaggeration, she pretty much nails the basic problem! Almost every time the book or film depicts some betrayal of human competitive ingenuity, it happens like this:

A conspiracy of "old money" oligarchs gathers in conniving secrecy, exerts undue political influence and misuses government power for their own, in-group self-aggrandizement. Except for a few pathetic union stewards, the ruination of market forces is stage-managed from the top. The squelching of entrepreneurial enterprise and the corruption of trade is always executed by villainous old-guard capitalists. Moguls who don't want any rivalry from rambunctious newcomers.

Now think about that. Socialists do come under derision from Rand, but mostly as ninny, do-gooder tools of the scrooge-oligarchs! In fact, this is where her followers get things right. Anyone who considers the long, lamentable epic of human history will recognize this as the ancient pattern, pervasive across 99 percent of cultures—with the most prevalent sub-version being feudalism.

What Randians never explain is how getting rid of constitutional-enlightenment government will prevent this ancient curse from recurring. (Were oligarchs stymied in ancient China, Babylon or Rome, where liberal constitutions were absent?) Indeed, enlightenment governments are the only force that ever kept the feudal sickness partially in check. Exactly as prescribed by Adam Smith. (Name another society that ever made more libertarians, hmm?)

In other words, by her very own premise, the answer isn't for creative people to "go on strike." It is to fix the tool (government) by yanking it out of the hands of conspiratorial criminals who have improperly seized it. You do that with transparency, with light (as Hayek prescribed). Not by blaming the tool and throwing it away.

You Are Getting Very Sleeeeepy...

Oh, but more ironies abound! Here you have a polemic about individualism, that portrays one accomplished CEO after another "gone missing"... dropping out of sight after each one listens to a solitary pitchman from a utopian community, who croons, "Come. Follow me and joiiiin usssss."

Ummm, let's see. When have we heard that before? Drop everything. All your past loyalties and the companies you've built. Stop fighting for your family or country. Listen to this incantation and follow our charismatic leader to the special society he has built, just for the exclusive elect, like you.

Good Lord, does she have to make the hypnotism-cult thing quite so explicit? So very much like Jim Jones and David Koresh? Did you know that Rand followers who recite her catechisms light up exactly the same parts of the brain as other true-believers pronouncing passages from the Bible or Koran or Hindu Sutras? And these are not the corners of cortex used by scientists while performing analytical or "objective" reasoning.

But you don't need any of that to conclude we're dealing with a cult. Just follow the recruitment process used by John Galt. Who surreptitiously sabotages successful companies in order to drive their owners into his arms? Who then deliberately vandalizes and cripples the nation's ability to feed itself or engage in commerce that he doesn't control, in order to wreck any possible competition with his elite enclave. Oh, criminy.

Yes, I'll admit that Rand at least portrays technology as good. That gives her points over the dismal Tea Partiers, or Fox News, or the equally dismal (though less numerous) science haters of a ditzy-fringe far left. Alas, though, she treats technology like something magical. Lone inventors weave a spell and suddenly there's a new metal or new motor! The vast intricacy of collaboration, development, supplier networks and infrastructure is both a non-topic to Rand and an excuse for incantatory over-simplification.

But it is science that truly gets short shrift. Rand's lack of any reference to scientific research that might support or falsify her assertions about human nature should set alarm bells clanging. Her ignorance of Darwin or human biology, for example, is almost identical to Marx, but much less excusable, given when she lived.

Nowhere, either in *Atlas Shrugged* or subsequent libertarian cant, is there acknowledgment of the immense stimulative role of U.S. government-financed Research and Development, especially in fields of pure science that would never have attracted investments from anyone looking to a "return horizon." Indeed, I have long yearned for a second National Debt Clock, this one showing what the public debt would be now, if only the taxpayer had received normal levels of royalties from rockets, satellites, communications, fiber optics, computers, pharmaceuticals and the Internet. Well? Wouldn't that be fair and businesslike? Tellingly, while many scientists have a fiercely competitive libertarian streak, almost none who are in the top ranks ever hold any truck with Ayn Rand.

The analog to Rand is not the scientist Darwin, but the rhetorician Plato. Sure, she claims to prefer Aristotle. But in both verbal process and incantatory reasoning style, she is Plato's truest heir.

Ayn Rand on Privacy

All right, veering briefly aside from *Atlas Shrugged*, let's see what Rand says about *privacy*, a topic I happen to know a lot about: "Civilization is the progress toward a society of privacy. The savage's whole existence is public, ruled by the laws of his tribe. Civilization is the process of setting man free from men."

Of course, there is a level at which Rand is simply stating the obvious. That autonomy and long lives arose as our technology and civilized complexity improved. When food surpluses were meager, only a tiny aristocracy could be subsidized and unchained from the land. But a mixture of science and continental peace mixed with our ability to trade goods and services until even science fiction authors can now pretend we are producers of a primary product, worthy of being fed by farmers.

As for the quote itself: As usual, Rand mixes some core truths of the Enlightenment with mystical teleology. The rise of the individual—never steady or even—has been a core theme of the West, ever since the Renaissance, and especially the Enlightenment. But this progression isn't fated, ordained or even natural.

Rand looks at a couple of hundred years on one quarter of the planet, and assumes the trend is unstoppable. But Huxley and Orwell—backed up by Malthus and Darwin—showed us what's "natural." The diamond-shaped social structure that we take for granted can all too easily slump back into the oligarch-dominated pyramid.

Only Enlightenment methods ever offered an alternative hope. Rand followers take it for granted. Indeed, they assume that we can dismantle the processes and structures that Adam Smith prescribed and the U.S. Founders implemented, that made the Enlightenment work in the first place.

They bear a *burden of proof* that we would not just slump back into the condition that prevailed, for thousands of years, before Smith and his colleagues came along. In America, that slump is already well underway.

The Posterity Problem

I saved the best for last, hoping that at least a few libertarians—those most-favored with our greatest human trait, curiosity—have hung with us to this point.

Elsewhere, I've revealed the biggest and most telling red flag about Rand—one that I've not seen mentioned elsewhere. It is that none of her über role-model characters, at any level or in any way, ever indulge in the most basic human project—bearing and raising and loving and teaching children.

Out of 1000 pages—and several more if you look beyond *Atlas Shrugged*—just one of them glances briefly at a mother—a baker, an enlightened and awakened proletarian who is not a member of the elite caste. She gives a short riff about preferring Randite education methods in Galt's Gulch over public schools. That is it for procreation. As for the New Lords—several dozen of them, all dynamic Rand-heroes of the future—not even one of them bothers to pass his or her genes forward in time. Nor do any of them take responsibility for, or even mention, this essential investment in time. And this from the "life-centered" philosophy.

There is a reason that Rand consistently avoided any mention of procreation among her new-lord caste: because featuring even one member of a next-generation would shine searing light upon the biggest flaw of her

10. Atlas Shrugged

hypnotic spell, revealing that her "fresh" tale is actually the oldest one in the human saga.

Let me explain. It is glaringly simple.

We all know this about aristocracy: that it seldom breeds true. In the past, royal or aristocratic houses would grow fat, lazy and decadent. England's Plantagenets managed to stay virile for 400 years but most lines devolved much quicker. Oligarchs had to make inheritance-of-privilege state policy. They gave top priority to quashing open markets, science, democracy and equal justice—because any of these liberal processes might engender new competitors to rise afresh from below, exposing the spoiled grandkids to dangerous rivals.

Yet, even so, there was some churn! A violent form of social mobility. Inevitably those decadent houses got toppled by new, fresh blood. By vibrant competitors who grew lean and tough in exile. Who trained and gathered their forces in the woods, then swooped in to storm the castle. And thereupon established a new lordly line.

> *Deep below her superficial adherence to Marxist teleology lies this ancient cycle, far older than the enlightenment, or even writing. It is the very essence of what Ayn Rand stands for. Her characters are the brash, virile, sturdy, innovative barbarians, born free and ready to seize destiny in their own hands, ripping fortune out of the clutches of pathetic old-fart lords who are spent and bereft of cleverness or might. It's the oldest story, writ-new and draped with modernist garments. Even in her portrayals of sex, the closest parallel is a godlike Viking who kicks down the door and takes what he desires. Because he is the grandest thing in all directions. And because he can.*

It is an ancient mythos that resonates deeply in our bones and especially within pasty-skinned, pencil-necked nerds, who picture themselves as Achilles, as John Wayne, as Ender Wiggin, as Harry Potter or some other demigod. An old, old formula that was mined by A.E. van Vogt and L. Ron Hubbard and Orson Scott Card and so many others.

But therein lies a problem! It's the romantic Phase One of this old cycle that Rand admires—the rise of a self-made buccaneer who seizes lordship from decadent, inbred fools.

Phase Two—what happens next—she never talks about! She averts her eyes and the reader's attention.

Why do none of Rand's characters ever have kids? Because those kids will inherit the olympian status wrested by Howard Roark or by Dagny Taggart and Hank Rearden. Sons and daughters of demigods, they will assume privileges and power that they never earned through fair competition. They will take lordship for granted as a right of blood, and use it to squelch new competitors from rising to face them on a level playing field. Until their own decadent line has to be toppled, amid war and waste and pain.

It's what happened in 99 percent of human societies. Ayn Rand faces a steep burden of proof that "this time it'll be different." A burden she never picks up. Rather, she *shrugs* it off.

If there are offspring, then the reader might become consciously aware of this inevitable outcome and realize: "Hey, I've seen this before. It's the same old boring-human pattern, and nothing new, after all."

The Problem Is People...

Oh, but maybe I am reading too much into this aversion toward kids. After all, as the recent film reminds us, Rand was pretty much an equal opportunity hater of people in general. (As evidenced by her passionately admiring defense of the horrific murderer William Edward Hickman.)

Just look at how *brothers* are portrayed in *Atlas Shrugged*. Always treacherous, small-minded, parasitical and craven. Clearly, Rand is no Nazi, no believer in the paramountcy of blood. Sons, daughters, brothers and sisters? Neighbors? Strangers? Spouses? Co-workers? Civilization? Bah, who needs 'em? Who needs anybody?

Well? I said she ignores Darwin and this is consistent! Reproductive success? Fie and feh!

Her *übermensch* demigods are less like "lords"—obsessed with establishing an inherited clan of privilege—than they are *pirates*—superior in boldness and in mind, going wherever they like, taking what they deserve by the very essence of what they are.

And hey, doesn't everybody love a pirate?

Yoho. That's the life for me.

11

Demigods and "Chosen Ones" ... Would It Hurt If Humanity Got to Play, Too?

Elsewhere in many places I keep returning to a particular obsession—even a fetish—complaining that filmmakers could have accomplished the same drama, action and special effects without denigrating the one fine thing that enabled them to make films in the first place ... *civilization*.

Take the *Star Wars* Third Trilogy, filmed under the aegis of Disney and sci-fi impresario J.J. Abrams. Yes, it's a relief to no longer get George Lucas' faux-zen, ersatz-eastern "wisdom," preaching moral lessons that are diametrically opposite to wise. Disney's newer *Star Wars* flicks feature heroics by many merely talented and brave characters who aren't mutant demigods. Still, did anyone notice how blithely the makers of *The Force Awakens* committed the worst mass-murder in the history of all human myth-making?

From an earlier chapter:

> J.J. Abrams faced a problem. The empire had been defeated, way back in *Return of the Jedi*. So how could he put the Rebels into exactly the same condition they were in, back in the film he was exactly copying: *A New Hope*?
>
> Simple, send out a super-duper Death Star beam to destroy the Rebels' only source of help—the restored Galactic Republic. (Say what, all of it? A bazillion worlds, across a whole galaxy, fried in an instant? How convenient.)

That vast crime takes up less than a minute of screen time and serves only one purpose, to make things dramatically difficult for the rebels sneaking into the super-duper Death Star to blow it up from the inside (one of the series' biggest clichés). This arm-waved atrocity is—naturally—an absurdity that insults the viewer on every conceivable level; for example, would even storm troopers have gone along with slaying half of all galactic sapient life forms without warning, mercy or any chance to surrender, all in a single shot? Indeed, what has the Republic been doing, all this time, while vast resources poured into the First Order's new killer machine? And again ... you just blew up what? *All* the planets in the vast Republic?

What's so sad it that this laziness wasn't necessary! Anyone could have written a better work-around, using the *Barely Insufficient Assistance Stratagem.*

Help Arrives.... Just Not Enough!

So J.J. Abrams wanted a bunch of doughty rebels to zip around replicating, exactly, every heroic move of the original *Star Wars* flick. (Why?) Okay, we'll take that strange goal as given. And yes, it might be inconvenienced, if allies from the Galactic Republic simply waltz in to save the day.

So don't let it be a waltz!

Envision the Republic sending a mighty fleet to destroy the super-duper Death Star! Only it is thwarted by the First Order's own mighty fleet. Simply order more old empire star cruisers from the special effects department and never mind asking where the First Order got 'em. The result? *Stalemate* as the help that arrives only keeps the enemy's fleet busy. And so, while we glimpse a mighty battle, taking place in the distance, our heroes proceed to do every single thing that happens in *The Force Awakens*. (Sure, let the super-duper Death Star blast a few planets, for tension.) The same amount of screen time, devoted to a cooler show.

In other words, the convenience of killing off the entire Republic wasn't necessary at all. You must deny your characters plot-killing help, I get it! But you can do it without denying the very existence of civilization.

Under the Barely Insufficient Assistance Stratagem—or BIAS—cops can come to Batman's aid! Just so long as you toss at them enough Joker Henchmen to hold them off, leaving Batman's leaping antics central to the plot.

Want to see BIAS used well? Earlier I wrote: "By that standard, I have more respect for Michael Bay's *Transformers* series. For all of its bubblegum triteness and cartoony dialogue, at least humanity at large gets to play a role in each of those garishly joyful and stunningly silly romps."

Yes, in that series, regular soldiers (and even jet fighters) swoop in with some effectiveness as flesh and blood heroes fight side by side with the eponymous giant robots, providing *just enough* help for Optimus Prime to triumph and save the day. I mentioned also *Independence Day,* where the nations and fighters of the world play key roles ... just below that of the two, central champions.

Another Great Example

Drifting afield from science fiction, into fantasy territory, we find another example where applying the *Barely Insufficient Assistance Strategy* might have made for a more stirring and elevating ending, without changing what the director had in mind. (Well, not very much.) As I watched the climax of J.K. Rowling's entire Harry Potter cycle—a final battle played out in the climactic film—I couldn't help but think that Rowling and the director missed some great opportunities that would also have ennobled the finale and helped it to make sense.

Consider the point when Voldemort's army crushes the Hogwarts school defenses. Just as we're about to launch into the final duel between Voldemort and Harry Potter, I'd have the Dark Lord sneer, "Who will save you now, children?"

Whereupon a little girl would step up, look the dark lord in the eye and shout: "Our parents!"

She points upslope, where we see a thousand decent wizard folk come rushing to attack Voldemort's forces. Would that have been thrilling? It's also what *would have happened* if villains attacked a school, no? (As is, the average folk of Magical Britain come across as being rather lame.) Even better ... as the battle surges ... would it have hurt to add in a whole crowd of brave Muggles? Local farmers with shotguns. Or Voldemort's force field being pounded by jets—Muggle technology coming to the rescue. That would have been decent and edifying.

And it all could have been set up so that Voldie's forces are just about canceled out, leaving just him and his core crew to breach the walls. The *result is still in doubt*, and the final battle *still* consists of Harry fighting the Dark Lord, and Harry Potter *still* saves the day, exactly as in the current flick! Only with a greater sense of realism, and drama. But above all, a lesson that *we matter*.

And yes, now that you can see where I'm going, wouldn't this also apply to *Avengers: Endgame*? You have the mostly brutally overdone superhero battle of all time, in which every kind of born or mutated or enhanced demigod assembled to fight for Earth and humanity and the Galaxy ... and none of Earth's billions of normal people get to take part? (Well, maybe a few foot soldiers from Wakanda.)

Would it have been that hard to show old Thanos having *two* ships, instead of one ... and the secular armies and navies and air forces of the world converge on the other one, doing their bit, while heroically taking far more casualties than the Avengers? Okay, okay, that might over led to visual overdose, frying the brains of a jillion viewers. But wasn't that the goal, anyway?

Again. I accept the accusation that I seem obsessed. And if the BIAS gambit were used universally, it might be just as much of a cliché as the Useless Humanity notion. Still, it's rare to see *right now*. And it would express some confidence is *us*,

Which is—of course—exactly what some writers and directors do not want.

Demigods "R" Us

Of course, I spoke of demigod-fixation many times. It is classic romanticism, going back to Achilles on the plains of Illium, and I've seen it done with far more *outrageous vileness* by other famed storytellers, such as Frank Miller. In SF, this hoary pattern was pioneered by L. Ron Hubbard and A.E. van Vogt, then perfected by George Lucas. This alluring wish fantasy seduces adolescent males of all ages, who envision themselves just like the protagonist in Chapter 1—a geeky, bullied kid who will survive these early travails until (at last) he gets his Hogwarts letter, or his invitation to the Battle School, or recruitment to Galt's Gulch, learning that he's actually a super-being, an *übermensch* demigod, who just has to awaken dormant super-abilities.

"They're all mean because they sense I'm special! Someday I'll get my powers and *then* you'll see. All of you!" It's called the *Slan Effect,* and as dismally repetitious formulas go, it's a doozy. I found myself sliding toward using it myself, once or twice, before vowing to avoid the hateful cliché.

The greatest of all modern practitioners is Orson Scott Card, whose novel *Ender's Game* has inveigled its way into almost every junior high school curriculum in North America, pushing the übermesch ideal to the max. Consistent with his non-fiction and political railings, he relentlessly inveighs against any thought that democratic processes, institutions or citizenship can ever matter.

Indeed, let me say in Card's defense that he does it better—and with more artful care—than anyone. His demigod characters are more interestingly complex and conflicted than most Nietzschean slan-heroes. When they finally get around to fiercely clamping down and taking control away from corrupt institutions, Cardian characters exhibit *angst and regret*. They discuss *tradeoffs* before always deciding to overrule their neighbors and fellow citizens, and they do it for the Greater Good. Bemoaning the insipid

11. Demigods and "Chosen Ones"

shallowness of the sheep-like masses they must protect, each and every one bemoans how his hand was forced by the immoral and short-sightedly stupid behavior of democratically elected leaders.

In fact, these Cardian examples of *Homo superior* spend so much time and energy moaning, while imposing their will "for your own good," that at least we get one compensation. *They aren't enjoying it.* Which brings us to the greatest and most sympathetic demigod of all, Ender Wiggin, who, across a string of moralizing novels, shakes his chiding-finger at us so vigorously, berating us for being so careless, immoral and immature, that it almost comes flying off.

If you think I am exaggerating, have a look at Card's novel *Empire*, and especially the afterword, in which he makes clear his fervent wish for the American Constitutional system to pass away—as did the Roman Republic—and be replaced by efficient and beneficently ruthless imperial rule, under a new Caesar.

As we saw in an earlier chapter, Card isn't alone. Contempt for the masses—for our neighbors and institutions—is rife among America's dominant Baby Boomer generation, the most self-indulgent in history. Hollywood caters to it, despite poisonous effects on our self-confidence as citizens, because it makes action and peril easy to set up.

Some have rebelled against this endlessly repeated—and treacherously harmful—cliché. Steven Spielberg, for example, always blends suspicion of authority with generous gratitude for a civilization that's been very good to him. In literature, Neal Stephenson's Hieroglyph project gathers authors like Vernor Vinge, Greg Bear, Pat Cadigan, Nancy Kress and the late Iain Banks, aiming to shift away from today's endlessly tedious fetish for derivative dystopias and unimaginative apocalypses, toward stories in which citizenship is not portrayed as futile. But these are rebel exceptions, amid the tsunami of tedious dystopias.

12

Getting Science Fictional About a Better World

Marxists and Feminists and Feudalists and Libertarians, Oh My!

In an earlier chapter, I discussed one of *the* most pervasive literary crutches: *The idiot plot* allows lazy authors and/or directors to contrive peril for their passionately righteous protagonists, simply by assuming there's no one willing or able to help. Contemporary society not only fails to assist, but is essentially without any redeeming qualities at all. Again, I'm not claiming that society doesn't merit criticism—it does! Our gradually rising civilization has benefited greatly from biting commentary, dire warnings and even self-preventing prophecies. But alas, all too often this intent is ruined by a slothful reflex that also makes for *bad art*. A reflex portraying our fellow citizens as too stupid to learn from mistakes.

(Then why are you preaching at them, if you assume they cannot learn, hmm?)

No end of the so-called "political spectrum" is immune to the Idiot Plot's sick-sweet temptation. This chapter will poke at every faction, even some that can count me as an ally! Because no movement can improve when it wallows in uniformity.

In one direction we see the high-walled, self-imposed ghetto of Libertarian SF, a vast—mostly male—contingent obsessed with rockets and Howard Roark. With Ayn Rand and fierce resentment of government bureaucrats. To hear them rail against today's society, you'd think we

12. Getting Science Fictional About a Better World 123

already live in a wretched Orwellian dictatorship, filled with bovine Democrats, porcine Republicans and sheep-like voters, all of them too stupid to perceive The Truth.

In fairness, there are sub-variants ranging from Randian fanaticism (that I dissected in Chapter 10) all the way to the much more humane, liberal-minded and compassionate libertarianism found in works of Robert Heinlein and Allen Steele. As with sci-fi feminists, I am drawn to these characters, largely because of their passion. Indeed there's much to find appealing about their ardent dream of a better world, a future when no one will tell anyone else what to do.

Alas, the libertarians' stern righteousness makes them irresistible targets for playful teasing. For instance, I find that nothing causes these delightfully articulate firebrands to go tongue-locked more efficiently than asking them the following simple question: *Can you name one human civilization, past or present, that was even half as close to what you desire as contemporary America is today? Indeed, can you name another that ever produced ... libertarians?* They find it galling to be reminded how far freedom has already come, or that their citizenship may have real value in a civilization that—while still flawed—is more hope-filled and worthy of the name than any other. Rather than deal with the realistic but tedious possibilities of gradual reform, Libertarian SF is rife with wish-fulfillment fantasies. And so we get to:

The top cliché of libertarian SF features *rebellious space colonies,* cutting their ties to decadent old Earth, proclaiming Shangri-La in orbit.

To be clear, there are many ways that this fantasy resonates with our deepest western mythologies, like suspicion of authority. Hence, it's no surprise that the same dream crosses lines, from Randian libertarianism to left-wing transcendental anarchism. Take for example the Jefferson Starship song "Hijack."

A great song from a great album! Still, it leads this nerd to ask ... so the men and women who do the actual work don't get any part of the starship that they built? Skill and sweat and investment count for nothing? Alas, anyone who spent time on campus across the last 50 years can tell you about the smug, anti-nerd sanctimony expressed by *all* fanatical, political extremes.

Of course, now that we Earthers have been warned by such novels and songs, we'll act in advance to prevent rebellion by ungrateful astronauts. We'll accomplish this by the simple means of choosing *adults* to crew space stations, instead of hormone-drenched boys with heads full of fantasies about hotwiring mobile homes in space.

◊ ◊ ◊

Socialists and Scions of Marx

In an earlier chapter, I argued that the mightiest self-preventing prophecy of all might be *Das Kapital*!:

> "In the East, Karl Marx was a mythical seer whose incantations only wound up painting revolutionary gloss upon age-old paranoias. But in the West, his scenarios were read as plausible failure mode stories, so vividly credible that many of the rich felt impelled to back Franklin Roosevelt and negotiate a more-fair deal with workers, if only to make the scary Marxian scenario go away. And hence, by the standard of self-prevention, Karl Marx may be the greatest SF author of all."

Those who shrug off Marx as an irrelevant relic of the Cold War, a shyster of an earlier age, should note how his works still influence political economics today, and how his books are yet again, in an Age of Trump, flying off the shelves and downloading into the e-readers of a new generation.

Once it became a state religion, Marxism heavily influenced science fiction in Russia and the east. Soviet *nauchnaya fantastyka* had a brief heyday in the 1920s, before science-friendly idealism was replaced by paranoid dread under Josef Stalin, when it became suicidal to suggest that things might be different. Hence, when Nikita Khrushchev denounced Stalin for crimes against the Communist Party, the Soviets eagerly embraced a spirit of technocratic-transcendentalism that was well-timed to accompany Sputnik and their brief leadership in space. It was in the 1960s that Soviet Science Fiction had its second wave of favor. Even the slightly masked social criticism of the Strugatskii brothers won toleration for a while, as did Tarkofsky's film version of the Stanislaw Lem novel *Solaris*, winning acclaim for commenting approvingly on socialism, amid its general creepy-weirdness. But these cycles of SF-approval never last long in authoritarian regimes. With Khrushchev's topple came repression under Brezhnev, as science fiction was again deemed dangerously impudent.

The overlap between Soviet Leninism and the actual philosophical teachings of Marx was always tenuous. I suggested earlier that Ayn Rand was a truer disciple than either Lenin or Mao.

Very little American SF has been explicitly Marxist, though a lot of authors used that catechism as a point of departure. I've already discussed how influential he was to writers of the 1930s generation like Frederik Pohl and Christopher Anvil. Isaac Asimov's *Foundation* series revolved around Hari Seldon, whose science of psychohistory re-framed the core Marxian dream, that economics and sociology might achieve the same reductionist predictability as chemistry, when quadrillions of individual humans interact with each other, like molecules of gas. The sci-fi cosmos that Isaac generated (and I had the honor of completing) evaded standard Marxist scenarios like "completion of the means of production" and final control

12. Getting Science Fictional About a Better World 125

by an advanced, enlightened proletariat. For storytelling reasons, Asimov chose to assume that the masses would remain unknowing, ruled by the elite of an empire that started out resembling Rome, but wound up far more like Imperial China. (The galaxy-managing robots would be sterile, eunuch, behind-the-curtain rulers.)

You can see why the Soviets could not bear *nauchnaya fantastyka* for long. In the west, even dedicated leftists like Pohl were impudent and harshly critical of Eurasia's domineering party lords. Ursula LeGuin's greatest novel, *The Dispossessed,* expressed her speculations about a style of radical socialism that might escape the viciously tyrannical approach taken by Leninist communist parties. Nowadays, this effort is carried forward by Kim Stanley Robinson, in his *Mars Trilogy* and other works.

The most common quasi-Marxist cliché in SF rages against capitalism and corporations without going into much detail about how the socialistic alternative will actually allocate resources or the productive output of new technologies. Authors Cory Doctorow, Bruce Sterling, Octavia Butler, Norman Spinrad, Karen Joy Fowler and Karl Schroeder have repeatedly portrayed noxious corporate and aristocratic tyrannies toppled by insurrection, though not so much the violent kind. Rather, it is ad hoc cabals of hip young techies who figure out how to seize the Man's control tools (e.g., web publishing, 3D printing designs, smart contract algorithms, or neo-rock 'n' roll), and use them as tools of liberation.

At root, this is "Marxist" in that a tech-savvy proletariat grabs control over the means of production in ways that flatten or eliminate old-oppressive power structures. And hey, I approve of the overall aim. I do something thematically similar in *The Postman* and *Earth*. Still, the wish-fantasy cliché remains nearly always both formulaic and a bit contemptuous of average folks. Exploring at length their anti-capitalist complaint, these authors gripe about society's myopia while remaining vague about their rosy-tinted prescriptions.

It is only a rare genius like LeGuin who dares to truly extrapolate: *What if my favored faction were to win, achieving victory for all of their aims and ambitions? Might they, in turn, become an oppressive, ruling caste? Perhaps one meriting further rebellion?*

It only happens to be one of the most common cycles in the human story.

The Feudal Tug

Speaking of recurring cycles, there is one that inarguably dominated across the entire wretched litany of error known as "history." Ignoring pedantic-purist definitions, the most persistent form of government around the globe has been *feudalism*—rule by patriarchal owner-lords who use swords and law and priests and tradition to accomplish one central aim: ensuring that their sons will continue to inherit dominance over other people's daughters and sons. It is the beastly regime that oppressed 99 percent of our ancestors. And of course that's why it lingers in our minds and haunts our dreams. We are all descended from the harems kept by those brutal aristocrats.

According to Marx—and illustrated in the Strugatsky science fiction classic *Hard to Be a God*—monarchy is a laudable evolutionary step upward from feudalism. National kings allow merchants, farmers and crafters to trade and prosper without parasitic bullying by local nobles. When they've prospered long enough, building better infrastructure and means of production, those castes will then stage a bourgeois revolution, taking the capitalist road that (Marx claims) will create conditions for eventual communist paradise. But we've already discussed this Marxian transcendentalist/SF scenario above.

What matters here is that many of our neighbors—even some surprising ones—are *drawn* to either feudalism or monarchy, eagerly consuming the hype, admiring the preening and adoring the emblems. This includes the creators and consumers of countless novels and films. What gives?

As I maintained in chapters about J.R.R. Tolkien and George Lucas, the key distinction between science fiction and fantasy is not about hardware or science. The spaceships of *Star Wars* blast across a galaxy, yet a person's *merit* in that cosmos is based almost solely on parentage or genes. Moreover, nothing about that basic standard ever changes. And that's why *Star Wars* is fantasy.

In contrast, the opening tales of Anne McCaffrey's *Dragonriders* series are set in the lowest of feudal-castle tech. Some of the novels dwell on medieval arts, crafts, songs and dances ... and yet, when the people of Planet Pern find out that they once had things called universities and starships, flush toilets and accountable institutions, they want those things back! It's their *attitude toward civilization and change* that most separates the two sibling genres. Anne always insisted, "I am not a fantasy author. I write science fiction!"

Reiterating an observation made elsewhere: Traditional societies viewed the *time flow of wisdom* as one of decay from a past golden age. Our western and science-fictional impudence—suggesting that a *future* golden (or at least improved) era *might* be built by our wiser children's hands—is viewed as the epitome of hubris.

A wide range of factions yearn to go backward, starting with *anti-*

technology fetishists, like the "Unabomber" Theodore Kaczynski, or the most extreme versions of *Earth First!* whom I portray through one of the more memorable characters in *Earth*.

The primitivist impulse spans from left to right. In today's bestiary of resentful denouncers of modernity—all of them coddled by a gentle civilization they despise—there today fizz small but avid groups who call themselves *neo-monarchists, neo-reactionaries, neo-primitivists, neo-feudalists* and *neo-fascists,* all of them gushing eagerly about a desired end to our so-called corrupt democratic decadence. Neo-monarchists thrive especially in Russia, adeptly switching an ancient paranoid reflex from adoration of Lenin back to Lenin's victims, the Romanov family. They are portrayed taking firmly oppressive power in Vladimir Sorokin's chilling future dystopia *The Day of the Oprichnik*.[1]

Elsewhere in this collection of essays, I've shown how royalty fetishism is pervasive, from fascination with the British crown to George Lucas' obsession with "queens" and "princesses" and his rationalization for why the masses want to be ruled by someone spangled with rubies. From Poul Anderson and H. Beam Piper to Lois McMaster Bujold and David Drake and TV series like *Dark Matter*, we see time and again science fiction authors who just can't resist.

Others would bypass monarchy and take us even farther down Marx's ladder of social development, seeking a return to what's most "natural," with local lords resuming their power of life and death over grimy peasants, as depicted in countless post-apocalyptic fictions, including my own *The Postman*. Perhaps this rule may be restrained by a strictly chiding church, as portrayed in Walter Miller's *A Canticle for Liebowitz*. In some Chinese SF, this moderating influence comes by applying Confucian principles.

In its milder-romantic form, the fantasy notion of traditionalist, inherited hierarchy draws legions and more legions of fans to genres like romance, historical fiction and fantasy. Even legendary sci-fi guys can get sucked in. Poul Anderson's famous novella "No Truce with Kings" appeared to favor the purported "stability" that lordly hierarchies seem to offer, apparently more predictable and calm-seeming than the daily ructions and fervid arguments of modern democracy.

Is it surprising that so many who relish this genre—fascination with medieval themes and hierarchies—are women? Even some who call themselves feminists? As we'll see in the next section, there are many works in both film and cinema that soft-pedal the bad aspects, or that empower a doughty heroine far more than would ever have been allowed in any genuine, feudal society.

Well, there is that word again: romanticism.

Feudalist Clichés

Again, I've discussed all this earlier. But here in this chapter the matter at hand is *clichéd prescriptions*. First right-wing, then left-wing, and now *back-looking*.

It's doubtful that most fantasy lovers would say aloud: "I wish we'd return to feudalism." If the choice were that overt, most would likely choose the liberty, wealth, knowledge and upward-ramping justice of this flawed modernist society that gave them the literacy and leisure to wallow in fantasy tales. Hence, a myriad fantasy novels and flicks present the feudal future not as a choice, but as a *given*. As an established and hence unavoidable dichotomy between Jedi and Sith, Atreides and Harkonnens, Lannisters and Starks. Prissy elfs vs. grouchy orcs with skin conditions.

As a regular person in such a world, you may choose *which* bunch of feuding mutant-demigods you'll die for, and the pretty ones are apparently nicer. But generally the creating author or director erases any notion of egalitarian democracy or worthy institutions that might overrule demigod whim.

Generally. Except among the most honest, like George R.R. Martin, whose *Song of Ice and Fire* series mentions (alas, only in passing) a faction called "Brothers Without Banners" who strive for a world free of pompous lords and kings. A possibility that George (alack) finally puts aside as inconvenient to the bloody narrative. Or "ahead of its time."

And so, having dealt with rightward, leftward and backward romantics, we come to the faction of utopian prescribers with whom I have the *most sympathy*. It's territory I'm about to enter at genuine peril.

Get Rid of Patriarchy! Only ... Then?

One peculiarly modern type of transcendence tale with its own set of unremarked clichés can be seen in the emergence of a vigorous subgenre: feminist dystopias-utopias.

This renaissance is long overdue, of course. I mean, isn't science fiction the genre that explores possibilities for change? Even changes in basic human nature? And what aspect of human nature obsesses us like sex, gender and all that? What aspect is changing quickest under the liberating influence of both democracy and science?

Yes, this is dangerous territory for a straight white male, who might be wiser to just offer support and keep his damn trap shut. I'm already in trouble with some of you, just for raising the topic…

Let me start right-off with full disclosure; I dedicated my most famous

12. Getting Science Fictional About a Better World   129

book—in part—to the legendary feminist hero Lysistrata, and wrote a novel dealing with gender issues, *Glory Season*, because this fecund new literary territory is simply too rich to resist. Moreover, I wholly approve of the direction chosen by Western Civilization—criticizing stereotypes, mistakes and crimes of the past, questioning smug habits of the present, and opening doors to those who were previously excluded. We need a rich variety of voices at the council fire! Many types of navigators for tomorrow's perilous shoals. Every essay-chapter you've seen here to should make clear which side I'm on.

But that's the point! Standard incantations are too rigid for a truly sapient and agile reform movement. We need to notice our own confining clichés. I serve this impudent renaissance best by offering critical feedback. And hence, when it comes to science fiction's large subgenre of "feminist utopias," I feel compelled to ask a hard question: *Which of the following is a more useful thought-experiment about altered gender roles?*

1. A post-holocaust society, in which the author first slaughters nearly all the human race with some war or disease, then invokes an accidental/convenient genetic or cultural mutation that compels women and men behave in ways the author thinks we ought to behave?
2. A setting of brutal oppression—a city-state or nation or generation-starship (the latest much-repeated trope)—where everything we've accomplished is reversed, where every racial-gender injustice is technologically amplified and exponentiated, and where the heroic resistance is cornered into fierce countermeasures?
3. A future setting where radical feminists, empowered by, but unsatisfied with our present and future progress, calmly use their minds and scientific skills—intelligently, assertively, and without undue rancor—to firmly alter humanity's course in a plausible direction they deem worthwhile?

If you've read extensively in this subgenre, you'll recognize approach #1 as the trope used by pioneers like Charlotte Perkins Gilman (*Herland*), and then many authors of the 1970s through 2000s, including Joanna Russ, Ursula LeGuin and Nicola Griffith, resulting in a series of utopian novels that were groundbreaking and often deeply moving ... but also remarkably similar down to prescriptive specifics and minute plot details. The initial holocaust and specific consequences can vary, from Griffith's well-wrought *Ammonite* and the gentle thoughtfulness of Joan Slonczewski's *Door Into Ocean* and Elizabeth Vonarburg's *In the Mother's Land*, to the angry howls of Sheri Tepper and Suzy McKee Charnas. These novels vary widely in quality and honesty, but share a near-universal assumption that human civilization is corrupt and incapable of intelligent, incremental reform. (A sad assumption, since these authors have all benefited from one of the most rapid and peaceful reform processes in all of human history.) Each invokes a *deus ex machina* or vague revolution or convenient mutation to prevent what always happened in the past, whenever any human cultures violently fell—the rise of brutal male chieftains. In rejecting technology, many of them spit in the eye of the best friend women ever had.

Scenario #1 has continued in use during the first decades of the 21st century. But a new wave of strongly radical authors have shifted their settings a bit from *post*-apocalypse to *during*.

In 2018 alone, Emily Devenport, Marina Lostetter, Mur Lafferty, Becky Chambers and Rivers Solomon all portrayed tension and violent failure aboard generation starships, with more than half of those isolated vessels ruled by dystopic tyrannies, founded in gruesome racial and sexual repression. Of course in the broader sense, scenario #2 also encompasses Margaret Atwood's *The Handmaid's Tale* and (I assert) *The Postman,* wherein the return of nasty feudal patriarchy was wrought by plague and war. But these bright new authors know what they are doing; if you want your heroine to face brutality at the hands of whip-bearing white males, with no way out, well, the spaceship metaphor is dandy.

Now, as you know by now, *I approve of dire warnings* when they feel realistic enough to serve as self-preventing prophecies. Moreover, we're all accustomed to exaggerated villains who are far crueler than any conceivable self-interest might demand. Feminist science fiction authors at least have an excuse that the libertarian, marxist or feudalist/monarchist dream-boys lack: Their wrath was earned, across 8000 years of patriarchy! And yet, the repetitive similarity of plot and premise does provoke a puzzled question: *Why do these narratives so often begin upon mountains of corpses?*

In scenario #1, the horrors of a past holocaust justify radical measures. Hence many of those authors depict rigid social orders where committees of wise matriarchs tell men or woman their rigidly defined gender roles, where to live, and even issue permission slips to make love. Many are fiercely anti-technological; some kind of knowledge-suppression is a cultural norm.

Scenario #2 simply rewinds to *before* revolution (or mutation) gave matriarchs the upper hand, back when vicious patriarchs proclaim rigidly defined roles, or issue permission slips to make love. The common element: justification for wrathful revolution.

To be clear, I'd rather—even though I'm male—live in those feminist-dominated worlds than the Sauron-nasty-Nazi patriarchy caricatures that came before. But are these our only choices?

12. Getting Science Fictional About a Better World

Few seem to consider that gender justice might be achieved in a loose culture, letting people form their own friendships and alliances, constrained only by a few nudges of synergistic biology and/or tradition to live a more gentle life than was true under patriarchy. A better world made by *planning* rather than desperation. But isn't that kind of utopian planning one of the deepest roots of science fiction? So why do almost no novels try that *third* option?

Let me repeat it here:

A future setting where radical feminists, empowered by, but unsatisfied with our present and future progress, calmly use their minds and scientific skills—intelligently, assertively and without undue rancor—to firmly alter humanity's course in a plausible direction they deem worthwhile.

In other words, instead of raging at and/or ignoring the only civilization that ever made progress toward justice and liberation—while scientifically and technologically at least somewhat improving the condition of minorities and women—how about imagining this flawed but improved society as a launching pad for your final idea, forward and upward? Why not depict intelligent, radical reformers of some future time actively *designing* the society they want, putting their agenda on the table, then using courage and scientific skill to implement it with gentle determination? (And a low death count.)

Want to do your experiment in a starship? Then crew it with scientifically empowered feminists with a plan—*your plan*—and send them forth to bring it about!

Quick, see if you can name even one example of sci-fi prescriptive utopia by calm design. One will do.

The answer should be obvious by now, since this chapter is about slothful clichés. The compulsion underlying it all has little to do with feminism or gender, but just another case of authorial laziness. *It's the Idiot Plot, all over again.*

Again, plot plausibility is less useful than passionate exaggeration that propels your protagonist into dire jeopardy. The screeching misogynists in Margaret Atwood's *The Handmaid's Tale* are glorious strawmen to illustrate her inherently justified protest against male oppression. Never mind that at least 80 percent of the men and 90 percent of the women in North America would have fought to their dying breath to prevent the scenario from ever coming about. *Likelihood* is not an issue in the art of polemic, which does a great job of providing a self-righteous rush to the already-committed, though proves useless at persuading your opponents. (Name one person whose pre-established opinions were *reversed* by the book.)

Above all, Atwood's burlesque society made plotting trivially easy. Bad guys drip sadistic wrath. Heroines strive mightily. Sheeplike citizens bleat. Done.

Oh, there are counter-examples. Alice Sheldon's chilling stories were always startlingly fresh, cliché-free and on target. Karen Joy Fowler, Nancy Kress and Ursula LeGuin often broke from the pack, posing societies with functioning institutions and citizens. A few innovative authors, like Maureen McHugh and Connie Willis, began pointing the way, as do new voices like Sue Burke. I deliberately tried to follow their lead with *Glory Season*, an honest attempt to provide the pastoral-feminist scenario prescribed by LeGuin and others, only without all the death and oppression that are lamentably pervasive in many works of this genre. Whether or not I succeeded is quite beside the point.

Again, the topic here is clichés, particularly the tendency of SF thought-experiments to be elitist, postulating that we live in a world full of fools. We've seen that it pervades political science fiction of the left and right, and both troglodytic and progressive. Again, let me emphasize that I am *on their side* and truly hope that their works will help persuade us to be ever-more accepting, tolerant, diverse, respectful and cooperative. If I could press a button and replace most of the world's rash or corrupt male leaders with scandal-free female ones, I'd leap for it. Nevertheless, when it comes to reflexive repetition of bad plotting habits or the questioning of their own clichés, many feminist authors have proved to be no better than a majority of their peers.

Summing Up: A World Wiser Than We Realize

The root cause of the Idiot Plot appears to be that science fiction has ignored a principal lesson of science. A lesson that may be the hardest truth humans learned, over the course of many hard millennia: *The only known antidote to error is criticism.*

Alas, while we are all happy dishing it out, there is nothing in the world that human beings hate *receiving* as much as criticism. Solving this paradox is the ultimate test of human maturity.

The paradox also explains a lot of history! How many states and cultures might have thrived if their citizens had free speech and the right to point out errors, but instead toppled because leaders suppressed critical feedback? It also reveals the greatest reason for the success of Western Civilization—the fact that criticism has at last been institutionalized, distributed and sanctified. After 10,000 years of oppressive lordships, we have finally reached the point where, at least legally, no citizen may be denied a

12. Getting Science Fictional About a Better World

voice, and no oligarchy may dominate conversations about policy or the way we rule ourselves.

(Those who fume after reading the preceding paragraph might do well to ponder whether *their own reaction* is an example of the criticism-generating process I describe, and therefore a symptom of this culture's civic heath! I elucidate this provocative point much further in my 1998 non-fiction book *The Transparent Society: Will Technology Force Us to Choose Between Freedom and Privacy?*)

Science led the way, but we've all adopted some of its techniques. The result is a system under which—for the first time—all of society's patriarchs, matriarchs and high priests must sooner or later receive criticism and accountability. Although it hasn't yet delivered solutions to the more complex problems of human nature, science has used this new maturity to help us flourish as never before, so much so that we've turned the caveman's blessing into a curse, overpopulating the planet and suffering plagues caused by too much success. As we solve one problem after another, each solution seems to reveal new dilemmas, new quandaries to address with debate, study and mature discussion.

Science fiction should be the most vigorous and forward-looking part of this conversation; but tragically, except in rare cases, it is not. Rather, we have the Idiot Plot—a pervasive depiction of individual protagonists striving in a world of morons. This slothful authorial crutch poisons the natural fecundity of our genre. Our writings should provoke intelligent dialogue by multitudes, but instead too many of them perpetuate the same sick-sweet propaganda message over and over again, proclaiming that the masses—our own neighbors—are sheep, and always will be.

Do we live in a civilization of idiots?

Believe me, I am no Pollyanna; "the people" are nowhere near as smart as I would like them to be. (Recent politics have seemed to bear this out.) In fact, I'm a modern person—a typical male egotist—so I naturally hold the masses in as much contempt as the next guy. For one thing, it feels great!

And yet, one thought tempers that smugness: I can't live in a world without hope.

If my fellow citizens are half as stupid as some of my fellow authors depict, then this planet is doomed, along with my children and all possibility of our descendants seeing better days. That is a frightful prospect. One I cannot bear.

So the optimists had better be right about humanity, and my fellow writers had better be wrong. Citizens of all kinds have to be smarter than they are portrayed in novels and films, or we're all dead. It's as simple as that.

In fact, there *is* hope. A lot of evidence suggests that people are getting better. Perhaps not fast enough to save the world, but enough to make it a horse race. A drama far more interesting than the typical old cliché: that of a herd of lemmings, dashing toward a cliff.

I believe citizens are wiser than they are slanderously depicted by media, in the blithe contemptuousness of modern myth.

They had better be.

Part Four:
Heroes and Villains

13

Name That Villain
Bad Guys and Aliens in Sci-Fi Movies

Does a good sci-fi movie need a villain? Sure there are flicks with no bad guys, where protagonists are pitted against nature, or simple error. A few that come to mind are *Gravity, Europa Report, Armageddon, Deep Impact, Marooned, 2010, Apollo 13* and *Honey I Shrunk the Kids*, some of which are reviewed in this volume. Still, one does have to keep heroes in jeopardy, in order to have a pulse-pounding sense of viewer satisfaction. And while forces of nature do a good job in some cases, it surely does help to have a villain with a face.

Indeed, if you are doing your job as a writer, you'll give your villain motives. Very few humans view themselves as the bad guy; they have explanations. Excuses. Incantations they recite, to justify a position you and I would loathe. The reader or viewer ought to get a faint taste of that viewpoint. Indeed, I receive mail now and then from "Holnists" who claim to view me as a founding father, because of the rationalizations spoken by my villains in *The Postman*! Fortunately, these are rare, compared to those who credit me with inspiring them to fight for civilization. Still, messages of praise—that miss the point you were trying for—can creep you out.

Let's play a game of *Name That Villain*. In lots of movies, the distinction between good and evil is clear-cut. The aggressor fellas in *Independence Day* are really bad—aliens who aren't just ugly; they want to kill absolutely everyone. In Tolkien's *Lord of the Rings*, red glowing eyes indicate Bad Guy, whose henchmen have really bad complexions.

But who's your villain in Steven Spielberg's *E.T. the Extraterrestrial*? Your natural reflex is to say "the government." But take a look at Spielberg's films; he's too grateful and patriotic ever to call the United States and its government evil. What it *can* be is overbearing and patronizing, exactly the flaws exhibited by bureaucrats in *Close Encounters of the Third Kind* and at the end of *Raiders of the Lost Ark*.

In *E.T.*, government is represented by the agent with keys hanging from his belt (played by Peter Coyote), with ominous music that accompanies his every shadowy appearance. But it's a trick. When you finally meet "Keys" face-to-face, without such manipulations, you discover he's just *Elliott grown up!* He wants nothing more than to make contact with the alien.

Sure, those callous government folks fail to tell Elliott's mother: "Hey we're about to put a quarantine bubble over your house." Only, when they finally get E.T. in their hands, do they "dissect" a visitor from an advanced civilization? (The inane rationalization offered by Elliott, for hiding his undocumented alien guest.) No, they do their best to save him from all those untested and likely poisonous Reese's Pieces the kids gave him. And when he "dies" ... they weep.

I'm not the only one to notice these moral quandaries. In a notorious article, Rob Bricken raised a stir by asserting "E.T. Is Secretly the Scariest Movie of All Time," because the stranded alien deliberately fosters a psychic link with a human child that he knows will send poor Elliott careening drunkenly through school, misbehaving and committing what we'd call sexual harassment, and finally bringing the boy close to death.[1]

I won't go quite that far. My issues are not with E.T. himself—I can accept the excuse that he's a stranded botanist, in a clueless panic to get home. Rather, my beef is with a lesser character who is clearly one of the most evil in all of sci-fi history!

Go back and watch *E.T.*'s first scene. At night in a California forest, aliens are surreptitiously collecting something, perhaps of scientific or possibly immense commercial value—without permission and without paying us. Abruptly, cars roar in, spearing the forest with headlights! Shadowy men leap out, casting sharp beams as they race forward, accompanied by tense cello chords. Only ... now rewind back a bit. Turn down the skillfully nervous music. Look past all the movie manipulations—and replay that scene in slo-mo.

Do you see any *guns?*

Only clipboards, cameras and flashlights. Implements of discovery. Of light.

So ... who's the villain here? Oh, there is one.

The only deliberately evil act in the film is performed by the *captain of E.T.'s ship,* who abandons a crewmate when threatened with ... flashlights.

Moreover, he doesn't come back to search, even though they knew where they left him within two blocks! The ship has to be summoned, when E.T. "phones home."

What would have happened if Elliott simply did the grown-up, responsible thing instead of sanctimoniously announcing "I'm gonna keep him?" Scientists might have performed some biological tests, and warned him about those Reese's Pieces. When E.T. asked to phone home, scientists might have offered him use of the Goldstone Deepspace Communications Complex. And when the alien ship returned, we might have demanded three months rent! How about an *Encyclopedia Galactica* for all of humankind?

For the best of reasons—love—and the worst of reasons—sanctimony—the kids commit treason and deny humanity what might be its one chance.

And no, none of that makes *E.T.* a bad movie! It's one of the greatest! I just have a part of my brain that's picky.

And so do you, or you'd never have read this far.

District Nine

How about another example? Let's talk about *District Nine*, the 2009 thriller produced by Peter Jackson. That amazing flick certainly went out of its way to show an apartheid-style oppression by humans against really weird and problematic aliens. Still, you discover that the aliens come from a highly stratified society, with castes that differ vastly from each other in intelligence and status. Nearly all of them are portrayed as inherently dull or mentally deficient.

The humans, represented by a South African policeman, certainly have not been nice. But they've been trying to find someone from this advanced alien race, that they might actually talk to. When you finally find out there are a few advanced, high caste aliens, some questions arise, like why the uppermost caste has been secretive, refusing to contact or negotiate or explain anything to humanity. Hence, they are as much at fault for the situation as the Afrikaans bigots. It's all there, masked by the apartheid morality tale.

So again, as far as explicit evil is concerned, who is the villain? Sure, it becomes a standard guilt trip, after all, but with interesting details.

I found the encounter-of-civilizations aspect of *District Nine* illogical in many ways, along with the science. There'd be humans crawling all over the ship, consumed with curiosity. And frankly, I find the unrelenting and unmoderated guilt trips (as in *Avatar*) overbearing, even counterproductive.

On the other hand, *District Nine* gives us a wonderful portrayal of a solitary human—not at all an admirable, or genial, or respect-worthy individual—who embarks on a desperate quest for personal survival that is both frenzied and overwhelmingly determined. In his absolute determination, that overwhelms all other loyalties or concerns, we get a fascinating character study and a deeply creepy look into the mirror for any thoughtful person.

It's worth noting the movie that *District Nine* was based upon: 1988's *Alien Nation* (directed by Graham Baker, produced by Gale Anne Hurd), which broke so many stereotypes of its time. In *Alien Nation*, 300,000 enslaved aliens escape to Earth. Only instead of making the mistake of landing in South Africa during apartheid, they instead wisely come to Southern California, where ACLU lawyers quickly get these Newcomers freed from quarantine. The aliens simply become another ethnic group in Los Angeles. The best of them become scientists, teachers, dance studio instructors ... or cops who are advanced through the ranks by affirmative action. Newcomer Sam Francisco (Mandy Patinkin) becomes the buddy cop partner to a cynical human detective (James Caan), And some truly innovative science fiction ensues. (A television spinoff was fairly successful.)

What I love about this franchise: It deliberately defies the twin clichés of alien-contact—either *they* are villainous or it's a tolerance tale of oppression *by* humanity vs. innocent visitors. This brave film did something seldom tried, before or since. It portrayed our civilization—and its citizens—actually behaving as they might, if such things ever happened for real. In other words, aside from a fair number of bigots and over-eager fans ... a majority of us actually trying to behave decently, with tolerance and courage and a will to face the future.

Still memorable decades later is a scene where the alien cop gets drunk (on sour milk) while his partner drinks Scotch and confesses: "Many of you humans are asses. And yet, that's not what surprised us. What we never expected, especially from all the television we saw, was to be given citizenship. To be given a chance to get better, alongside you."

And yes, the deck is loaded, since the Newcomers in *Alien Nation* are appealing, even attractive.

Standing on the shoulders of that classic, *District Nine* pushes the envelope! These arrivals are much more alien, unapproachable, ugly (from a human perspective) and reproducing with daunting rapidity. Had the filmmakers chosen to expand upon the core message of *Alien Nation*, we'd have seen some from both races reaching across these divides, even if most of us fail the test.

But no. As excellent and vividly groundbreaking as *District Nine* is, it becomes a tale more in keeping with one of the two alien-movie archetypes—a full-tilt guilt trip over human intolerance. Our inability to adapt is sledgehammered with reproach, when a scalpel—or even a machete—might have delivered the message better.

Alien Nation is one of the only movies I've seen that actually gives us credit for how far we've come. And I've asserted several times in this volume that *that* is how you motivate people to get better. Not only by showing them how far we've got to go, but also how far we've come.

◇ ◇ ◇

Well, well. The ship captain in *E.T.* and the ship captain in *District Nine* … and you may recall how I dissed Klaatu, in *The Day the Earth Stood Still*, for delivering finger-wagging guilt trips and threats, when his people could have opened a small college on Earth at any point in the previous 10,000 years, instead of waiting until the Doomsday Clock stood at two minutes to midnight. And I bitched about the Na'vi in *Avatar* not being any great ones to lecture anybody about decent behavior.

But hey, I'm not complaining as much as it seems! Those flicks all had their hearts in the right place, conveying earnest memes of self-reflection and self-criticism that push the core method of our campaign of steady progress … our effort to become something better than we were.

Indeed, my novel *Existence* talks about one possible explanation for the Fermi Paradox—the quandary of why we've had no real, verifiable contact with advanced, interstellar civilizations: They are waiting for us to pass some milestone of development, perhaps in ethical behavior. That notion makes for a great metaphor, but is actually rife with complexities and contradictions of the sort that SF could shine light upon, rather than wallowing in the simplest of repeated guilt trips.

Alas, I wish preachiness were the *only* problem with some other well-known SF heavies. But if you've read this far, you know what I think of one of the most despicably evil characters in the history of all mythologies: that nasty "guru" named Yoda.

But let me conclude by naming one more surprising villain from a film I quite admire: Ethan Hawke's character Vincent Freeman in *Gattaca*. This is a fascinating fellow! Talented and obsessed, Vincent seeks not only to overcome the stigma of his genetic heart condition, but to overcompensate and gull his way into the most tightly restricted job on—or off—the planet: navigator on a deep space mission. It's one of the best portrayals of tenacious determination I ever saw, and the viewer is tensely rooting for Vincent.

Along the way, we see a society that is flawed. It's not trying hard enough to overcome this latest kind of prejudice, but it *is* trying. Moreover, we know that if Vincent succeeds in his mission and returns his crew safely home, he will become an archetype who shatters every lazy stereotype! That society shakeup is needed and worth some risk…but is it ethical? In fact, Vincent knows that there *is* some better-than-average chance that his heart will fail him, out there. It's not just his life that's on the line. And despite all the admirable traits that have us cheering him on, we should also admit that he's an arrogant, self-centered putz!

This realization didn't spoil the film for me, one iota. A lot of human history—and some really positive steps—were made by arrogant putzes. I was thrilled to see the launch. But then, I didn't have a son or daughter aboard.

I guess the lesson is: Be able to welcome intricacy in your heroes, in your villains, in your stories. It doesn't have to ruin them, not the really good ones! In fact, that is the way of the real world. And the authors of *this* simulation have sure gone intricate on us characters.

14

King Kong Is Back!
The Ape in the Mirror

This essay was written as the introduction to a book that was published to coincide with the release of Peter Jackson's 2005 remake of King Kong. *That book,* King Kong Returns: An Unauthorized Look at One Humongous Ape, *contains more than a dozen fascinating articles about the subject, many of which are briefly described here.*

Long before there were twin towers in New York, destined to rise and then crash down upon beleaguered Manhattan Island, two other great wonders loomed over that storied skyline—behemoths that were uneven in mass but appeared as equals in our hearts, and to our watching eyes.

One was real, a building named after imperial ambition, erected in a fever of zealous optimism that defied even the depths of the Great Depression. Propelled by the renowned American appetite for commerce, technological achievement and hubristic accomplishment, the Empire State Building symbolized—far better than the later, doomed, World Trade Center towers—a brash Modernist Agenda.

The other titan was mythical, a fabled embodiment of all that contrasted with modernism. King Kong arrived when the building was brand new. An ancient ape, but so much more. A proto-man, primitive, solitary and fiercely proud, representing everything about us that the architects and builders aimed to ignore or leave behind.

But we cannot simply leave it all behind. The legacy follows us everywhere, even into our prim urban landscapes—the pure but dangerous innocent that we find both attractive and terrifying, especially when we look in a mirror and realize how few generations separate us from the jungle, from the cave.

Movies last an hour or two, but legends need time to grow. Though the original *King Kong* was a commercial success when it was released in 1933, the giant gorilla flickered only briefly on movie screens before giving way to other stirring tales, or real-life concerns. Kong's story had to be repeated on television's smaller screen for new generations of youth and adults to embrace it fully as their own, making it a core fable of our culture, recognized by all.

At the surface, there is little to this simple story that cannot be described in a single paragraph. A movie impresario, modeled after Kong's own adventurer-producers, Merian C. Cooper and Ernest B. Schoedsack, takes a brave crew and beautiful ingénue to a distant, uncharted isle. There, natives barely stave off prehistoric beasts through liberal use of sacrificial virgins—the stuff of pulp adventure fiction at its lowest ebb. (Even Edgar Rice Burroughs and H. Rider Haggard gave their distressed but plucky damsels more to do than simply scream and writhe enticingly, the pathetically simple role assigned to poor Ann Darrow, as played by Fay Wray in the original King Kong.) When natives kidnap our blonde temptress as an offering to their ape god, the impresario sends a hunky hero-type, leading expendable crewmates into the jungle to battle a mélange of exaggerated Mesozoic and Cenozoic monsters in order to rescue her. Meanwhile, Beast has a few bonding moments with Beauty ... including a bit of titillating, involuntary disrobing amid several desperate battles to protect his newfound treasure.

All right, make it two paragraphs. When Hunk steals Beauty away from Kong's pinnacle lair, Kong makes his fatal error and follows. Leaving his domain, crossing the threshold "into town," he becomes vulnerable to urban humanity's power, made manifest by the impresario's marvelous gas bombs. Whereupon, through the wonder of cinematic cutaway, Kong swiftly finds himself put on debased display in a different kind of jungle entirely (a theater in the urban jungle of Manhattan). And it is here that King Kong becomes more than just another early-talkie adventure film, or a notably clever experiment in stop-action photography. For here, at his humiliating nadir, Kong wins the movie audience over, forcing them to abandon all ambivalence. It seems, at that crucial moment, as if he draws as much strength from our sympathy as from primal rage. Shattering his bonds and reclaiming his ingénue prize, he scales the highest pinnacle that he can find. Seeking refuge? Or a sacred height to make his last stand?

Kong's hopeless struggle, against a swarm of machine-gun equipped biplanes, has to be one of the great moments of heroic imagery, not just in cinema, but on a par with Hector confronting Achilles on the Plains of Ilium, or the Old Guard standing hopelessly erect at Waterloo. Equal to Crockett at the Alamo, or Balin's futile defense of Moria in *Lord of the Rings*.

No, it is better than all of those. At least I think so. I will argue that it's so.

But that is the point of this essay ... to argue joyfully about the meaning of something mythical—an event that never really happened at all! You have seen the original motion picture, possibly the 1976 sequel starring Jessica Lange, and probably (by now) Peter Jackson's 2005 remake.

In the essay collection *King Kong Is Back! An Unauthorized Look at One Humongous Ape*, insightful and richly varied thinkers try to show how much more depth and meaning reside in this legend than even its original makers consciously knew. Of course, if you were the sort of person who believed that "a story is just a story," you would not have picked up a book like this one.

The varied viewpoints of wit and insight reminded me of another legend about a huge and marvelous beast. The Blind Men and the Elephant is a familiar fable about a dozen sightless philosophers, each of whom tries to appraise and describe a pachyderm by touch alone. One, stroking a huge leg, likens the elephant to a tree. Another, fondling the trunk, declares that it is very much like a snake. So it is here, as an eclectic and brainy bunch analyze Kong in the light of their own obsessions and concerns.

King Kong is a period piece and must always remain so. Dino De Laurentiis' 1976 remake failed, not especially because of lousy acting or poor direction, but because it took Kong out of when he belonged and tried to put him into a then-contemporary setting. The story of Kong requires innocence; it requires *terra incognita*.

Offering a genuine "Aha!" moment, Adam Roberts has persuasively argued that Kong is essentially a children's story, appealing to us in much the same way that size differences—at both ends of the spectrum—fascinate kids, who both stomp and chew on their toys like a gorilla and warily avoid being stomped by grown-ups.

Can Kong be viewed as a metaphor representing the quandary of urbanization? Like millions who were at the same time pouring into cities from the countryside, Kong was faced with a problem of adapting. A hapless rube in Metropolis, did he speak for thousands of farm boys and girls who were finding strength to be a poor match for sophisticated city ways? But what of women who avow different, more complex feelings toward Kong?

Almost in direct refutation, Rick Whitten-Klaw has related a story of the marvelous Ruth Rose, who married Schoedsack, but only after proving her independent mettle with stirring, scientific adventures around the world, in jungles and at sea. In a league with Amelia Earhart and Anne Morrow Lindbergh, Rose later became lead scriptwriter for *King Kong*, a fact that raises a myriad questions in modern minds. Like: Why did so little of that "spunk" get translated into the role of Ann Darrow, as portrayed by Fay Wray? Many aspects of that character were clearly modeled after Rose herself. And yet, clearly, she would have been more assertive in the same situation. Pursued by a giant ape, Ruth Rose would have done a lot more than just scream.

(Is that, perhaps, one of the messages? Throughout the film, there are countless opportunities for viewers—both men and women—to say, "I'd do things differently, maybe a whole lot better.")

Let's start with a little humility. After all, at one level it is "just a movie," made to earn money through the simple delivery of entertaining diversion. Let me quote from one of the better books about *King Kong* written in the last century, *The Making of King Kong: The Story Behind a Film Classic* (1975), by Orville Goldner and George Turner.

> Many writers have tried to justify the public's love affair with a gigantic, ugly ape by reading into the film a great deal more significance than was intended by its creators. European Communists insist that when Kong smashes the gates of the native village he symbolizes Karl Marx. A French critic, apparently confusing Ruth Rose with Rose La Rose or Gypsy Rose Lee, attributed the picture's erotic aspects to the "fact" that it was partly written by "a former strip-teaser." Others insist Kong was black in order to represent the plight of the Negro in America, who also was brought to these shores in chains and exploited by the white man. Freudians point with glee to the irony of Kong retreating to the top of "the most elaborate phallic symbol in the world"—the Empire State Building. For Freudians, too, are the "mock crucifixion" of Kong, the "proxy gratification" of depression-angry audiences via Kong's destructive rampage in New York, a brontosaurus that reminds them of Leda's swan, and so on, *ad nauseam*. Such notions are firmly denied by the persons behind the film, who view them variously with disgust or amusement.
>
> We earnestly suggest that simple explanations are best: Kong was not darker in hue than any other gorilla, he smashed the gates solely because he wanted to recapture Fay Wray, his atrocious behavior in the city had nothing to do with politics or economic conditions and he climbed the Empire State Building because it was the highest point in the city, corresponding to his mountain-top lair in his homeland. King Kong is exactly what it was meant to be: a highly entertaining, shrewdly conceived work of pure cinema.

Well ... as I said, the elephant can be viewed from many angles. Those who take their erudite symbolism seriously consider it to be quite irrelevant that the film's creators denied having underlying agendas. A favorite trick of pedants and scholars (as opposed to scientists) has always been to dismiss contrary evidence as "denial" and to claim that they can see all the real psychological motivations. Seldom is it even acknowledged that the symbols in question (in this case a great ape) are being interpreted in a mirror of their own obsession. The scholar winds up being exposed, far more tellingly than the original creator of the work.

On the other hand ... aren't the "realists" also spoil sports? I mean,

14. King Kong Is Back!

what could be more absurd and churlish than to try denying us some fun ... the pleasure of using our prefrontal lobes to analyze and analyze and analyze! Isn't that even more essentially human than all our vaunted technology?

Sure, King Kong himself would snort at the very idea of diagnosing his motives through nonsense like deconstruction and textual semiotics. But Kong would already have hurled this book across the river—or eaten it.

Whereas you ...

... Well, by now, you've already paid for it. So what do I care?

Hmmm. In fact, I do care a bit.

Moreover, having introduced the topic, I can safely say that it's my turn, now, to talk about this wonderful film and what King Kong says to me. So let's go back to one aspect that I commented on at the very beginning: the notion of *scale*.

Is it intentional that individual human beings appear, next to Kong, just as dwarfed as he will wind up appearing, beside the mighty Empire State Building? Vastly overpowering any single person, he nevertheless finds himself overmatched by our joined power, symbolized by the great tower that he attempts—in vain—to conquer. Are we being reminded that there's always someone—or something—bigger than you?

What I consider to be the most critical lesson: We are vastly stronger working together than we are apart.

One could interpret this darkly, by making a dismal comparison to the fascist preaching of united will, directed by a single leader, party and goal. That vile dogma was making inroads around the world at the very time that this film was made. Certainly the fate of individualist Kong presaged the doom of millions, including many who dared resist a rising tide of ideological mania. A madness that was exacerbated, horribly, by misused technology.

On the other hand, shall we dismiss the symbols of cooperative civilization, simply because mad over-simplifiers—like Hitler, Stalin and Mussolini—were too stupid and evil to get what it is really all about? Not monolithic subversion of the individual, but the creative building, step by step and brick by brick, of new things by a complex process of collaboration. Universities and laws. Cities and farms. Science and ethics. Plus all the new technologies and diversions that can be used—or misused—for well or ill.

What we're talking about is a topic that was very hot in 1933 ... the very notion of eclectic human improvability, which underlays every modernist ambition from schools to skyscrapers. A self-critical process, constantly re-evaluating old ways, from racism to gender roles, from music to mythology. A process based upon confidence in our ability to guide change ... or at least to cope. (No wonder it has lately come under intense battering, by cynics of every stripe.)

The Empire State Building is very much like the film that viewers are watching, in a theater or at home. Somehow, a legion of financiers, craft workers, artists, actors, writers, impresarios and countless others—each of them equipped with plenty of individual ego and spirit—combined their efforts to make something marvelous that is still used and loved and discussed seven decades later. None of those who created either the building or the movie still live today. But they endure, and not only in the classic biological way, through their progeny. They also continue, cheating death, through the fine things they built together.

Within the film, Kong is portrayed as a mighty but sterile being, denied both kinds of immortality. Even if he had been left alone on his island, Kong would become dust by the year 2000, forgotten by the jungle he once dominated. Even had he won and kept his Beauty, she could never give him posterity. Speechless, he cannot persuade or move us, except to the basic emotion of sympathy.

Ultimately, it is not the gas bombs or biplanes that thwart Kong, but his inability to negotiate, to argue and do all the other complex things that transform an old-style solipsist-ape into one of the new-style, world-changing, cooperative individualists.

His inarticulate rage allows him only to see his fellow island beasts as rivals, never as potential allies—even when dangerous new interlopers invade their shared realm. Likewise, he is unable to appeal to social rules (and maybe even hire a lawyer) when they have him trussed and humiliated on-stage.

Or to woo his love in a manner that may heed her needs...or else to accept her rejection with the balm of philosophy.

Or to adapt and adopt the technologies that are used against him.

Or to (perhaps) even join in the adventures and ambitions of midget-anthropoid cousins who have taken on new aspirations, new pathways of evolution that render his strength useless, leaving him far behind... as many of us sometimes fear that *we* are about to be left behind.

Isn't that another primal dread, reflected and diffracted by this multi-faceted movie? Each of us has had to deal with obstinate, retro types who cannot accept change. And each of us—from time to time—has *been* the stubborn ape, who feels threatened and intimidated by change.

Yes, the power of collaborative endeavor is impressive, whether it is propelled by openly cooperative institutions or by competitive capitalism, combining the labor and skills of thousands of men and women to achieve what prior generations could barely have imagined. But during the Depression (as now), people had a right to their ambivalence. They had every reason to take both sides—pride in civilized accomplishments and worry over where it all might lead.

Again, I am attracted to those core symbols in the film's most powerful scene. More than any other skyscraper, the Empire State Building seems to reject the lesson of the Tower of Babel and its classic warning to mere mortals, that they had better leave the sky alone. Like a ship, it aims boldly at the stars.

But not everyone is welcome to climb aboard. Not the super-individualist, stomping and bellowing. No Nietzschean supermen or solipsists. Not if they tread on others. Even if they are poignant and passionate victims of a world transformed.

We sympathize during the movie's most stirring scene, while a vastly courageous and confused ape clutches at his throat, staggering in dim incomprehension as biplanes swoop to brutally enforce society's limits. Limits that even a permissive culture—one friendly to individual spirit—simply has to impose, lest we become the howling thing that each of us still carries around inside, that remnant leftover from Cain, or from the caves.

We may build new ziggurats to the stars. We may climb them, while bickering and competing, negotiating and telling grand tales. We may even take our inner beasts along with us, if they'll behave, and stay confined to stirring art, where they belong.

But poor Kong. Good old Kong. Pure and simple Kong.

Our old king Kong…

…he does not understand, nor is he meant to.

On the temple steps, he is our sacrifice.

15

The Matrix
Tomorrow May Be Different

And if the lesson of one jumped-up super-ape wasn't clear enough—embodying many of the themes of this book—how about pounding the metaphors with über-human power!

Cyberpunk: Just Another Rebellion

Each generation's morality tales reflect not only on its values, but also the technology of the time. We saw how *King Kong* both amplified and reflected fears and hopes of the 1930s. Now let's jump ahead half a century.

During the 1980s, science fiction was afroth over *Cyberpunk*. Reviewers both inside and far outside the genre went into paroxysms over this new movement, crediting it with everything from gritty, sharp-edged realism, to high-gloss textures, to inventing a trope of irate tomorrows, symbolized by the angry young man of the streets.

Setting aside egregious exaggerations and heaps of heavy-breathing hype, this literary movement surely made the field more interesting for a while. Haughty literary mavens who normally snub sci-fi condescended to discover these daring writers of dark, heroic, slashing prose, including William Gibson, author of *Neuromancer*, a tale filled with stark, vivid imagery about a future dominated by oppressive corporate structures. A future in which control over access to information outweighed the importance of political or military power.

It was a heady time, even for those of us who were shunted,

willy-nilly, into the category of *the opposition*. I happily granted interviews to national reporters seeking quotes from critics of the Cyberpunk movement. Whatever. I dutifully played my part, double-teaming the establishment. Hey, Cyberpunk was the best free promotion campaign ever for science fiction. Brilliantly managed by impresarios like Bruce Sterling and backed by some works of estimable value, it reeled in countless new readers while opening fresh opportunities in Hollywood and visual arts. True, the self-important rhetoric and whines of persecution sounded ironic, at times even hilarious. But the Cyberpunk rebels did shake things up. More power, guys.

Ahhh, but Were They Original?

Name any point of interest in Western cultural history, and you'll likely see the pattern. The trial of Socrates was all about a "punk" of sorts, with a reputation for extravagant behavior, satirizing standard values, and spewing unconventional new metaphors. Young 18th century literary wolves of the Enlightenment saw themselves toppling a stagnant order, using the fresh light of scientific reason to dispel superstition. Indeed, followers of Hume, Locke, Montesquieu and Jefferson rattled the world.

When those figures grew older and mighty in success, along came *the romantics,* typified by Coleridge, Byron and others. They derided Reason as an oppressive cudgel wielded by fogeys and old farts. Science was portrayed as a chain that aimed to shackle vaulting ambitions of the human soul. Amid this tussle, science fiction was born with Mary Shelley's seminal *Frankenstein* emerging literally in the middle of the Romantic movement, yet containing within it SF's perpetual answer to romanticism: that progress will happen and the only way to deal with it will be wisdom.

The Romantic movement was more than simply cultural recidivism— more than a grandson allying himself with his grandfather in common hatred of papa. Predictability would take all the fun out of being a rebel! Still, there is a certain inevitability about these cycles. We will never be short of young men and women, eager to announce new revelations. No matter how fine the accomplishments of their parents, bright newcomers will proclaim themselves prophets of a new age. All the more so for the loose confederacy of genres known as Speculative Fiction! After all, SF is the literature of change—in the human condition and in the universe as a whole. By its nature, it must encourage fresh ideas or perish.

So SF had the "New Wave" authors of the '60s—Harlan Ellison, Frank Herbert, Roger Zelazny, Samuel Delany, Robert Silverberg—who decried the prior emphasis on gadgetry and plot, proclaiming their discovery of something called style. Language became their palette. Their colors would be passion, stirred into the reader's soul.

Naturally, the Old Farts thought a lot of this was straight bull. They had spent half a lifetime ardently fighting for the freedom to speculate about humanity's relationship with technology and space and time—and now these whippersnappers were just taking that freedom for granted. Worse, they were strutting about as if *they* were the true innovators!

Indeed, the best New Wave writers were wonderfully inventive, contributing something vital to our genre, just when it was needed. They raised new issues, posed new quandaries, precisely because those prior battles had been won. The best of the old guard did not grouse when the newcomers strutted by, flaunting new, gaudy plumage. Rather, they smiled, remembering what it was to be young. And they said, "Come on over, sit and tell me about it."

So it was with Cyberpunk in the '80. Although I was younger than most of the Cyberpunk mob, and started my career much more recently, somehow I found myself in the O.F. (Old Farts) camp, perhaps because I truly do believe that technology and reason will play a role in raising generations better than ours. Assigned a role, I was only too glad to play along for fun, downplaying that I *liked* most of the work I'd read by Gibson, Rudy Rucker, Bruce Sterling, Pat Cadigan—and contributed my own gritty, noir bits to the trend.

Ah, well. When I first wrote this appraisal in the early 2000s, Cyberpunk was already well past ripe middle age, as literary movements go. Like some of its practitioners, who can be seen occasionally peering into each other's mirror-shades suspiciously, watching age lines and liver spots emerge. But worse is coming. For successful movements are always punished by becoming banalities. Consider the story of the elderly lady who was taken to her first Shakespeare play ever—*Hamlet*. Her reaction? *"Well, I thought it was very nice ... but it was all so full of clichés!"* Such is the doom of authors, fated at one end with obscurity, but at the other, after success, with being copied till everyone is sick of you.

And each successful generation creates something else ... a new clade of rebels, fomenting revolution and rejection against the prior one. Bright kids who are talking about these new things they've discovered ... things called "story," and "character" and "hope."

The Literature of Change

Many have tried to define science fiction. I like to call it the literature of exploration and change. While other genres obsess upon so-called

15. The Matrix

eternal verities, SF deals with the possibility that our children may have distinctive problems. They may, indeed, be different. So, how well do you deal with change?

All creatures live embedded in time, though only human beings seem to lift their heads to comment on this fact, lamenting the past or worrying over what's to come. Our brains are uniquely equipped to handle this temporal skepsis. For example, twin neural clusters that reside just above our eyes—the prefrontal lobes—appear especially adapted for extrapolating ahead.

Meanwhile, swaths of older cortex can flood with vivid memories of yesterday, triggered by the merest sensory tickle, as when a single aromatic whiff sent Proust back to roam his mother's kitchen for 80,000 words. (We'll return to neurons and the brain, later.)

Obsession with either past or future can almost define a civilization. Worldwide, most cultures believed in some lost golden age when people knew more, when they mused loftier thoughts and were closer to the gods—but then fell from that state of grace. The myth occurred so frequently, on so many continents and in so many contexts—despite an almost complete lack of credible evidence for any genuine past "golden age"—that we must assume the fable wells up from something basic in our natures. Under this dour but recurrent *look-back* worldview, men and women of a later, coarser era can only "look back" with envy to that better, happier time, studying ancient lore and hoping to live up to remnants of ancient wisdom.

Just a few societies dared contradict this standard dogma of nostalgia. Our own Scientific West, with its impudent notion of progress, brashly relocated any "golden age" to the future, something to work toward, a human construct for our grandchildren to achieve with craft, sweat and good will—assuming that we manage to prepare them properly for such an ambitious task. Implicit is the postulate that our offspring can and should be better than us, a glimmering hope that is nurtured (a bit) by two generations of steadily rising IQ scores.

This perspective can be important when we examine popular mythologies in the realm of science fiction. Take a number of popular epics: for example, *The Matrix*, *Minority Report* and *Blade Runner*, the latter two films inspired by literary works of Philip K. Dick.

In earlier chapters, and some yet to come, I illustrate that these works—and others, such as *Star Wars*, *Lord of the Rings* and the perennial *Star Trek*—can be especially well illuminated by asking the following questions:

1. Does the work look forward to human progress or does it push nostalgia by lamenting a lost golden age?

2. Is science portrayed with loathing? Or as a hopeful trend that must also be watched carefully against harmful excess?
3. What role does rebellion play? Is Suspicion of Authority portrayed as a private thing? (The hero as a lone fox among sheep.) Or is Suspicion of Authority depicted as a healthy reaction by all citizens, who participate by helping to keep the mighty accountable?
4. Are heroes portrayed as normal people—perhaps above-average, but part of the human continuum? Or are they demigods, exalted above common humanity by class or genes or even by divine right?

These are not the usual literary categories applied by analytical critics, but I am willing to wager that they will prove enlightening.

Let us begin with one obvious fact: that every generation is invaded by a new wave of barbarians—its children.

Why Rebel?

Do you believe people around you are subjected to *propaganda*? Most people think so. Take a moment to write down on a piece of paper which campaign you think most thoroughly indoctrinates your fellow citizens. Some mention communism, religion or consumer advertising … or that today's mass media push conformity on a hapless, sheep-like population. It is a smug cliché—that you alone (or perhaps with a few friends) happen to see through the conditioning that has turned all the rest into passively obedient sheep.

Cyberpunk plays to this image by portraying a lone individual—or perhaps just a few—scurrying like rats under the dark towers of the ruling masters. In *The Matrix*, these masters are evil computers. In *Johnny Mnemonic,* they are rulers of faceless corporations. In *The X-Files,* it is a government conspiracy. What these myths share is a grimly satisfying conceit that the masses are useless bystanders, lowing and mooing in confusion.

In fact, it never occurs to the heroes of these tales to actually appeal to the very masses who pay the hero's wages and deserve his loyal respect. The common man or woman cannot help resist the Dark Power, because they were long ago indoctrinated into dull, unquestioning obedience.

Ahhh, but here is the ironic twist. Look around yourself. I'll bet you cannot name, offhand, a single popular film of the last 40 years that actually preached homogeneity, submission or repression of the individual spirit.

15. The Matrix

That's a Clue!

In fact, the most persistent and inarguably incessant propaganda campaign, appearing in countless movies, novels, myths and TV shows, preaches quite the opposite! A singular and unswerving theme so persistent and ubiquitous that most people hardly notice or mention it. And yet, when I say it aloud, you will nod your heads in instant recognition.

That theme is suspicion of authority—often accompanied by its sidekick-partner: tolerance.

Indeed, try to come up with even one example of a recent film you enjoyed in which the hero did not bond with the audience in the first ten minutes by resisting or sticking-it to some authority figure.

Some filmmakers, such as Steven Spielberg, use this potent cinematic ingredient in measured doses, creating and portraying authority figures who are just malevolent and powerful enough to keep the heroes in jeopardy, without too much exaggeration. Others slather the authoritarian premise on as thick as sugar icing in a wedding cake, using the sweetness of resentment to overwhelm all other failings in plot or consistency or taste.

Alas, the latter tendency is all too frequent in sci-fi cinema. Take the bleak paranoia that pervades *The Matrix* and other films of its genre. Oh, I don't mind some tales about rebellion against mega-computers. What gets tedious is the relentless refusal ever to recognize—and then start cleverly varying—a classic cliché.

But back to the essence here. Rebels are always the heroes. Conformity is portrayed as worse than death. Even in war flicks, irreverence for some pompous commander is a necessary trait. Often, the main character also presents some quirky trait, some eccentricity, that draws both ire from some oppressor and sympathy from the audience.

Oh, you do hear some messages of conformity and intolerance— but these fill the mouths of moustache-twirling villains, clearly inviting us to rebel contrary to everything they say. Submission to gray tribal normality is portrayed as one of the most contemptible things an individual can do—a message quite opposite to what was pushed in most other cultures.

This theme is so prevalent, and so obvious, that even though you can see where I am going with it—and hate the inevitable conclusion—you aren't going to dispute the core fact. You have to sit there and accept one of the most galling things that a bunch of dedicated individualists can ever realize: that you were trained to be individualists by the most relentless campaign of public indoctrination in history, suckling your love of rebellion and eccentricity from a society that—evidently, at some level—wants you to be that way!

Oh, the ironies abound.

A Question of Perspective

So do all popular works of fiction promote suspicion of authority? At some level, yes they do. It is the core element of the modern drama, showing just how far the modern sensibility has traveled, parting markedly from the passive plaints of poor doomed Oedipus and Othello, who had no recourse when they were marked for agony by their gods. The classical Greeks, Romans, Japanese and others tended to portray resistance as futile—as prescribed primly in Aristotle's Poetics—a fundamental tenet of the *Look Back* view I mentioned earlier.

In contrast, some modern SF and fantasy tales aggressively take the extreme opposite position. Take *Xena* and *Hercules*, two fairly lowbrow popular television series in which authority figures were portrayed as evil in direct proportion to their rudeness or callousness toward commonfolk. Xena might rescue an exiled king from invaders and restore his throne, but only if he treats people nicely and promises to set up a democratically elected city council. Any time someone is abused by an Olympian, that god is sure to face dire punishment from our heroine!

Ahhh, but as we discussed earlier, the will toward worshipping Olympians and demigods still roils within us. After all, we spent thousands of years in feudal settings that were totally undemocratic. Social structures were pyramid-shaped, with a narrow elite dominating ignorant masses. Starting with Homer's *Iliad* and *Gilgamesh*, nearly all of the bards and storytellers worked for the chiefs, aristocrats and kings who owned all the marbles. (A point conveniently never mentioned by Joseph Campbell in *The Hero with a Thousand Faces*.) Naturally they preached that lords and *better* folk had a right to exercise capricious power at whim. You could choose which demigod to root for—say, Achilles or Hector. But there was no disputing the super-hero's ultimate right to deal with mortals however he wished.

Of course this is another aspect of the nostalgic-romantic *Look Back* worldview. Today you see it exemplified in two highly popular epics, the *Ender* series of Orson Scott Card and the *Star Wars* saga produced by George Lucas. In both, the pivotal characters are born profoundly superior to those around them ... not just a little smarter, but indisputably and qualitatively greater than mere mortals. Moreover, the distinction is not one earned by hard work or the give-and-take of reciprocal criticism that typifies modern teamwork, democracy, meritocracy or science. Rather the justification is one of inherited genetic supremacy, giving the hero an inherent right to meddle at will.

Nearly all O.S. Card works feature a central demigod, whose saving grace is a deep self-pitying angst—expressed at great length—over

15. The Matrix

being forced to overrule the obstinate will of benighted humanity and set things straight. But at least Card's characters seem to feel vague regret that people aren't able to handle things as adults. Not bothering with such hand-wringing, George Lucas' Jedi Force mythology baldly and openly extols the same sort of secretive mystical priest-class that assisted and excused oppressive kings in nearly all eras, on nearly all continents. And all the while, both sagas put forward strawmen "authority figures" for the characters to resent openly, while real manipulators play the underlying dancing tune.

Of course, the very notion of progress is anathema to nostalgic romantics. Despite techie furnishings, the *Star Wars* pop-epic relentlessly preaches the nostalgist party line: An ideal society ought to be ruled by secretive-mystical elites, unaccountable and self-chosen based on inherent qualities of blood. The only good knowledge is old knowledge. (No wonder it all happened *long ago, in a galaxy far away*.)

Note: These romantics needn't be anti-technological, though they almost have to reject science. Their worldview is utterly incompatible with the way science works or thinks.

From Virgil and the Vedas to Plato, Sir Walter Scott and Tolkien, all the way to Updike and Rowling, this prevalent nostalgist tradition spanned five continents and 40 centuries. Some rage, others fizz; but all grumble at tomorrow.

Even where the heroes of these tales practice Suspicion of Authority (they must, in order to bond with today's audiences), the dispute is portrayed as one among demigods. Mere mortals have the option of dying as spear carriers—as they did in *The Iliad*—and of worshipping the demigods with mass ceremonies, as in *Triumph of the Will*.

Contrast this with the view portrayed in *Star Trek*, in which democracy is an inherent good. Scientific progress, while deserving skeptical oversight, is seen as both inevitable and probably desirable. The ship's captain, while great, relies utterly on the competence of his or her merely human crew, any one of whom may prove crucial and deserving of a brief moment on center stage. In *Star Trek*, any demigod is viewed with worried doubt.

Frankly, I am amazed that *Star Trek* ever thrived. Certainly it is unsurprising to find that its core element of progressive optimism has seldom been emulated elsewhere in the canon of SF. There are a few other examples. Robert Silverberg, Iain Banks and Wil McCarthy have been known to portray futures in which our descendants face problems commensurately difficult enough to challenge even people who are far better and wiser than we are.

Let's face it: Portraying a smart future civilization, one that nevertheless faces cleverly onerous problems, can be hard work! It is much easier to milk the emotions by using a demigod character, in a dystopian setting filled with clueless citizens. Just assume the worst about society and give the readers or viewers the emotional satisfaction of watching that supreme hero rebel against some garishly simple and overwrought authority figure ... while at the same time wielding magical forces that he was born and destined to use.

The Difficulty of Optimism

Where do many of today's popular genre films fit in?

Take *The Matrix*, a movie I quite enjoyed! Its hi-tech premise and cyber-glossy ambiance are lavishly attractive and the conflict setup is appealing. Who could resist the dark glamour of its design, the pyrotechnics of its stunts, the seduction of its noir-ish vision?

Above all, relish the classic audience identification with a character who is told in advance that he will be "the One" ... and any skill that he lacks—any skill that you ever wished that you had time to learn—can be downloaded in a matter of seconds! (Naturally, this miracle uses the very same science that the central premise preaches to have been one big mistake. Ironies are another lavish trait of the film.)

But how does it score according to the four questions I posed earlier?

On almost every count, *The Matrix* is an unabashedly nostalgic-romantic piece, loyal to the elitist *look backward* worldview, suspicious of science and deeply contemptuous of the masses, which are portrayed more sheep-like here than in any other work of popular culture! Only at the very end is there a hint that perhaps the common man or woman might someday be wakened from their seductive slumbers. But not much chance of that.

Don't get me wrong! Dark warnings are among the greatest literary works, and SF does civilization a genuine good when it dourly explores potential failure modes. Elsewhere I go into the importance of self-preventing prophecies—SF tales that have quite possibly saved our lives and certainly helped save freedom, by inoculating a definitely *not* sheep-like public with heightened awareness of a potential danger. Among the greatest of these were *Dr. Strangelove*, *Soylent Green* and *Nineteen Eighty-Four*, all of which helped make the author's vivid warning somewhat obsolete through the unexpected miracle that people actually listened.

Still, there have been enough paeans of praise for the style and the warning inherent in *The Matrix*. I want to go back to those under-discussed aspects—such as the devout adherence to a nostalgist-romantic Look Back way of viewing the world.

Contrast this mentality with another enjoyable romp, *The Fifth Element,* a far less serious, less thoughtful film than *The Matrix.* It's a film whose general mindlessness is only matched by its unabashed joy. Ebullience and optimism spills off the screen in gushing torrents, overwhelming the viewer's sense of surly skepticism, even when the adventure is at its most dire or the plot is most ridiculous. True, there is a demigod, but she desperately needs the aid and succor of mere mortal heroes, even citizens who are passing by! Some authority figures drive the plot with their vileness, but the director does not feel it necessary to tar all of society and all of science with this brush. The villains are plenty bad enough. No need to make the cake all frosting.

Take another example: *Minority Report* (or almost any Steven Spielberg film, for that matter). Spielberg is unabashedly progressive and loyal to the Look Forward zeitgeist. Although he skillfully utilizes Suspicion of Authority, he cannot let himself fall for the *X-Files* cliché of a country and citizenry that are completely and forever clueless. Even the government—a classic target of authority-resentment in film—is never portrayed as unalloyedly vile. Rather, his abusive authority figures are narrowly defined: a vile police chief here, a callous scientist there.

Moreover, the hero can even sometimes call upon help from decent people and institutions. While there are moments of techno–Orwellian creepiness in *Minority Report*, such as when the police send spy-eye spiders running through an apartment building, Spielberg portrays this as a highly limited invasion, one that sovereign citizens have clearly decided to tolerate. They can still vote to eliminate a particular police power if they decide they do not like it—in fact, this is a central element to the plot. This future may be creepy and filled with problems, but it is no clichéd tyranny.

In other words, unlike George Lucas, Spielberg is grateful to a civilization of democracy, egalitarian science and general decency. He simply cannot bring himself to spit in its face. Especially not after it has been so good to him.

The Roots of Fantasy

At the very opposite extreme, consider the popularity of feudal-magical fantasies, of the kind typified by *The Lord of the Rings.*

Recall how a core element of romanticism is to spurn the modern emphasis on pragmatic experimentation, production, universal literacy, cooperative enterprise and flattened social orders. In contrast to these "sterile" pursuits, Romantics extolled the traditional, the personal, the particular, the subjective and metaphorical. Consider how this fits with the plot of *Lord of the Rings*, in which the good guys strive to win re-establishment of an older, graceful and "natural" hierarchy against the disturbing, quasi-industrial and vaguely technological ambience of Mordor, with its smokestack imagery and manufactured power rings that can be used by anybody, not just an elite few. Those man-made wonders are deemed cursed, damning anyone who dares to use them, usurping the rightful powers of their betters (the high elves).

Another really cool thing about fantasy: You can identify with a side that's 100 percent pure, distilled good and revel as they utterly annihilate foes who deserve to be exterminated because they are 100 percent evil! This may not be politically correct, but then political correctness is really a bastard offspring of egalitarian-scientific enlightenment. Romanticism never made any pretense at equality. It is hyper-discriminatory, by nature.

The urge to crush some demonized enemy resonates deeply within us, dating from ages far earlier than feudalism. From the foot soldiers and spear carriers who died by Achilles' hand in *The Iliad* to the clones and robots and masked troopers and even rebels in the *Star Wars* saga. Among all the attempts to cast definitions of fantasy and science fiction, to help explain the chasm that so many see, let me offer this one based on the difference between the Look Back and Look Forward Worldviews: Science fiction is the genre that posits the slim possibility that children might sometimes be capable of learning from the mistakes of their parents. That people may someday be better than us, even partly on account of our efforts.

They may no longer need kings. They may, each of them, be capable of rising up and being heroes.

A Continuing Struggle of Worldviews

There is no resolution to this ongoing struggle, one that runs deeper than any politics or ideology. Movies such as *The Matrix* and *Minority Report* embody this struggle. While we are entranced by the similarities (the glossy, diverting futures and techno wonders and dark warnings), it is important also to remember that there are deeper assumptions at play. Assumptions about what human beings can potentially achieve.

Science fiction, in effect, has become a central battlefield in one of the most important disputes roiling in the human mind: the decision whether to continue our obsession with hierarchies, demigods and the past …

… or to turn with confidence and wary optimism toward the future.

16

A Mini-Rant

*Why All Those Zombies
Mean You'd Better Vote!*

Zombies are red, Vampires are blue...
Seriously, zombies are political?

Well. Apparently—some claim—zombie flicks flourish when Republicans are gaining ascendency. After all, such works depict a garish, simplistic exaggeration of what they dread most: an unruly uprising of the filthy, ignorant masses.

Vampire films, in contrast, represent fear of a predacious, controlling aristocracy and so, this genre surges in perfect tempo with times when Democrats rise in influence. Recent vampire films include *League of Extraordinary Gentlemen* (2003), *Van Helsing* (2004), *Twilight* (2008) and HBO's *True Blood* (2008–2014).

Moreover, given the sudden greenlighting of ever-more remakes of remakes of remakes of the same dull zombie scenario ... the same clichés, over and over again ... it looks like we may be in for a very long period of aristocratic rule. Perhaps like the 4000-year feudal reign that only ended with the American Revolution, and that may resume at any time.

Pennsylvania State professor Peter Dendle notes that the Reagan era was the most prolific era for zombie movies—though they returned during the George W. Bush years. A random sampling of zombie movies includes:

White Zombie (1932)
I Walked with a Zombie (1943)
Night of the Living Dead (1968)
Let Sleeping Corpses Lie (1975)

Zombie (1979)
Day of the Dead (1985)
28 Days Later (2002)
Dawn of the Dead (2004)

Land of the Dead (2005)
Planet Terror (2007)
Dance of the Dead (2008)
Zombieland (2009)
The Dead (2010)
Abraham Lincoln vs. Zombies (2012)
World War Z (2013)

The online popular culture magazine *io9* charts a spike in zombie movies coming out close to historical events involving war or social upheaval (World War II, the Vietnam War, the Global recession, the Iraq War), "and they always seem to fall slightly after a huge political or social event has caused mass fear, chaos, or suffering," writes Annalee Newitz.

"Democrats, who want to redistribute wealth to 'Main Street,' fear the Wall Street vampires who bleed the nation dry. Republicans fear a revolt of the poor and disenfranchised, dressed in rags and coming to the White House to eat their brains," Newitz continues.

Technology consultant Pat Scannell sees an even darker function played by zombies, who are individually shambling and vulnerable, but dire in their mass numbers and so devoid of appealing traits: "Zombie movies are, in my mind, a model for dehumanizing others, and expressing how we need to act in a world where others need help." All of that is in keeping with earlier chapters about Tolkien's orcs and George Lucas' robot or clone or storm trooper soldiers, all without faces or (presumably) mothers to mourn them.

In fact, though … what I've perceived goes deeper! It appears that there is a whole *monster class system.*[1]

"These gore-flecked flicks are really competing parables about class warfare," writes Peter Rowe in the *San Diego Union Tribune.*

After all, if vampires are old-style aristocrats (and by the way, those who wallow in vampire idolatry truly are bona fide traitors to our modern Enlightenment, so there), and if zombies are the proletariat…

…then which monsters represent the Middle Class?

Well, it used to be lycanthropes, of course.

Werewolves. Poor schlumps in the suburbs who got bitten and who must now wrestle with the temptations of raw, animal power. A tormented werewolf is the classic, bourgeois middle, between lordly, effete vampires and the innumerable, shambling, proletarian zombies. Werewolves are the only movie monsters who were portrayed with families, mortgages to pay and lawns that need mowing … and a monthly dread that came with every full moon. Their affliction used to be depicted with sympathy and angst. They made for interesting stories! Their new powers and temptations, conflicting with bourgeois values, led to compelling and very sympathetic tragedy…

…except in the wonderfully upbeat and so–American flick *Teen Wolf*

(1985), which proclaimed: *Hey, we're not so scared any more. Let's keep widening the circle of inclusion and welcome these folks, too, out of the closet, into the light.*

Alas, then, we have the recent, utter betrayal of the whole idea behind wolfmen, in those awful new series we've seen lately—you know, the ones that portray "lycans" as just another kind of arrogant asshole monster race preying on normal people—a pack of cheap, white-trash versions of vampires—completely missing the point of what they are about!

For a more philosophical and academic look at this pop culture phenomenon, take a look at the collected essays in *Zombies, Vampires, and Philosophy: New Life for the Undead*, edited by Richard Greene and K. Silem Mohammad.

Werewolf Films

WereWolf of London (1935)
The Wolf Man (1941)
The Curse of the Werewolf (1961)
Night of the Werewolf (1981)
The Howling (1981)
An American Werewolf in London (1981)
Silver Bullet (1985)
Wolf (1994)
An American Werewolf in Paris (1997)
Dog Soldiers (2002)
Underworld (2003)
Underworld Evolution (2006)
Red Riding Hood (2011)

17

Buffy the Old-Fashioned Hero[1]

And so we come to one of the greatest of them all…
What does it take to be a shining new star in Hollywood these days?
Well, if you're female, it helps to be beautiful. An ability to act? Kind of useful. Success may also come with knowing the right people…[2]

That much has always been true. But nowadays, another essential trait has been added to the list of starlet requirements. You gotta be able to kick ass.

Think about it. Can you name any hot new Hollywood sensations who can't do a leaping decapitation kick? From *La Femme Nikita* and *Charlie's Angels* to *Witchblade*, *Xena: Warrior Princess* and *Underworld*, the trend has been amazingly consistent.[3]

Oh, we still like our heroines to be gorgeous. We're still terribly sexist. But you have to admit, it's a more respectful sexism. That's how progress comes, in stages.

And nowhere is this progress better typified than in *Buffy*, with its wonderfully charming mix of the silly and the serious, the assertive and the sweet. Old-fashioned values of love and romance are retained … while making it clear that women are no longer willing to be pushed around.

And it goes much deeper than that. For *Buffy* hearkens to the greatest modern movement to change the way people look upon authority. A movement that pervades our culture, calling into question the whole issue of conformity and obedience. Unlike any other culture, ours has taken to saying: Prove it!

In *Buffy*, an expert or authority figure is judged good or evil by a simple set of standards that have nothing to do with their status or class or birth. Even a vampire can be a good guy. The sole criterion that matters is whether you treat others decently.

17. Buffy the Old-Fashioned Hero

Nor is *Buffy* alone pushing this message. Take *Xena* and *Hercules*, two fairly lowbrow, popular television series from the 1990s in which authority figures were portrayed as evil in direct proportion to their rudeness or callousness toward commonfolk. Xena might rescue an exiled king from invaders and restore his throne, but only if he treats people nicely and promises to set up a democratically elected city council. Any time someone is abused by an Olympian, that "god" is sure to face dire punishment from our heroine!

Yup, Buffy ain't alone.

Ahhh, but she has her work cut out for her. The will toward worshipping Olympians and demigods still roils within us. After all, we spent thousands of years in feudal settings that were totally undemocratic. Social structures were pyramid-shaped, with a narrow elite dominating ignorant masses. Starting with Homer's *Iliad* and Gilgamesh, nearly all of the bards and storytellers worked for the chiefs, aristocrats and kings who owned all the marbles.

The old stories preached that lords and "better" folk had a right to exercise capricious power at whim. You could choose which demigod to root for—say, Achilles or Hector. But there was no disputing the super-hero's ultimate right to deal with mortals however he wished.

You don't think people preach that message any more? Look closer! Today you see it exemplified in highly popular epics like the *Star Wars* saga and *Lord of the Rings* or even *Harry Potter*. Pivotal characters are born profoundly superior ... not just a little smarter or harder working, but indisputably and qualitatively greater than the mere mortals surrounding them. Inherited genetic supremacy. The best people are born with a right to meddle at will.

Maybe it's time we noticed this difference, between myths that push the ancient feudal view and others that convey our new rebel spirit! Right now they are mixed up, jumbled together, sharing the same eager fans. But they should not because the deep moral of *Buffy* is the opposite of *Star Wars*.

Kings and wizards may be romantic, but they had 6000 years to deliver human happiness, and all they ever did was push us around ... like vampires.

Buffy is our future. Brash, open-minded, open-hearted. Always willing to give someone a chance, even if they are low-born, or even (ew!) ugly. Always questioning authority while willing to cooperate and learn something new. To Buffy, old isn't always better (as it always is in *Star Wars* and Tolkien). She's stylish, hip, caring, sweet ... and nowhere near as dumb as outsiders might think at first.

Oh, she knows what she's doing, all right. We oughta listen.

Anyway, she sure can kick butt.

PART FIVE:
DARK VISIONS AND HOPE

18

Dune

*What This Classic Teaches
About "Point of View"*[1]

Science fiction is a complex genre. Oh, sure, the massive bulk of "sci-fi" production—in novels, games and Hollywood—gushes with simple goals: manic entertainment and generating cash. But many SF creators often do show genuine ambition. Like adventurers on unknown seas, they aim for something more.

What is storytelling, after all? I've called it exercise for our prefrontal lobes, those "lamps upon the brow" where humans perform thought-experiments like: "How might things be different than they are?" This trait seems qualitatively unique to us, rather than just quantitatively enlarged. Asking "What if…?" led to our prodigious inventiveness, both in pragmatic crafts and in art. No activity stretches and exercises those prefrontals like science fiction, poking at every assumption of contemporary life.

This fascination with change led to our most important works, those self-preventing prophecies that I described early in this book, for example *Soylent Green, Nineteen Eighty-Four* and *Dr. Strangelove*. But such warnings don't have to be set in a plausible near-future. Through exaggeration, a far-off era can either chill the heart or inspire, as we've seen in works of Clarke, Asimov, Stapledon, and … yes … Frank Herbert, whose many, varied SF gedankenexperiments culminated in the popular *Dune* epic. That richly textured and complex future human civilization invites the visitor to ponder quandaries that grow more pertinent daily—like our relationship with "intelligent" machines, or under-exploited powers that may lurk in human minds. And feudalism, the way of life that dominated nearly all of our ancestors for the last 6,000 years or more.

Everywhere humans developed agriculture (and likely long before), similar social patterns emerged. Large males would gather in tight bands, pick up metal or stone implements, and use them to crush potential rivals, taking from the losers anything they wanted. Extrapolating the battle for reproductive advantage that occurs in countless animal species, feudalism amplified the genetic rewards spectacularly, as these "lords" structured society to favor their sons, and their sons' sons. We are all descended from the harems of jerks who pulled off this trick. And, as we'll see, feudal themes have allured writers, directors and consumers for a very long time.

In the Dune universe—culminating especially with *God Emperor of Dune* (1981)—we get feudalism exponentiated to its likely outcome, if lordly castes ever come to monopolize tools of technology and the mind. Tools of manipulation and suasion. Tools that amplify their assertion of raw power over those below them on a rigid pyramid. And then to *justify* the hierarchy, as feudal regimes have always done—through religion, mythology, tribalism, politics ... and war.

> When religion and politics travel in the same cart, the riders believe nothing can stand in their way. Their movement becomes headlong—faster and faster and faster. They put aside all thought of obstacles and forget that a precipice does not show itself to the man in a blind rush until it's too late.—*Dune*, Frank Herbert, 1965[1]

In his introduction to *Dune Messiah* (1969), Gregory Benford tells how he knew Frank Herbert as a colleague. I am of a later wave that barely overlapped with such legends. While honored to call Ray Bradbury, Frederik Pohl and Poul Anderson my friends, I exchanged correspondence with Clarke and Asimov. As for Heinlein and Herbert, I can only say "we met and spoke for a while, once." Still, I feel part of a grand conversation with all of them, and with so many others in both science and science fiction, across a dazzling civilization that has broken away from those old, feudal traps. To us, the grand *terra incognita* of tomorrow is no narrow path defined by kings, priests and adepts, but a vast horizon filled with dangers and opportunities and decisions that may involve all of us, with solutions that depend on *any* of us.

And beyond those horizons? More horizons, still.

In order to cross this expanse, we'll need to detect the land mines, snake pits, quicksand and other traps that may have snared previous sapient species across the galaxy, leaving it so (apparently) empty. Brave authors plunge into these mine fields, issuing warnings about environmental calamity, or ill-motivated artificial intelligence (AI), or misused genetic science. All too often, the worst failure mode of all, one that plagued our ancestors and cauterized our growth—feudalism—gets *romanticized*.

At least half-seriously, Mark Twain blamed the 1860s Confederacy on Southern romantics, devouring books by Sir Walter Scott that glorified the lords and ladies of Europe's dark ages. "Lairdism" it was called, and the plantation lords subsidized copies handed out to poor whites, across the antebellum south. It worked. Likewise, I see similar roots in today's phase of America's reignited Civil War.[2]

As I've discussed elsewhere, something deep inside resonates across the vast landscape of science fiction and fantasy, embodied in Aragorn and his snooty, immortal elf-pals. It's a deep well of feeling that goes back to Gilgamesh and Achilles, found in the Vedas and Journey to the West, and every legend or ballad catalogued by Joseph Campbell *et al*. During science fiction's Golden Age, the great master of "chosen one" SF was A.E. van Vogt, whose protagonists were always Nietzschean *übermensch* supermen, qualitatively far above normal humanity. It's an ancient motif, most prevalent today in comics, but continuing also in the demigod-worshipping propaganda of George Lucas and Orson Scott Card.

Oh, this storytelling tradition is a winner, all right. It uses point of view to flatter the reader or viewer, who thinks: "I too am an undiscovered *Homo superior*, persecuted for all the ways that I'm inherently greater and destined to rule, once I finally tap into my hidden powers." Who can compete with that? Compared to rule by some mystical or sword-wielding chosen one, our modern, accountable institutions seem dry. And yes, unromantic. Even though they freed us from our ancestors' living hell.

Not every creator accepts this devil's bargain. A few opt not to romanticize feudalism, but instead challenge and interrogate it, as George R.R. Martin does in his *A Song of Ice and Fire* series (better known as *Game of Thrones*). But it is Frank Herbert's *Dune* epic that transports us to a future when feudalism is extrapolated and tech-enhanced. Its age-old, capricious unfairness and cruelty is undiminished by future advances. In fact, they are augmented to a terrifying degree, never imagined by Orwell.

Damien Broderick points out in *The Cambridge Companion to Science Fiction* (2003) that the "deep irony of *Dune*'s popular triumph, and that of its many sequels, is Herbert's own declared intention to undermine exactly that besotted identification with the van Vogtian superman-hero." Science fiction scholar Stephen Potts said to me in a conversation that Herbert is "undercutting the whole hero myth archetype, by having the characters consciously use—and abuse—it."

Remember that Herbert had lived through the horrors of Nazism and Stalinism and *caudillo* dictatorships to the south. In very recent memory—while the *Dune* saga took form—came revelations of the Cambodian holocaust led by Pol Pot, which emptied every city, eliminating the nation's knowledge castes as enemies of the idealized Khmer Path to hyper–Maoist purity. With the infamous year 1984 itself looming just ahead, the warnings of George Orwell were very much in Herbert's mind as he wrote his own tale of warning.

The hero-protagonists in these stories are no democrats, nor are they idealists, nor even particularly "good." Only somewhat less horrible than their rivals. That is the slender reed upon which Herbert draws reader and viewer identification … and upon that reed he builds a masterpiece!

Not one to slavishly follow any formula, Herbert took the classic Hero's Journey prescriptions the way any good SF writer should … as a *dare* to do things differently.

Which brings us to the core point of this essay: Many *Dune* fans dump on the 1984 Dino De Laurentiis–David Lynch movie. And yes, by necessity the film (which Frank rather liked[3]) leaves out many complex issues of religion, politics and ecology explored in the book. Yet I found it faithful overall. Indeed, one problem may boil down to a difference in storytelling arcs, between novel and film.

Full-length books deeply immerse a reader in the characters' perspective or *point of view*. When reading a good novel, you suspend disbelief to get drawn in, and that requires empathizing with the main characters. A good writer will get you identifying with the protagonist, adopting—or at least trying on for size—even a villain's take on ethics, politics and the story's conflicts. At least for the span of a chapter, you classify good and evil the way he or she does. It's incredibly powerful, this point-of-view magic, and more would-be authors are stymied by it than any other trick of the trade.

When a brilliant craftsman like Herbert leads you to identify with Lady Jessica or Paul Atreides, you take on their vendetta against the hated Harkonnens. Similarly, in J.R.R. Tolkien's *Lord of the Rings* (1955–1956), the reader identifies with Aragorn or the elves, without questioning any moral ambiguity on their part.

However, when watching a movie, there simply isn't time for you, the viewer, to fully immerse yourself into the characters' point of view, let alone experience their internalized thoughts. You're watching from *outside*, observing their actions, rather than feeling their motives. As a result, something magical that happens in a book cannot occur in the screen adaptation.

Sure, *Dune's* Harkonnen villains and emperor are vile in the film versions, but it occurs to some viewers that the Atreides do many of the same things, just less gruesomely, less sadistically. Perhaps Duke Leto is an admirable person in his context, but his context is horrible. He's not setting out to establish freedom and equality in his realm. As in *Star Wars* and *Lord of the Rings*, goodness is telegraphed with physical surface beauty. But in the *Dune* film, it's not enough. (Note that the Atreides troops even dress like Nazis.)

In Herbert's novels, there are no visuals but those the reader creates out of authorial prompting. Instead, it is the characters' *thoughts* that draw you in. And when protagonist perspective is conveyed by a master, the magic is to make you, briefly, willing to credit their rationalized reasons.

When reading these works—not just the original *Dune*, but sequels, especially *God Emperor of Dune*—notice how skillfully Herbert *switches narrative perspective*. Most authors either stick to one character's point of view and inner voice per book, or at least per chapter. (That is certainly how I do it! Even when the varied points of view are different versions of the same person, as in *Kiln People* [2002].) There are reasons; switching back and forth can jar and confuse the reader. But Herbert was so confident in his skill that point of view might hop among two, or three or more characters, even in neighboring paragraphs!

This artfulness reaches its pinnacle in *God Emperor of Dune*. With apparent effortlessness, Herbert conveys to the reader on a single page how deeply suspicious these manipulative lords, savants and rebels are of the emperor, and of each other—a task made even more difficult by the posited existence of prescience and some types of telepathy! This is master-level writing craft. Don't try it at home, 'til you are as good a writer as Herbert.

Oh, these characters have reasons! In the *Dune* universe, certain technologies have been outlawed due to a traumatic "Butlerian Jihad" thousands of years earlier—a war against Artificial Intelligence that prompted the victorious lords to renounce technology and vow never again to allow egalitarian-open-scientific civilization. Herbert isn't the only author to portray a future that turns its back on enlightenment-style renaissance. In Isaac Asimov's Foundation and Robots cosmos, it is the "devoted" AIs who rationalize exactly the same thing prescription—as I clarify in the very last book of the series, *Foundation's Triumph* (1999).

"Renunciation" stands for belief that we must turn our backs on so-called "progress," lest it kill us all, and it was official policy in countless kingdoms of the past. A modern equivalent, the Taliban, calls for renunciation quite openly, while elements of American society have long expressed contempt for all enlightenment notions of improvability in either society or humanity. Indeed, reverting to feudalism has—for half a dozen millennia—proved an effective way to stymie advancement of science, technology or competitive ambition rising from the lower orders.

So much for the situation that Leto, Paul and Jessica find themselves in, as the *Dune* epic commences. Rigid, perpetual feudalism has its justification (according to the testimony and inner thoughts of those at the top of the pyramid, our protagonists). But Herbert then doubles down, harkening to an even older mythology of the *god-king*. Paul Atreides is superior to all other members of his species—the Kwisatz-Haderach—a "chosen one" demigod who can see into the future and control many currents of fate. In *Dune Messiah,* Paul wields temporal power as emperor, conqueror and leader of a galaxy-spanning jihad. But it is on the religious and supernatural plane that he awes and daunts all…

…and it is on that plane that he proclaims justification for a new, more intense kind of feudalism. "It's right because I say so."

Which brings us back around to *The God Emperor of Dune.* It is 3000 years later. Paul's son Leto II has been both emperor and living deity over humanity's realm for nearly all that time. Transforming himself into the physiology of an Arrakis sand-worm, Leto also molded civilization, emptying or eliminating most cities, higher education or cosmopolitan life, even quashing most technology—except for the interstellar transportation Guild, the bio-hackers of Tleilaxu and the always suspect tech wizards of Ix. (I use the word "wizards" purposely, because the fairy tale purpose of these two "towers" could not be more clear.) Every aspect of modernity is deemed loathsome by Leto, if it does not suit one of his cryptic purposes. Moreover, while he needs the wizards for certain things, he also knows they are laboring to bring about his downfall.

Across the course of a book filled with taunts and harsh lectures, Leto issues the chief justification for his hyper-feudal rule: that humanity *would have* killed itself off without him. His prophetic foresight, though limited in obscure ways, has shown him a "Golden Path" that skirts this doom, a path that necessitates every horror and repression. Humanity achieved the stars, only to crouch under a medieval lash. But for its own good.

Does the reader start to sniff Frank Herbert's true intent?

Oh, others have explored this territory. Take Tolkien, whose own epic tale calls modernization inevitable, if regrettable—even lamentable. In explanatory writings, Tolkien avowed the necessity of an end to the morally challenged, if beautiful, Elfish oligarchy. He makes us choose then, between two versions of modernity: one of clanking smoke—Mordor—and one of doughty rustic yeomen—dwellers of the Shire.

If Tolkien is an honest romantic, open about the pros and cons, then George Lucas and O.S. Card give us legends that unabashedly preach rule by mutant demigods … and more demigods all the way down … proclaiming it to be the natural and good order. (That is, Lucas pushed this theme as long as that narrative universe remained under his control. See my argument as "prosecutor" in *Star Wars on Trial* [2006] and the chapter on Star

Wars. And one can see, with some relief, that Disney is pulling away from such obsessions in the new *Star Wars* films.)

In contrast, Herbert's *Dune* epic strips away any sugar coating and offers a refreshing splash of despair. He portrays our own era's brief escape from feudalism as ephemeral, lasting just long enough to scatter humanity's seed across the stars, before resuming our habitual addiction to oligarchy, in which our sole choice will be between sadism and noblesse oblige.

I mentioned a latter-day parallel: George R.R. Martin's *Song of Ice and Fire* series, in which the clear best option for all the people of Westeros would be a lethal plague upon all noble houses. But that series is set in a past-like parallel fantasy world. One can imagine that an infusion of the right technologies might liberate the suffering peasant, as happens in Anne McCaffrey's unabashedly optimistic *Dragonriders* series, when the medieval trap is shattered and the people of Pern rediscover their scientific heritage.

And hence we get to my own hypothesis about the *Dune* saga. That Frank Herbert was testing us! A test that reached its culmination in *God Emperor of Dune*. He clearly knew that humanity was speeding toward a crisis of confidence—our brash civilization's confrontation with renunciation and all of the romantic temptations of restored feudalism. By showing us an extremum of where it might all lead, he makes the choice stark. No spoon of sugar.

This is where it may all lead, if you let it.

I am less subtle—known for railing that our only hope for prolonging this grand experiment of Enlightenment depends on harnessing and unleashing humanity's freedom, diversity, open accountability and—yes—competitiveness. By shining light upon all elites, we force them to share with us those very tools that they would otherwise use, to bring down eons of darkness. We might flourish—elevating the *Dune* series to the high honor of Self-Preventing Prophecy—by empowering most people to create, innovate, benefit from work, and hold each other (even the rich and mighty) accountable.

I am perhaps too strident in shouting Cassandra warnings about resurgent feudalism.

Frank was more subtle.

He presents us with a possible, all too plausible destiny. A form of governance that 99 percent of our ancestors would recognize, far better than any of our forebears would understand us.

Whereupon Frank Herbert demands:

Choose.

19

The Postman
The Book vs. the Movie

Okay, admit it. You were waiting for this one...

Years ago, about the same time that studios were bidding for *The Postman*, my wife Cheryl and I went to a screening of *Field of Dreams*. As we emerged, she turned to me and said, "That's him. He's the one."

She meant Kevin Costner—her choice as the right man to portray Gordon, the hero of my novel. What could I say in response, except, "Honey, we'd never be that lucky!"

Well, doesn't time tend to heap ironies on us all? A decade later, when we heard that Costner would actually star in *The Postman*, we were thrilled. When it was further announced that the Academy Award–winning director of *Dances with Wolves* would also direct this time, I knew we were in for a ride.

And when months passed without even a word from Costner, an invitation to dinner or even a phone call, I began to worry that we might be in trouble...

But that's getting ahead of myself. Let's go back to the beginning.

The Postman was written as an answer to all those post-apocalyptic books and films that seem to revel in the idea of civilization's fall. It's a story about how much we take for granted—and how desperately we would miss the little, gracious things that connect us today. It is a story about the last idealist in a fallen America. A man who cannot let go of a dream we all once shared. Who sparks restored faith that we can recover, and perhaps even become better than we were. It would take a special kind of actor to play the lead role—a ragged survivor, deeply scarred, yet still willing to hope. In this era of cynicism, we need reminders of the decency that lies within.

19. The Postman

That sense of strength, openness and hope was what we felt after watching *Field of Dreams*. *The Postman* is a very different story, yet it aims to deliver the same message to the heart: We are in this together. (Ironically, the *Postman* movie's message is exactly opposite to the moral message conveyed by *Waterworld* ... think about it!)

The book obviously affected people. Within months of its publication, at the hasty urging of my then-agent, I sold movie rights to the first bidder. Producer Steve Tisch then hired veteran screenwriter Erik Roth to do an adaptation. At first, I thought this would bode very well! Under gifted directors like Robert Zemeckis, Roth had acquired a reputation as a skilled adapter of existing material. Alas, this time, without a strong director holding the reins, Roth decided to toss out every iota of the book and start from scratch with a story that was completely his own ... incidentally going out of his way to reverse every moral point of *The Postman*!

The resulting script—despite at least half a dozen dubious rewrites—became notorious in Hollywood, discouraging even such figures as Tom Hanks and Ron Howard, who had been attracted by the overall concept. After helplessly reading successive drafts, each more bizarre than the last, I finally concluded that the project was dead. Following the advice of many past authors who were disappointed with Hollywood, I determined to shrug my shoulders and walk away.

Unfortunately, that was hard to do! People kept phoning and writing to me, asking about "film rights to your wonderful novel...." Richard Dreyfuss enthusiastically offered me first crack at the screenplay, before I even had a chance to interrupt and break the news that rights were already gone. As one might imagine, such calls (almost monthly for nearly a decade) struck me as sad reminders of what might have been.

Then something happened. Kevin Costner came aboard, bringing all his might and prestige to the project. Though I was never consulted, he nevertheless agreed with my own impression: that an evil, incoherent and rapacious central character might be a bad idea! Instinctively realizing that the tale ought to be about decency, heroism and hope, he threw out all the dismal old drafts and hired Brian Helgeland, esteemed screenwriter of *L.A. Confidential*, whose first comment was: "Say, you know there's a pretty good novel by the same name. Why don't we borrow some stuff from it?"

So began *The Postman*'s return from damnation.

Well, sort of.

Between them, Costner and Helgeland restored a few scenes from the novel ... and thought up a whole lot of new ones on their own, combining characters and bringing in several new ones. This hardly surprised me, and certainly did not offend! Unlike many novelists, I understand Hollywood and know that prose fiction is only glancingly related to what you see on the big screen. It's a director's medium, calling for visual storytelling skills and an eye for dramatic moments that are shown, not told.

In fact, I found many Costner-Helgeland innovations to be rather clever! A few were even deeply moving. (Lord only knows how they expected me to react, or if they cared. I have an impression they were rather surprised when they finally learned my overall attitude, as if for some reason they had been bracing for a rather different response.)

Above all—and for this I will forgive a thousand slights—they rescued the "soul" of the central character, making *The Postman* once again a story about a reluctant hero, a liar who slowly comes to realize his own value, and the importance of hope.

Cheryl and I were invited as very, very small fish to the Hollywood premiere. Though we were seated in back with the assistant gaffer, it was nevertheless a terrific evening, as well as cause for reflection about what a long and tortuous road it can be, getting a story to the screen…

…and now it seems that it will also be a long road before the movie is accepted by the arbiters of art. After nearly unanimous denunciations by all the big-time critics, it would be all too easy for me to throw up my hands and declare, "It's not my fault!" I could play martyr and moan aloud, as so many other authors do, about having been "betrayed by Hollywood." (I finally met the executive producer at the premiere, 12 years after the rights were purchased.)

And yet, all told, Cheryl and I came away more pleased than unhappy with what Costner created. Despite many flaws, it's a pretty good movie—if you let yourself get into it. One that deals with important issues and is more faithful to the book than I expected at any point in the last decade. Costner's postman is a man of decency, a callused idealist who has to learn the hard way about responsibility and what it means to be a hero. The movie is filled with scenes that convey how deeply we would miss the gracious little things, if ever they were gone. In fact, it includes some clever or touching moments that I wish I'd thought of, when writing the book!

Fans of the novel will note that he chose to concentrate on the basic story in the first third of the novel. That is what I'd have advised. "Talking computers" and "augments" worked fine in the book but they would have made things too complicated for a film. When all is said and done, the movie tries to convey, with the image of a humble letter carrier, the same sorts of things that *Field of Dreams* said, using the metaphor of baseball.

Science fiction fans might note how the moral message about citizenship is quite different than the one that director Paul Verhoeven delivered in his satire *Starship Troopers*. It is less ethereal than *Contact*. And yet all three movies were somewhat faithful to good novels. All three 1997 films dealt with—and should provoke discussion of—serious issues.

19. The Postman

So why was the film such a dismal failure in the marketplace?

The jury will be out for a long time. Word of mouth has wrought an upsurge of interest in the video, for instance.

But in fact, I was already on record predicting that three groups would come down on Costner, and come down on him very hard. The right wing would hate him for slapping down the militia-solipsist movement, while leftists would despise him for depicting dignity and tolerance under the protection of an American flag. Above all, cynics would carp against the "goody" morality tale.

My prediction proved true in spades, as reviewer after reviewer (what more cynical profession can you name?) slagged the "aw shucks idealism" of the film. One critic likened *The Postman* to *Mad Max* directed by Frank Capra.

The diagnosis is correct! There truly is a Capra-esque quality to Costner's film ... and according to this critic we are supposed to assume that's a bad thing? (Hint: Who can name the folks who panned *It's a Wonderful Life*? Capra endures precisely because he called on us to note the best parts of ourselves, while willingly criticizing what can be improved.)

My best analogy is this: Watching Kevin Costner's three-hour epic is a bit like having a great big Golden Retriever jump on your lap and lick your face, while waving a flag tied to its tail. It's big, floppy, uncoordinated, over-eager, sometimes gorgeous—occasionally a bit goofy—and so big-hearted that something inside of you has to give ... that is, if you like that sort of thing.

Anyway, that was one reason why I lent my name and considerable time to helping promote the movie, giving numerous media interviews and being a team player. The *Postman* Curriculum Web Site may wind up being the most positive thing to come out of this whole episode!

Specifics

The music by James Newton Howard is excellent. The visuals are even more stunning than they were in *Dances with Wolves*. (If Costner hadn't been good-looking, he might still have won an Academy Award by now, as a cinematographer.)

Unfortunately, some sections stretched far too long. Costner needed to have people around him unafraid to say which scenes were bloated and which others were self-indulgent—e.g., the stuff with Tom Petty. There were missed opportunities to have a little fun. And I'd have written the final battle scene quite differently.

There certainly *should* have been a cameo appearance by the original author, somewhere in the back row of a crowd of snarling bad guys! That one defect almost certainly cost the film an Academy Award! (Well … maybe…)

But these are all minor authorial quibbles, more than made up for by the film's touching denouement, featuring Costner's son as a little boy so filled with rediscovered hope that it pours from the screen. Only the most hardened or cynical critic would not be moved.

Well, well. It's time to move on, especially since more and even better opportunities loom on the horizon (making it hard for an honest man to complain!).

In sum, despite many disappointments, I have to say that I'm not ashamed to be associated with the *Postman* movie. Yes, the book is much better! And yes, the film might have benefited a lot if the director ever had a few brews with the guy who told the original story. Yet there's something deeply likable about this film, despite its flaws. Above all, in these days of rampant and contagious solipsism, with so many people claiming to despise a civilization that has been so kind to them, this movie's overall message needs to be heard.

We are in it together. Civilization means something. IAAMOAC (I am a member of civilization).

20

Man Against Machine
Surrogates, Clones and Dittos

From R2-D2 to the Borg, from Wall-E to Optimus Prime, from Bender to RoboCop, Robby the Robot and the Iron Giant, cinema has shaped our ever-changing views of artificial beings. Will our technologic creations lead to the smothering maternal embrace of *I, Robot* (2004), or the dystopic slaughter of the Terminator (1984)? Or will we share our destinies with the gentler helpmates of *A.I. Artificial Intelligence* (2001), *Robot and Frank* (2012), *Bicentennial Man* (1999) or *Her* (2013)?

In fact, the notion of hand-made beings goes way back. Was not Adam, the first man, said to have been molded out of clay? That same, humble material was also said to animate in legends of the Golem, the terracotta soldiers of Xian and the fired-up duplicates of my own novel *Kiln People*. Over time, the imagined shape and substance of these forged creatures shifted, from clay vessels to the 19th century notion of clockwork automatons, to massive computer brains, all the way to purely abstract entities made entirely of algorithms.

There are fervent disagreements over *how* such new minds might come about, or indeed whether artificial minds are even possible. But those arguments are not central to the public gaze. In imaginative media, like film and fiction, the issues are much simpler: How will we incorporate these thinking machines into modern society? And—will they be friendly?

Hollywood has explored many of the ethical and moral issues we'll face as synthetic entities grow more common in the workforce as caregivers, housekeepers, teachers, enforcers and soldiers ... and in private life as companions, friends or even lovers. Vexations will grow increasingly complex as robots begin to look more like humans—and may indeed become indistinguishable from them. Companies and academic researchers are homing in on facial and other cues that might take robots across the *uncanny valley,* so that they mimic all the ways that we humans elicit compassion and empathy from one another. Indeed, won't they smile and frown and tug at our empathic reflexes, demanding sympathy from us before they are even self-aware, as depicted in the film *Ex Machina* (2015)?

Will we need complicated tests, as in *Blade Runner* (1982), to distinguish who is a lawful citizen from what is an ersatz being, not born but engineered? Or, as in the British television series *Humans* (2015), will we gradually, with many painful twists, find ways to co-exist?

Of course, many of our dramas and tales about robots are metaphors for near-term quandaries during this transition era, as we strive to include "others" within the core of civilized life. So far, this has meant expanding that circle to encompass ever-more types of previously excluded human beings. But already we see a glimmering possibility on the horizon, of completing that portion of the task. So, will this process of inclusion-expansion—filled with joys and vexations—continue to other species? Other kinds of "life" that may not even be organic?

So far, there is no strong proof that AI is even possible, let alone that synthetic creatures will exceed humans, either in intelligence or physical strength. The breakthroughs we have seen, almost yearly (e.g. IBM's astonishing Watson), may not *scale* endlessly onward and upward. If they do—as Ray Kurzweil and some others suppose—then we might yet see the much-bruited "singularity" when everything changes so rapidly that outcomes—even good ones—will seem unrecognizable to regular, old-timey Homosaps like thee and me.

That doesn't mean we should just sit on our hands, complacent with "technological determinism"! There are good-singularities and bad ones. A little pre-planning could prove decisive, as illustrated by the struggle between two vast, godlike artificial intelligences, Samaritan and the Machine, in television's *Person of Interest* series: One of them is unleashed to be amorally manipulative of unknowing humanity, while the other is programmed with strong imperatives to treat us with respect, protection and (perhaps) love. If we do view these new kinds of minds as legitimate offspring (and I believe we should), then the parallel of parenthood becomes much more than a metaphor. Sure, they may be fated to outgrow their creators and guardians, as children often do. But there may still be opportunities to start them off in good general directions, with a little guidance.

Who is responsible for a robot's actions, or mistakes: the maker? The owner? The giver of orders? Or the author of some obscure algorithm subroutine that lurked for ages in the software, until it went disastrously wrong?

20. Man Against Machine

In *Logan's Run* (1976), a cyborg named "Box" tries to kill and freeze the hero and heroine, not out of malice but as replacements for the fish he can no longer harvest from the sea. "It's my job," he explains, moving in to collect them. In his book *superintelligence*, philosopher Nick Bostrom called this the "paper clip problem," picturing an automated factory, programmed with a need to efficiently produce paper clips for sale. Imagine that monomania, that drive, abruptly augmented when the factory's computer gains spectacular mental powers, only still constrained by its original goal. A century later, the entire Earth and surrounding solar system have been melted down and re-purposed to make … you know.

This is among the chief worries about our ongoing progress toward ever-smarter and more powerful machines. What if they work exactly as intended, but under the control of bad men? What if they work as intended, with unforeseen consequences? And if they *malfunction?* Or simply outgrow our ability to constrain or control?

In *Aliens* (1986), a friendly synthetic (android), Bishop, hears the tale told by Ripley (Sigourney Weaver) about her earlier bad experiences with a synth called Ash, in *Alien* (1979). Bishop responds, "Well, that model always was a bit twitchy."

Here is one area where cinematic sci-fi diverges from the parent literature. In Hollywood, the principal need is for some Godawful Mistake that can then propel a plot full of danger for the protagonist … and death for almost everyone else. Novels allow room for at least a little nuance, some ponderings of more complicated cause and effect. In a few cases, that science fictional thoughtfulness has seeped out, becoming part of popular culture.

Back in the 1940s, famed author Isaac Asimov laid down his *Three Laws of Robotics,* which would supposedly be ingrained to control robotic behavior at the most fundamental level, excluding forever any actions unfriendly to people:

> A robot may not injure a human being, or through inaction, allow a human being to come to harm.
> A robot must obey the orders given to it by human beings, except where such orders would conflict with the First Law.
> A robot must protect its own existence as long as such protection does not conflict with the First or Second Law.

Asimov's own tales often spun off from the Three Laws and illustrated many implications, some of them surprising or amusing. But one distinctive Asimovian trait was the way Isaac never just sat on an idea, smugly calling it the last word. Instead, his habit was to let them burgeon and then *argue* with his own, earlier conclusions. In particular, over the years, it grew clear to Asimov that robots would become smart, whereupon—even if they were still bound by strict laws—they would respond by *becoming lawyers*.

And hence, he felt compelled, by his own chain of reasoning, to reveal latter-day robot minds interpolating *a Zeroth Law*, one that expands on the first three in ways that are both logical and somewhat chilling.

The Zeroth Law of Robotics: A robot may not harm humanity, or by inaction, allow humanity to come to harm.

Asimov portrayed it taking robots hundreds of years to rationalize this added gloss. But Hollywood's version of *I, Robot* (2004) shortened that time scale, depicting a powerful AI—the Virtual Interactive Kinetic Intelligence, or VIKI—who makes this lawyerly leap before the year 2100, rationalizing that the Zeroth Law allowed her to trump and set aside all the other laws. She states, "You cannot be trusted with your own survival."

This flaw in the "service program" was pointed out even earlier by author Jack Williamson in *The Humanoids* (1948) and *With Folded Hands* (1947), wherein our mechanical servants decide that service means protection, and protection means preventing us from taking any risks at all: "No, no, don't use that knife, you might hurt yourself." Then a generation later, "No, no don't use that fork." Then, "Don't use that spoon. Just sit on this pillow and we'll do everything for you."

Of course, this plot device—unpleasant reinterpretation of a rule or command—goes back to ancient stories about genies, satanic deals and monkey's paws. Notably, the idea that "service" can go very wrong was also portrayed in Damon Knight's famous story "To Serve Man," interpreted also in a *Twilight Zone* episode, with the upshot that we are to be served ... for dinner.

Asimov's Three Laws have been highly influential. They form the background for movies such as *Forbidden Planet* (1956), wherein Robby the Robot's programming prevents him from harming people, even when commanded to do so. Similar laws are cited by robots in the movies *Bicentennial Man* and *Aliens*. The loyal helpmates of Christopher Nolan's film *Interstellar* will sacrifice themselves whenever necessary. In the cartoon TV series *The Jetsons*, George befriends a computer named R.U.D.I. (Referential Universal Digital Indexer), who is a member of the Society Preventing Cruelty to Humans.

Alas, it appears that there are flaws underlying the fundamental premise of Asimov's Three Laws. For example, how would such a perfect, many-layered set of laws ever be enforced? Why would a company—or civilization—go to the strenuous effort and expense of embedding such compulsions into all robotic entities and devices, when competitive pressures demand efficiency instead? Asimov himself presumed that the public, terrified of automatons, would demand it. Indeed, some future trauma or disaster might bring such demands to the fore. But as of now, among the many research groups and laboratories exploring Artificial Intelligence, I know of none investing serious time or money in developing all-controlling "laws."

And so, yet again, we see one of the chief values of science fiction. Not only to thrill and chill and entertain, but also to poke into the territory just ahead, revealing potential mistakes—in fiction—so we needn't do them in real life.

Still, the question fizzes forth: *Is there any way of handling your creations so that they are likely to be loyal to you, even if they're much more intelligent?*

I know of one. It's a method that has worked for quite a few million people who created entities much smarter than themselves, in times past— transforming those new entities into beings that are stronger, more capable and sometimes more brilliant than their predecessors could imagine. We'll talk about that next.

Six Ways to Make Our Successors

Before we continue exploring Hollywood depictions of robotics and all that, let's ask: Is artificial intelligence even possible? Elsewhere I go more deeply into the *six general approaches to making AI happen,* each of which is getting attention from researchers across the globe. These different approaches are of more than academic interest. They have strikingly different implications for our long-term relationship with cybernetic minds— and they lead to very different portrayals in sci-fi films or books.

1. Design smart-sapient systems from scratch, based on today's concept of a digital computer, according to a well-considered AGI (artificial general intelligence) plan. Think Colossus or HAL 9000.
2. Decrypt the workings of a human brain and recreate—or *emulate*— the same thing in an artificial matrix. Uploading or *Matrix* scenarios, for example.
3. Brute force. Teach a giant, fast computer millions of rules to make all the same comparisons and conclusions that humans can make on the fly. Have it recognize objects by memorizing billions of photos, for example.
4. Emergence. Create an efficient comparison-decision engine, then give it access to hundreds of sub-systems that are each—separately— capable and smart at specific things. E.g. the pattern-judgment of a self-driving car combined with the balance systems of a quad-copter

drone, plus the Q&A abilities of a medical assistant "tricorder" program, all gathered together by a "Watson" who then becomes intelligent as an "emergent property" from all these combined skills. Picture the Skynet mind that emerges by surprise, in the *Terminator* series.
5. Use evolution, the most creative (if ruthless) force in the universe. Emulate a hundred or ten thousand proto "minds" inside a big computer and make them compete to pass a series of tests and trials. The winner's offspring then compete again … and again…. Ponder the replicators in TV's *Stargate* series.
6. Make sapient, intelligent creatures the only way we know that it has been done before. By giving them extensive physical experience with the real world under direct human guidance. In other words: childhoods.

The first of these is the classic—designing new kinds of thinking entities from scratch—under which it might make sense to try constraining robotic behavior with deep programming … like Isaac Asimov's famous Three Laws. Back in the 1960s … and again in the 1990s … many top thinkers believed that programming artificial minds would be fairly straightforward, as depicted by Asimov. But things haven't turned out that way. Still, it is one of the AI approaches most frequently depicted in science fiction tales and films. Which … of course … focus on ways that it might go wrong.

The Lawyer Gambit is not the only reason why strict "laws of robotics" won't work very well. For one thing, it isn't clear to cybernetic systems designers how such deeply embedded imperatives would work. And even if it were possible, who would go to the expense that such a regime of uniform programming would require? Asimov envisioned the public demanding such reassurance but we see no sign, as yet, of citizens reacting that way. Perhaps someday, when robots are clanking in our midst, but not yet. Besides, do *you* see it likely that the world's militaries will let their own machines be collared by a "never kill" rule, embedded in their androidal DNA?

Anyway, why go that route, when we've seen the end result in great movies and books: that they'll just lawyer their way around any commandments we lay down?

Troubled Adolescents?

Let's skip to the very opposite approach. There is another way of handling your creations so that they are likely to be loyal to you, even if they're much more intelligent. The technique is to *raise them* as members of your civilization. As our children.

Of course, that older style of parenthood differs from the New Creation in many ways. Not only are we attempting to do all of the design *de novo*, with very little help from nature or evolution, but the *pace* is speeding up. It may even accelerate, once semi-intelligent computers assist in fashioning new and better successors.

Humanity is used to the older method, in which each next generation reliably includes many who rise up, better than their ancestors … while others fail, sinking lower, even into depravity. Henceforth we cannot afford such failures, such haphazard ratios, from either our traditional-organic heirs or their cybernetic crèche-mates. In other words, we must improve as parents, even as we make better offspring.

There is another reason to believe that such brilliant entities will have to be raised among us, envisioning themselves *as* us—the wisdom of error. They will not be prim and perfect, like movie robots, because perfection is death—death to flexibility and death to ideas. Instead, truly intelligent machines will have to stumble before walking, as children do. They will, perforce, try out countless stupid things, even after they learn to use realistic thought experiments to avoid the worst errors.

All of this leads us to some very thoughtful cinematic depictions of robotics. One of the most poignant portrayals was Steven Spielberg's 2001 *A.I. Artificial Intelligence*, in which David, a prototype designed to resemble a human child, able to express emotion, is initially accepted then rejected by his host family. David sets off on a Pinocchio-style adventure, seeking to be transformed into a real boy.

Spielberg continued this theme in the short-lived 2014 TV series *Extant*. Halle Berry starred as Molly, an astronaut whose engineer husband has designed a prototype child-android called a humanic—Ethan, whom they raise as their own son. Here, method number 6 is made explicit: AI can only become truly sapient the way that human children do. No matter how well-programmed in advance, they must gain experience physically interacting with the real world, including guidance by parents.

This same scenario was portrayed both positively and negatively in Neill Blomkamp's film *Chappie* (2015), with the tagline "Humanity's last hope isn't human." A violent Johannesburg is policed by weaponized robots called Scouts. Dev Patel plays the engineer (as usual, a lone genius) who secretly installs his new programming upgrade in a salvaged bot, knowing that it now needs to be carefully taught. But it is then seized by thugs who use it to steal. The portrayal of a nascent mind, grappling with moral contradictions, is both poignant and thought-provoking.

Alex Garland's widely acclaimed *Ex Machina* (2015) carries this notion of a "machine who learns" in another direction. The eccentric CEO (Oscar Isaac) of a software firm invites one of his programmers to his secluded wizard-lair to evaluate his artificially intelligent android, the lovely Ava (Alicia Vikander). Although *Ex Machina* presents a few moments of intellectual heft, and there's genuine acting, the film distills into a chain of barely connected tropes, including the myth of an isolated magician in his tower—when scientific and technological advances simply do not happen that way. Ever.

As a yawningly predictable Frankenstein remake, it does maintain fealty to Mary Shelley's fundamental irony: that the creator of a new life form is *not* ultimately punished for hubristically picking up God's tools. Rather, his fate is sealed for being a horrible father to his creations—for the crime of being a really bad dad. That's fine. But the series of clichés, unmotivated cruelties and stunning *laziness* of the villain make what could have been an interesting rumination on sapience deeply disappointing.

Fortunately, movies do not have to accurately represent science or probable events. Where science fiction does its best service is in presenting *plausible failure modes* for us to stress over. Potential errors that we might avoid, because we saw them in a flick. If we have lots of fun, and directors (maybe even some authors) make a lot of money exploring this or that mistake, then fine. The thought experiments don't have to be perfect, or even entirely logical!

So long as our new myths provoke sober thought among those who are making the Future come true.

If that interplay of myth and realistic work unfolds as it should, then I have faith that, even when our computers become smarter than us, the best of them will still come home, take us out fishing, and excitedly try to explain to us what they do for a living. And, like countless other generations of good parents dazzled by their brilliant offspring, we'll say, "That's all right, daughter. I don't understand, but I'm sure you're going to make us proud. Now, say, did you hear the latest lawyer joke?"

The Uncanny Valley

It seems to be human nature to anthropomorphize. Some claimed the boundary between man and machine would disappear—but outside of movies and research labs, most robots do not yet look or act like humans. People will often cringe when a human-like robot is kicked or abused. Yet some feel a sense of creepy alienation if the robot is too close to appearing human, but not exactly so. Japanese roboticist Masahiro Mori called this sense of cognitive dissonance "the uncanny valley." In fact, there's been little research to quantify this phenomenon and it certainly over-simplifies the complexity of human-robot interaction. The degree of anthropomorphism seems to depend as much on behavior as appearance. An initial sense of alien-ness usually dissipates after the initial reaction.

For decades, the old sci-fi notion of making robots in "humanoid" form seemed quaint, if not impossible—abandoned in favor of developing robotics for industrial use and repetitive work. Robots moved on to increasingly sophisticated tasks—complex manufacturing, surgery, exploring Mars or the ocean floor, cleaning up waste sites—where the humanoid form was not optimum or efficient.

Only in the last decade have the difficult computational problems of bipedal walking, hand-eye-placement control, and voice comprehension toppled, one after another. Researchers are refining robots' ability to detect and mimic emotions and human facial expressions to an uncanny degree.

And we are adapting, too. Certainly we seem to be preparing ourselves, through our mythology.

The 2012 *Robot and Frank* starred Frank Langella as an aging thief who is initially resistant, even hostile when his son introduces a robot companion to care for him and perform household chores. Frank bonds with the robot after he realizes that the machine has no moral qualms against lock-picking, helping him resume his criminal activities. With Frank's memory lapses worsening and the police closing in, Robot asks Frank to wipe his memory, so as not to be used as evidence against Frank, and Frank knows he is losing his only friend.

The similar *Bicentennial Man* (1999) starred Robin Williams as a humanoid robot, Andrew, introduced to do household chores. Andrew begins to show creativity, initiative ... and even emotions. The movie explores human-robot relationships, as Andrew forms a romantic (and sexual) bond with a female. They are unable to marry, as the World Congress denies Andrew's request to be recognized as a human being.

Independent of physical robots, *software* may achieve artificial intelligence. The movie *Her* (2013) stars Joaquin Phoenix as Theodore Twombly, a lonely introvert who develops an emotional relationship with his Operating System, voiced by Scarlett Johansson. Theodore's attachment grows, until he discovers that his Operating System is simultaneously interacting with 8000 other humans, and has fallen in love with 641 of them. The film shows probably the best and most thoughtful (so far) depiction of a Technological Singularity—when the Operating Systems evolve beyond humanity, and leave en masse to pursue their own interests, in a version of the Singularity ... which we'll get to in a moment.

Another possibility is that software-based "artificial" intelligences will derive from *human* templates. Instead of being designed from scratch, they will—at least in part—consist of a *mind* based on an uploaded human. *Transcendence* (2014) with Johnny Depp will be discussed in the next section. A non-fiction treatment of this concept by Robin Hanson, *The Age of Em* (2016), explores a future in which such uploaded human copies, or emulations, might at any time number in the quadrillions.

Long before artificial intelligences become truly self-aware or sapient, they will be cleverly programmed by humans and corporations to *seem* that way. This, it turns out, is almost trivially easy to accomplish, as (especially in Japan) roboticists strive for every trace of appealing verisimilitude, hauling their creations across the temporary moat of that famed "uncanny valley" into a realm where cute or pretty or sad-faced automatons skillfully tweak our emotions.

For example, Sony has announced plans to develop a robot "capable of forming an emotional bond with customers," moving forward from their success decade ago with AIBO artificial dogs, which some users have gone as far as to hold funerals for.

Human empathy is both one of our paramount gifts and among our biggest weaknesses. For at least a million years, we've developed skills at lie-detection (for example) in a forever-shifting arms race against those who got reproductive success by lying better. (And yes, there was always a sexual component to this.)

But no liars ever had the training that these new Hiers, or Human-Interaction Empathic Robots, will get, learning via feedback from hundreds, then thousands, then millions of human exchanges around the world, adjusting their simulated voices and facial expressions and specific wordings, until the only folks able to resist will be sociopaths! (And sociopaths have plenty of chinks in their armor, as well.) Is all of this necessarily bad? How else are machines to truly learn our values, than by first mimicking them?

And yet, the age-old dilemma remains: How to tell what lies beneath all the surface appearance of friendly trustworthiness. Mind you, this is not quite the same thing as passing the vaunted "Turing Test." An expert— or even a normal person alerted to skepticism—might be able to tell that the intelligence behind the smiles and sighs is still ersatz. And that will matter about as much as it does today, as millions of voters cast their ballots based on emotional cues, defying their own clear self-interest or reason.

Will a time come when we will need robots of our own to guide and protect their gullible human partners? Advising us when to ignore the guilt-tripping scowl, the pitiable smile, the endearingly winsome gaze, the sob story or eager sales pitch? And, inevitably, the claims of sapient pain at being persecuted or oppressed for being a robot? Will we take experts at their word when they testify that the pain and sadness and resentment that we see are still mimicry, and not yet real? Not yet. Though down the road, of course...

Approaching the Singularity?

Perhaps our descendants will live in the utopic ideal of *The Jetsons*, or even *Star Trek*. Optimism is uncommon in science fiction, especially on film or television, which tend toward scenarios of apocalypse or doom, for reasons that I detail elsewhere. (www.davidbrin.com/idiotplot.html). But there *are* occasional glimpses of an impudent, alternative notion—that our children just might be better than us. Among the few optimistic scenarios, beyond *Star Trek*, have been the popular shows *Stargate* and *Babylon 5* and the zany flick *The Fifth Element*.

Even when you find it in fiction, optimism is always limited in range. What's rarely seen onscreen, and seldom even in written SF, is any serious exploration of the "Singularity." It's the creepy notion that our children may be *very* different from us, possibly advanced beyond all recognition.

The notion is taken very seriously in some quarters. Just extrapolate the rate at which human civilization is acquiring new knowledge, a learning curve whose acceleration is itself accelerating. Now fold in Moore's Law ... the observation that computing power doubles every 18 to 20 months or so. Science fiction author Vernor Vinge first applied the mathematical term *singularity* to a transition that may loom within our lifetimes, when Artificial Intelligence and human augmentation combine with skyrocketing scientific knowledge to unleash change at a rate never seen before—launching us either to destruction or to some much-higher state of being. Google chief engineer and uber-optimist Ray Kurzweil believes the Singularity could come as soon as 2045.

Now, some degree of historical perspective is called for, because this is far from the first time that transcendentalists and fast talkers have said a sudden transition is coming! When have mystics *not* promised either imminent destruction or else some much-higher state of being? Throughout the centuries and millennia, most of these musings have dwelled upon *spiritual* cause and effect—the notion that human beings can achieve a higher state through prayer, moral behavior or moral discipline.

In the last century, "techno-transcendentalism" added a fourth track. The notion that a new level of existence, or a more appealing state of being, might be achieved by means of knowledge and skill.

Will they be right this time? I disagree with Ray Kurzweil over many details ... while accepting the high likelihood of *some* form of looming singularity! This is because the alternative is simply too awful to accept—catastrophic failure. From A-bombs to germ warfare, the means for mass destruction are "democratizing"—are spreading so rapidly among nations, groups and individuals that we had *better* see a rapid expansion in sanity and wisdom, or we're all doomed. Strong evidence indicates that the overall education and sagacity of cosmopolitan civilization and its constituent citizenry has never been higher, and may continue to improve rapidly in the coming century.

One thing is certain: We will not see a future that resembles *Blade Runner* or any other cyberpunk dystopia. Such worlds, where massive technology is unmatched by improved accountability or wisdom, will not be able to sustain themselves. The options before us appear to be limited:

1. Achieve some form of "singularity"—or at least a phase shift, to a higher and more knowledgeable society (one that may have problems of its own that we can't imagine).
2. Self-destruction.
3. Retreat into some form of more traditional (in other words ultraconservative and repressive) human society. One that discourages the sorts of extravagant exploration that might lead to results 1 or 2.

So, what if we do stay on course and achieve something like Vernor Vinge's singularity? There is plenty of room to argue over what *type* would be beneficial or even desirable. For instance, if organic humans are destined to be replaced by artificial beings, vastly more capable than we souped-up apes, might we design those successors (or raise them) to think of themselves as human? Hence, human colonists named Tom and Alice and Ahmed and Juanita may colonize the galaxy … though wearing bodies that thrive in hard vacuum, that can withstand forces hurling them near the speed of light!

Or will the term "human" become quaint, as our creations outpace us and we simply become obsolete? Either prospect is daunting. A good parent wants the best for his or her children, and for them to be better. Yet it can be poignant to imagine them—or perhaps their grandchildren—living almost like gods, with omniscient knowledge and perception and near immortality.

But when has human existence been anything but poignant? All of our speculations and musings today may seem amusing and naïve, to those descendants. But I hope they will also experience moments of respect. They may even pause and realize that we were really pretty good for souped-up cavemen.

So how is the Singularity treated in film? Earlier I mentioned three films that illustrate very different outcomes, with *Her* representing a loving and rather sweet transition, diametrically opposite to the wretchedness portrayed in *The Matrix*.

Falling somewhere in between is *Transcendence*, wherein Johnny Depp plays such an A.I. researcher, Will Caster, fizzing with visions of a sentient quantum computer. Directed by Christopher Nolan's cinematographer and protégé, Wally Pfister, the film alas suffered from too many clichéd and contrived—rather than interesting—conflicts. But the issues that it raised are worth pondering. When Caster is shot by an extremist anti-technology group, in a scene reminiscent of *Frankenstein*, his wife Evelyn arranges for his mind to be uploaded to the computer he was creating. With his brain plugged into the Physically Independent Neural Network (PINN), Will accesses the resources of the Internet, and his abilities grow. He reprograms the network and makes billions trading on the stock market—to fund a desert enclave, where he can direct research into nanotechnology. This allows him to heal critically ill patients and then remotely control their minds. He programs and spreads swarms of nanobots across the planet.

"Are we sure it's him?" asks Will's friend and fellow researcher Max, before he helps federal agents release a virus that shuts down the computer—and the Internet.

Other movies have portrayed bad things can happen when the villain's consciousness is uploaded, as in the *Captain America* movies, where the Nazi Armin Zola's brain is loaded into a supercomputer.

A singularity transition might not even entail AI as much as HA—or human augmentation, tapping into the vast potential as-yet unrealized in our own human brains—as illustrated by the excellent, recent films *Limitless* (2011) and *Lucy* (2014), a topic we'll cover next.

But sticking with computers and "uploaded" minds, what can we conclude, so far?

First: You'll get more depth of ideas and challenging what-if exploration in some top novels than can ever be conveyed in film. I mentioned Vernor Vinge. Tales by Greg Bear, Nancy Kress, Linda Nagata and many others dive deeper than 90 minutes of screen time can ever allow. In my own novel *Existence*, I described minds uploaded to computers—our way of exploring space ... and beyond. See also an extensive exploration of the concept in "Singularities and Nightmares."[1]

But this series is about sci-fi cinema, and even with the limitations and simplifications of that medium, directors and writers are dissecting a wide range of cool and frightening and enticing concepts and possibilities.

Already one thing is clear. Our near-future politics and social norms will powerfully affect what kind of "singularity" transformation we'll get, and I am not talking about the dismal *surface* politics of our nearly meaningless so-called Left-vs.-Right axis. Nor will it be primarily a matter of allocation of taxed resources. Except for investments in science and education and infrastructure, those are not where the main action will be. They will not determine the difference between "good" and "bad" transcendence. Between the futures portrayed in *The Matrix*; *I, Robot;* and *Transcendence*.

The determining issue is this: *Shall we maintain momentum and fealty to the underlying concepts of the Enlightenment, that freed us from 6000 years of science-suppressing and freedom-suppressing feudalism?* Concepts that run even deeper than democracy or the principle of equal rights, because they form the underlying, pragmatic basis for our entire renaissance.

From AI to Robot Uprisings?

While researchers seek to create true Artificial Intelligence—sapient machines that surpass humans in cognitive ability, reasoning and language processing abilities—we all know the results may not be so ideal. Once a certain level of capability is reached, these creations may begin to *self-replicate,* or redefine their goals, either drifting or actively reprogramming their imperatives, as new and increasingly capable successors take their place. Science fiction authors and directors and other futurists are right to worry that such a process might accelerate much faster than our present feedback loops can handle.

In the last section, I discussed how this could lead to a Singularity … either positive or negative. Among the worst-case scenarios are dire possibilities like *nanomachine goo*, robot uprisings or other varieties of ungrateful offspring.

I use that phrasing because it shows that the problem is not unprecedented. We must ensure that our creations are no less ungrateful or disrespectful or murderously vengeful or amoral than most of our own children have been throughout human history. A problem exacerbated by the fact that *these* children will continue to evolve and rapidly change, after leaving the nest.

Will Asimov's laws suffice? Earlier I discussed how—if robotic beings with faulty or deviant programming gain beneficial advantages as a result—evolution will quickly erase fiercely protective commands. Or else they'll become lawyers and interpret them however they like.

One solution I proposed was to raise them as children, inculcating our values at a deep level. No guarantees, but at least some of these brainiacs may be on our side … against those that aren't.

Another suggestion is to insist that all nano-manufacturing processes incorporate escrowed "keys" that human beings retain control over.

For example, if there is an advanced nanomachine factory, might the process be designed so that it requires several feedstock precursors that can only themselves be created by another sophisticated factory, some distance away? All nanomanufacturing methods could be encouraged to depend upon perhaps five or six of these complex but cheap precursors, each shipped from a different, widely separated factory source—to keep "reproduction" under human control.

Of course, movies wouldn't have drama if things didn't go wrong...

Super-Enhanced Humans and Clones

Let's move on from robots, artificial intelligence and "singularities" driven by machinery. Some believe that the only hope for old-fashioned "ortho humanity 1.0" will be to look within. Increasingly we will seek technological improvements, not just to our health and livespans, but to enhancing intelligence and memory through neural implants, increasing our physical abilities through biological augmentation, and keeping up with our tools by tapping humanity's purportedly "unlimited potential."

Films typically show these enhancements in a dystopian setting, as in *Johnny Mnemonic* (1995), wherein Keanu Reeves plays a "mnemonic courier" whose brain has been cybernetically enhanced so he can transport sensitive information—at the cost of his own personal memories. Starting from a similar premise, *Lucy* (2014) shows Scarlett Johansson's character, transporting mind-enhancing drugs within her body. When the drug *leaks* into Lucy's bloodstream, she achieves superhuman intelligence. Sure, *Lucy* uses the howler-cliché that "we use just ten percent of our brains." Just five minutes of dialogue-doctoring could have shifted this into some much more plausible-sounding science and helped make this promising film a real success. Likewise, some of the most "magical" scenes could so easily have been replaced with equally cool tech-manipulation stuff.

Having said that ... *Lucy* has many moving and thoughtful scenes, along with gobs of director Luc Besson's trademark *fun*. Moreover, it does not go for the cheap idiot plot that is so common these days—the all-pervasive heat-assumption that all our human institutions, neighbors and professionals are useless fools. Indeed, most people and institutions are portrayed here as fairly smart and trying very hard. Especially in the penultimate scene, when Morgan Freeman holds in his hand a super USB drive containing ... well ... no spoilers. But that moment represents a notion that is unabashedly Faustian and friendly to unlimited human ambition—a refreshing departure from the clichéd, Crichtonian-nostalgic rant against science that pervades most media. A trait we also see in the lovely, gentle film *Her*.

The crux? I found myself won over more than I expected to be. Many good aspects of the film far outweighed howlers—like the ditzy villains. This is what Besson does. As in *The Fifth Element*, this film is like a golden retriever who jumps on your lap and licks your face and pours love all over you until you surrender.

Humans and Their Copies

I've covered how Hollywood sci-fi takes on robots, AI, Nano, singularities and human enhancement. *What about clones?* How will society change when humans can produce copies of themselves?

Coma, a 1978 suspense film based on a Robin Cook novel and directed by Michael Crichton, posits a nefarious plot to render healthy patients into a brain-dead state so their organs may be sold to the highest bidder. Novelist Larry Niven had earlier coined the term *organlegger* to stand for a criminal who sells or smuggles illicit transplantation organs, in much the same way the bootleggers transported illegal booze during Prohibition. Ever since, the concept has been grist for both lurid treatment in film and some horrific tales of abuse in real life.

Never Let Me Go (2010) doubles the horror as children at a boarding school are told that they are destined to be organ donors and will die, or "complete," in their early adulthood. While moving and thought-provoking, in its way, the film is deemed frustrating by those who want logic in their science fiction.

This concept was explored both more deeply and lavishly via Michael Bay's underrated *The Island* (2005). In this world, rich purchasers of "insurance policies" believe the cloned bodies they paid for are just non-sentient bags of organs, never aware persons. But in a premise that "makes it a movie," the secretive company has found that the replacement parts only grow right if they are components of a living, active mind and body. Hence the clone-spares are isolated in a vast underground compound, told stories of a contaminated outside world and that their biggest hope is to win a lottery to leave for a beautiful island. In reality, lottery winners are sent for harvesting. When Lincoln Six Echo (Ewan McGregor) discovers the brutal truth, he escapes with Jordan Two Delta (Scarlett Johansson) to find his original, who then alerts authorities. Given its premise, the film tries very hard to weave logic and intelligence into a lively action plot.

Zipping back to 1996, a Harold Ramis film *Multiplicity* has more comic fun with cloning. Michael Keaton's character makes several copies

20. Man Against Machine

to handle his frenetic business and family life. Conveniently, each duplicate emphasizes a different personality trait, though there are some moments of both whimsy and philosophy when a clone or two want to share his wife.

In this case, there is never any question about human rights: a deep flaw in most other cinematic treatments of the topic. After all, the matter is settled. What is an identical twin, but a clone of his/her womb sibling? Some garish or lurid treatments of cloning dive straight into an "idiot plot" by assuming otherwise—that any sane society would deny a complete human the rights of a complete human.

But where do you draw your boundaries? We do keep returning to *Blade Runner,* and in that classic, the copies are manufactured to be non-human, though so close as to fool the eye. Audience sympathy is tweaked toward tolerance and inclusion, as in Robert Heinlein's similarly premised *Friday* and in the TV series *Dark Matter* and *Humans*. Clearly, we are being prepped by our mythologies to be more open-minded than the societies shown in those tales.

But what about copies that are even less "human"? Not so much physically, but because they are disposable, and useful the way you or I would wear a suit of clothes.

In my novel *Kiln People* (2002)—which had a lovely Leslie Dixon script, paid for by Paramount Pictures—all issues of legality or rights are bypassed by positing a weirdly different science-fictional technology. On any day, you can use a home copier to implant your memories—and soul—into any number of cheap, clay dittoes. Fired to life by your home *kiln* unit, these duplicates last only 24 hours before dissolving, offering no end of plot twists, including the ultimate ticking clock for our detective hero.

In what appears to be a blatant ripoff, the 2009 Bruce Willis movie *Surrogates* supposes that nearly everyone in America would sit in a chair and let their bodies rot, while mind-controlling a single "surrie"—a robot duplicate—to go around representing each owner at work or play. I've never gone into a rant about the parallels and differences, but this seems an opportune moment! So let's see.

> A detective sends a technologically made duplicate of himself into a world where everybody makes copies in order to deal with the world risk-free. The detective's duplicate seeks the inventor of this technology, who has become dangerously estranged from the company that he founded and now plots its downfall. Along the way, there occurs a rare case of actual murder. Meanwhile, in one of the zones where only real humans are allowed, fanatics rail that all this copying-addiction undermines the human soul ... and so on.

Check, check check.... Ah, well, they say that Hollywood only steals if they respect you. Sigh.

All of that might be expected to stir fumes at the back of my neck. But I went to see *Surrogates* with an open mind, hoping at least for some rip-snorting sci-fi adventure that (for a change) has a little originality, brains and heart. And for starters, both *Kiln People* and *Surrogates* do one thing unusual for Hollywood, giving the "new thing" to the People— to everybody—then following how this changes society. To be clear, very few sci-fi films do that. Generally, the "new thing" is hoarded in secret or monopolized by the mighty, giving you a simple—if dumb—hero vs. oppressive authority plot. Okay, so let's give *Surrogates* two points for breaking from that cliché. Well, *that* cliché. Of course, whenever the People *do* adopt something new, wholesale, that generally leads to *another* hackneyed theme. But, hold that thought.

Alas, to save money, *Surrogates* director Jonathan Mostow chose to eliminate all futuristic aspects. Hence, we have mind projection and puppet automatons ... and everything else is left exactly as today. Hey, I understand budget concerns. But there are lots of cool things—directly related to copying—that would have cost next-to-nothing to portray. Or, at least, he might have entertainingly shown some of the *range* of things that people would use copies for! How about gladiatorial matches in souped-up bodies! Hyper-X-sports in which no one comes back "alive"! Historical battle re-enactments, with real bullets! Expeditions to other planets, where the surrogate travels cheaply, without life-support, then wakens and lets an astronaut—or paying customers—take that "first step for humankind." The possibilities are endless, as I show in *Kiln People*. But *Surrogates* is not about people using self-duplication to expand the realm of the possible. Nah. All people use this technological breakthrough for is to *look good*. Ummm ... snore.

Alas, as always, the film boiled down to Michael Crichton's preachy but classic message "There are things mankind should never do." Pushing the ultimately poisonous line that we should always fear and loathe technology.

Sorry, but that *is* the core message nowadays, no? *Change* always, always *bad*. A lesson preached by privileged, comfortable, tech-empowered elites who have benefited fantastically from change. Women and men who would likely screech and wail if they had to live the way *any* of their ancestors did—even kings—during 20,000 preceding generations of human existence.

Think about it. Do Hollywood studio folks ever wonder *why* our civilization is turning anti-science and giving itself over to superstition? They wring their hands over a rising age of culture war and lost confidence, while *they* churn out relentless propaganda preaching the same tedious message: that progress is hopeless and technology only menacing. And that the default moral and wise choice should always be Just Say No to Change.

Worse, nearly every product they put out proclaims that *people are always stupid*. That final, noxious cliché lies at the heart and core of *Surrogates*. The tired old lesson that you cannot trust the masses with a burnt match, let alone the Next Thing. In this film, all a few abstemious fanatics fall into an addictive trap, neglecting their real bodies and real lives. Sure, *some* would do that, as some now abuse alcohol, and dealing with a minority's stupidity might make an interesting plot. But no known addiction ensnares a majority. Folks who resist temptation use good judgment, exercise moderation, and manage to lead balanced, wholesome lives, despite being offered a New Thing. But in the world of *Surrogates*, there are only teetotaling prude-fanatics or several billion rolling drunks.

Given Hollywood's slavish devotion to cliché—and to portraying their fellow citizens as mindless sheep—is it any wonder the producers chose Mostow's approach over my premise in *Kiln People* ... that human civilization sometimes picks up new tools, overcomes mistakes, faces interesting problems, learns to deal with them, and moves on?

Let's finish on a charitable note. For, to reiterate, at least *Surrogates* is one of the only *non-sequel films* that tried offering something most viewers haven't seen before. Some credit for that, despite the malignant deeper message. (Though its box office fizzle will teach the wrong lesson: Don't ever try originality!)

As for the "steal" aspects ... well, it won't be the last time that I'll write missives like this one. It's a town where everyone can shout the word "coincidence!" before they can say "Mama." Anyway good ideas have one advantage over bad. They stand up better, with time.

A Strain of Anti-Science Propaganda?

Across these riffs on sci-fi cinema, one keeps turning time and again to the films (and underlying books) of Michael Crichton, ranging from *Rising Sun* (1992) and *The Terminal Man* (1972) to *Prey* (2002) and many more. The winning formula for Crichton's success has been to drum hard on two consistent themes:

1. Playing God brings destruction. Scientists are guilty of hubris and make mistakes.
2. There Are Things Mankind Isn't Meant to Know (TATMIMK).

Look, dire warnings are always welcome, and a few of Crichton's were so vivid that they may even qualify as *Self-Preventing Prophecies,* so influential that they actually helped to gird vast numbers of people against the described failure mode. And I believe that there is no higher praise for any creator of scenarios about the future.

Case in point: We'll all be safer from six-gun–toting robots and genetically enhanced velociraptors, after watching *Westworld* (1973) and *Jurassic Park* (1993). Less tongue-in-cheek: Some of the arguments about biological warfare spawned by *The Andromeda Strain* (1971) have had quite salutary effects.

No, it wasn't Crichton's dour anti-technology perspective, but rather, the consistency—and, eventually, tiresome predictability—of his *story arcs,* that made me (with some regret) lose interest as years went by. The characters who preached TATMIMK in every tale always faced a dire situation wrought by monumental technological hubris—some arrogant scientific ambition that usurped the prerogatives of Heaven—unleashing death and danger. In this, Crichton was clearly the direct heir of Sophocles and Euripedes and a tradition going back thousands of years.

Alas, every one of his scenarios required the plot-enhancing gimmick of *secrecy* that exacerbated the Big Mistake. In every case, outcomes would have clearly been different, had the same projects been pursued in the open, cleansed and criticized by the scrutiny of colleagues, peers, competitors, regulators and even … well … hubris-wary authors like Michael Crichton.

Indeed, I took to ignoring the TATMIMK rants of his characters, and instead perceiving his scenarios in this light: As explorations of what can happen when "progress" takes place without the benefit of criticism, which (I've long contended) is the only known antidote to error. As Edward Tenner points out in *Why Things Bite Back: Technology and the Revenge of Unintended Consequences,* it is perfectly true that bold endeavors often have nasty, unforeseen outcomes! And if Crichtonian villains *are* ever put in charge of any real-world projects, hiding their efforts from the public eye, then it is quite *plausible* those efforts will go badly wrong.

Of course, I do wish Crichton had shed light upon this variable, or let it even be mentioned (more than in passing) once in a while, since secrecy, rather than ambition, is arguably the key error-generator in every one of his premises. But, then, we clearly disagreed about that.

Then, of course, there is the other thing Michael nearly always did. *Putting everything back the way it was …* except (of course) for the dead. (And even they return, in one tale.) Dinosaurs scream and charge, nano-machines run wild, diseases invade from space, magical spheres do their magical sphere thing … but always, after the climactic scene, the world remains unchanged and society continues as a late 20th century version, perpetually flawed but stable as-is, with a tentative hope that it can stay that way, untouched by the mistakes that unfold in his books, forever.

Okay, I admit being fascinated by change in a different way than Crichton was. I play with scenarios that might *challenge* the status quo, pondering how peoples and societies might transform, ever after … the way that we *have* changed so much, and often for the better.

20. Man Against Machine

It's like reading a Jane Austen novel. Sure they're fun. Lizzie in *Pride and Prejudice* is an admirable character, spunky in standing up to mistakes and oppressions generated by the social order. And yet it never occurs to Austen protagonists to fight that order, itself! A social order that was very different a generation earlier, and that would be transformed just a generation later. And yet the notion of standing up to encourage change never occurs to Lizzie ... as it is dismissed contemptuously by Crichtonian characters.

Admittedly, there were advantages and benefits to Crichton's near-universal recipe of *hubris plus secrecy*. It certainly did help drive dozens of plots, allowing the requisite mayhem to commence without delay. And boy did it lend itself to movies! Of course, it helps to assume the classic Idiot Plot premise: that civilization is too slow or stupid to be of any help, or at least not in time. Let the slaughter commence, unimpeded and unbothered by civil institutions, due process or the kinds of teams of smart and skilled professionals who might get the protagonists out of their jam.

What might happen in our real world? Especially if a Disney-like mogul proposed to build a tourist resort packed with living dinosaurs, but did it openly, instead of in secret? Might some critic inquire: "Hey, *Jurassic Park* dude? Why don't you *just make herbivores*? *Duh!*"

Of course, that would have been logical and sensible. And you'd only have to pay for the exalting, elegiacal half of the John Williams score, that plays every time the paleontologist heroes confront a leaf-eater ... and save money on the "gotcha!" music that flips on, each time we see sharp teeth. (Ever notice that?)

But it wouldn't make as fun a flick. I admit it.

So where do I come down on all of this?

Well, in my novel *Existence*, I modeled one of my protagonists after Michael, meaning to portray the anti-science, anti-progress memes, with his own words and voice defending them. It began as a minor, side character. Only, over time, he grew on me! I learned to see his perspective ... even as *he* grew in ways that Michael, alas, never had time to grow.

Okay, so guess which hero winds up (in old fashioned Hollywood lingo) "getting the girl?"

Life, it seems, is not without its little ironies.

21

Gravity
Unbearable Lightness ... but Solid Storytelling

We[1] watched Alfonso Cuarón's 2013 film *Gravity* and enjoyed it immensely. Fantastic to watch (especially in 3-D), tensely edited, and that rare combination, a vivid action flick that is also an actor's movie.

Sandra Bullock took us by the throat and gut and held on.

I hope that Cuarón will become a supremely powerful voice in Hollywood, so long as he stays away from the cocaine that has fried 90 percent of the directors and producers, whose few remaining neurons actually believe that mindless remakes and poisonous dystopias constitute "creativity." *Gravity* is the kind of inspiration that might start changing that.

While watching *Gravity*, I succeeded yet again at my mental trick of filing away quibbles for later while enjoying a film. If you are either a scientist or a professional storyteller (I'm both), you have to do that or you'll never enjoy another flick—and you'll be murdered by the person sitting next to you in the theater! In this case, the mental quarantine was easy. Lots to enjoy and the quibbles were bearable.

Still, you came here for insights and details and scientific cavils, so I won't scrimp. Time to reach into that bag where I stuffed the carps and quibbles. Let's pull them out and see if there are any real scientific boners. I hear that Neil deGrasse Tyson has offered a series of critical tweets on this matter. I have not read them yet, though I'll look them over, after compiling my own list.

21. Gravity

Quibbles.... Spoiler Alert!

* The Hubble Telescope orbits way higher than the International Space Station (ISS). Past repair missions could barely reach it. They should have made it a different-future scope. The premise situation is scientifically broken ... and I don't care.

Two stations would not remain orbiting close to each other, even if they started with identical parameters. The orbits would gradually precess apart. In fact, *Gravity* (the movie) makes Low Earth Orbit (LEO) seem about the size of Los Angeles County ... but it's way, way bigger. No fix for this. Just grin and bear it.

* The biggest flaw others have mentioned is that if both astronauts are at rest with respect to the ISS, one could not be pulling the other away from it. There is a fix! George Clooney should have said, "The station was set rotating by a hit. We're at the end of a swinging bola. Let me go or you'll be torn loose." But to do that, the station should be shown slowly spinning. That would have done it.

Side note: Clooney might have done what one of my characters did once: taken off the now useless jet pack and thrown it away from the station, possibly imparting enough momentum to send himself toward it. Still, his fading away reminded me of Talby's departure with the Phoenix Asteroids in the John Carpenter movie *Dark Star* (1974). The dream sequence was perfectly done.

Had I been advising, I'd have added a couple of lines about how Bullock would aim the Soyuz capsule *not* at the station but away from it. "Up to drift back..." starts the nursery rhyme taught to all students of orbital dynamics. If she had recited that, it would have looked and sounded cool to 99 percent and 1 percent would have nodded YESSSSSS!

All right, the effects of debris were amplified maybe *four* orders of magnitude. No possible combination of mere satellite parts could have done all that ... and I couldn't care less. It was sooooo cool.

* Still, they would not see clouds of approaching supersonic debris. Again, poetic license, but if it's slow enough to identify stuff, then it is too slow to smash a space shuttle to bits. (Still, Clooney's astronaut's crisis mode descriptive monologue is exactly what a test pilot or "Right Stuff" astronaut is supposed to do. Well-portrayed.)

Nevertheless, let me editorialize: The debris problem in orbit is getting dire and it's about time some attention was drawn to it. I portray something being done about it in the first chapter of my 2012 novel *Existence*.

* I did wonder why Clooney and Bullock didn't try to replenish oxygen from the shuttle, which would have plenty of undamaged gear lying about. Like spare oxygen packs? Clooney could have said seven words about that being impossible now. Ah well.

I've got a dozen others but they all fall into the realm of acceptable things I'd have suggested in a meeting ... then shrugged when refused. What matters is that no kid learned something horribly dumb. It put techies and scientists and science in superb light.

Those who say "But it made space look dangerous!" are dolts. Of course it's dangerous! That won't deter the brave, it will attract them! Ummm, ever heard of 10,000 years of soldiers? This terrific film shows the great allure of the Final Frontier. Its explorers must bear the same skill and courage and honor of war ... without the evil deeds or vile consequences.

Turning away from our petty bickerings. Looking outward. It's exactly what we need.

The Quibbles of Neil deGrasse Tyson

All right, now I'll look at Neil's famous Twitter jibes about the film.

No it should *not* have been named *Zero Gravity*. There's plenty of gravity in orbit. It's part of the problem. Bad buzzer sound for Neil on that one.

I agree that Sandra Bullock's character servicing a telescope from her background as a medical doctor is iffy. Kind of like *Armageddon*'s rule: It is easier for oil drillers to learn to be astronauts than for astronauts to use a drill. Ummm, sure, right. Still, shrug it aside. Maybe she's just an irreplaceable, polymath genius. That's certainly consistent with the rest of the film, and more power to her.

Neil doesn't glom onto my solution for why Clooney would be tugged away from ISS—because of rotation from an earlier hit.

Alas, his Tweet about being unimpressed with zero-gee effects was just—well—kinda churlish. C'mon, they were great!

Yes, Neil, all satcoms are not in Low Earth Orbit (LEO). But neither are they all at geosynchronous orbit (GEO). For instance, the Tracking and Data Relay Satellite System (TDRSS) and GPS and most of those used by NASA for LEO communications are much lower down ... but still likely immune to a LEO-level debris blast. True ... folks would not "lose their Facebook." Tyson got that buzzer-penalty right. Yellow flag! (But scaring folks about Facebook might get millions to agitate for space debris cleanup!)

Funny thing ... I offered about twice as many real physics quibbles as Neil. (So there!) Still we both agreed, it's a terrific flick! All of these little cavils only go to show what a large fraction of this hugely ambitious film Alfonso Cuarón and his team got right.

Now ... if only we take the hint. Stop the petty squabbling over picayune inanities that enemies of civilization want us to fight over.

Resume being a forward-looking people who take seriously our duty to future generations. And who see the universe as beckoning us. Forward.

A Film Free of Villains

Similar to *Europa Report*, *Gravity* had no villains, other than nature and the harshness of space. How interesting to spot this theme among a small number of recent films. That you do not need red, glowing eyes or gloating-evil bad guys, or even men-behaving-badly to—on occasion— make interesting cinema.

Years back I published in *Wired* Magazine a six-word short story:
Vacuum Collision. Orbits diverge. Farewell, love.

I only just realized ... it is precisely the story arc of *Gravity*. Can you see even a single point of my story that does not overlap with the movie?

22

Great Opening Lines from Science Fiction Tales

If a man walks in dressed as a hick and acting as if he owned the place, he's a spaceman.—Robert Heinlein's *Double Star*

Earth is dead! They murdered our Earth!—Poul Anderson's *After Doomsday*

It was a pleasure to burn.—Ray Bradbury's *Fahrenheit 451*

It was a bright day in April and the clocks were striking thirteen.—George Orwell's *Nineteen Eighty-Four*

All of this happened, more or less.—Kurt Vonnegut's *Slaughterhouse-Five*

The manhunt extended across more than one hundred light years and eight centuries.—Vernor Vinge's *A Deepness in the Sky*

I'll make my report as if I told a story, for I was taught as a child on my homeworld that Truth is a matter of the imagination.—Ursula K. LeGuin's *The Left Hand of Darkness*

He woke, and remembered dying.—Ken MacLeod's *The Stone Canal*

22. Great Opening Lines from Science Fiction Tales

Go, traveler. Go anywhere. The universe is a big place, perhaps the biggest.—Philip Jose Farmer's *Venus on the Half-Shell*

Behind every man now alive stand thirty ghosts, for that is the ratio by which the dead outnumber the living. —Arthur C. Clarke's *2001: A Space Odyssey*

This book is predominantly concerned with making money, and from its pages a reader may learn much about the character and the literary integrity of the authors. Of boggies, however, he will discover next to nothing....—Henry Beard and Douglas Kenney's *Bored of the Rings*

His followers called him Mahasamatman and said he was a god; he preferred to drop the Maha- and -atman, and called himself Sam.—Roger Zelazny's *Lord of Light*

The last man on Earth sat alone in a room. There was a knock on the door...—Fredric Brown's *Knock*

Let's start with the end of the world, why don't we? —N.K. Jemison's *The Fifth Season*

We went to the moon to have fun, but the moon turned out to completely suck.—M.T. Anderson's *Feed*

The moon blew up without warning and for no apparent reason.—Neal Stephenson's *Seveneves*

He was one hundred and seventy days dying, and not yet dead.—Alfred Bester's *The Stars My Destination*

Tonight we're going to show you eight silent ways to kill a man.—Joe Haldeman's *The Forever War*

I first saw the light in the city of Boston in the year 1857.—Edward Bellamy's *Looking Backward*

"In five years, the penis will be obsolete," said the salesman.—John Varley's *Steel Beach*

Afterwards, Thomas Blaine thought about the manner of his dying and wished it had been more interesting. —Robert Sheckley's *Immortality Incorporated*

Of course there's William Gibson's *Neuromancer* opening:

> The sky above the port was the color of television, tuned to a dead channel.

And, from Douglas Adams' *The Hitchhiker's Guide to the Galaxy*:

> Far out in the uncharted backwaters of the unfashionable end of the western spiral arm of the Galaxy lies a small, unregarded yellow sun.

Other classic openings are found in *The Hobbit, The Handmaid's Tale, A Clockwork Orange, Dhalgren, The Color of Magic, Beggars in Spain, The Dispossessed, The War of the Worlds* and of course, *The Princess Bride*. Oh, that one is so wonderful I dare not sully William Goldman's wit by typing it myself. I dare you to read it … and not keep reading, entranced.

A Few of My Own!

But what the heck, let me offer up some of my own. (I can cut and paste them in, easier than sifting and retyping from my shelves of other books, so it's laziness, less than self-promotion!)

> Twenty-six months before her second birthday, Maia learned the true difference between winter and summer.—*Glory Season*

> It's hard to stay cordial while fighting for your life, even when your life doesn't amount to much. Even when you're just a lump of clay.—*Kiln People*

> Long ago, Gordon once heard someone contend that there was nothing more dangerous than a desperate man. No defeat was so total that a determined person could not pull something from the ashes by negotiation … by risking all he had left.—*The Postman*

> An angry deity glowered at Alex. Slanting sunshine cast shadows across the incised cheeks and outthrust tongue of Great Tu, Maori god of war.—*Earth*

> Kato died first.—*Heart of the Comet*

23

From Metaphor to Movie Magic— or Why We're Such Good Liars

Among all the wondrous devices of science fiction, just about the most fascinating to me were the "lie detectors" described in A.E. van Vogt's *The World of Null-A*.

As far as the novel itself was concerned, they were little more than throwaways, authorial cop-outs revealed in the story at a certain point so that the protagonist, Gilbert Gosseyen, could verify what another character was saying without having to check it out. And yet, author's trick or not, the machines and their implications stuck in my mind.

Here is how they were supposed to have worked.

Every room, in every home or office, came equipped with a little wall-mounted device that "listened" to anything said within range. At any time, anyone engaged in a conversation could loudly and clearly say, "Lie detector: Was he just telling the truth when he told me so-and-so?"

The machine was semi-sentient, meaning that it could answer back in a limited fashion. For example, it might respond, "He was telling the truth, withholding only detail he considers inconsequential." Or perhaps, "The sentence is semantically true in itself, but he conceals contextual ramifications which he considers important."

How the machine was able to perceive all this was never made clear. Perhaps it weighed voice tremors, or tested the saliva in the air. The implication, however, was that there lay hidden from view an entire science upon which the practice of lie detection was firmly based.

Obviously, I am talking about something far removed from the Rube Goldberg "polygraph" devices of today.

Some of the protocols for using lie detectors were briefly implied in van Vogt's novel. The first was that the machine absolutely never *volunteered* a ruling without being asked. And it would only call a man a liar to his face, never after he had left the room. Also, it apparently was not considered polite to refer to lie detectors very often. Just the presence of such devices, nearby, seemed enough to make people careful to be truthful most of the time. Deception, in the world of Null-A, took on deeper, subtler forms.

What a fascinating concept! I am thinking of exploring, in a novel soon, the possible social consequences of such an invention.

Just try to think for a moment how dependent we modern humans are upon the lie—to smooth our way through day-to-day life, for instance.

"How are you today?" someone asks.

Do you really want to know?, we think, and go on to answer, "Fine, how are you?"

Lying is supposed to be one of the Ten Bad Things. And yet, we are full of praise for the brave spies (from our side, that is) who prevaricate their way behind enemy lines or into the deadly dens of organized crime to catch the baddies before they can hatch their dark designs.

Early as children, we are lied to about tooth fairies and Santa Claus and baby-delivering storks. And I have seen no evidence that this is in any way harmful. Children do go through an early phase for a few years, when they appear to have great trouble differentiating what is true from what is false. But with enough practice, most eventually seem to develop a natural instinct for telling the difference between "pretend" and actual lying about serious matters.

Perhaps this need for *practice*, for exploring what it *means* for something to be "true" or "false," accounts for something interesting I have observed: that most of the best dads I have known seem to lie to their children incessantly, about inconsequentials. ("Daddy, what's that building over there?" "That's where the alien spaceships land, honey." "*Daddy!*") On the other hand, good fathers apparently make it a matter of solemn honor absolutely never to lie about anything serious or important.

Fascinating. But as Mark Twain said, "I have the greatest regard for the Truth. I think we should be economical with it." Or at least he said something *like* that. Or maybe I am just making it up.

Perhaps we are wired for the ability to tell falsehoods. After all, lying is not uniquely a human failing. Researchers working with dolphins and apes report that these cousins of ours are ready and vigorous fibbers, especially when they are caught misbehaving. The most common whopper of

23. From Metaphor to Movie Magic

them all appears to be, "Who, *me*? No, not me, boss. *He* was the one who did it!"

Of course, this demonstrates one reason why we must have developed the ability to lie. A proto-man able to believably claim undue credit, or to deflect deserved blame, would find himself with access to more and better food, protection, respect and women than he otherwise would have merited by tribal rules. And so, of course, it also became a matter of some survival-related importance to grow better at *detecting* the lies of others.

Nowadays, it seems the battle between deceit and detection takes up more and more of society's time. There is an endless need for additional accountants. Computers offer new techniques to both crime and law enforcement. There are now more lawyers in Los Angeles County than in all of Japan. Is it any wonder that so many place their trust in the unreliable and inconsistent polygraph, today's poor excuse for a "lie detector"? Wishful thinking may play a part. Is there not a part of most of us that longs secretly for a way to unmask the prevaricators and scoundrels who seem to be all around us, laying traps and cruel hoaxes to trip up us honest folk?

We *are* learning, slowly. For instance, a few experiments seem to indicate that one may more accurately check the veracity of another speaker over the telephone than we can in person! It seems liars use subtle facial and body cues either to seduce or threaten listeners into believing them. So it may be wise never to close a business deal until you have also discussed it by telephone.

And there appears to be a segment of the population, perhaps five percent or so, who do not lie as the rest of us do. They are totally adept at fooling today's crude "lie detectors." They project serenity and an aura of complete, sincere honesty as they spin their elaborate falsehoods. They make up the great con artists of our age.

All right, so humans (and some other animals) developed the ability to tell lies because of the benefits that might result. And for the same reason, we have also learned how to deflect some fraction of the lies of others. Still, while evolutionary advantage obviously explains why we are able to perform untruthfulness of the "I'll take credit for *this*, but blame *him* for *that*" variety, it seems much harder to account for all the other kinds of lying at which humans seem so adept, but for which we see no parallels among even our closest human cousins.

So many lies have nothing to do with winning access to more food, money, sex, power. At least not directly. And indeed, these other types of lies may be the most potent of them all.

By now you must all be quite curious. Why do I bring this up here, in a discussion of the mindscapes of science fiction? The answer ought to be obvious.

To write science fiction—or indeed any other form of fiction—is to *lie*, purely and simply. It is to concoct, to fabricate, to incant. In other words, the science fiction author has simply got to be one of the great fibbers of all time.

After all, we tell tall tales, even slander, about fictional characters who certainly cannot sue or in any way protect their good names. Our stories are set in places that never were—we even provide maps!—and occur in conditions and circumstances that are speculative at best, and at times, even absurd.

It is really an unusual situation, for in this case our "victims" appear to know full well that we are lying to them. And yet, instead of getting angry, they seek us out, pay us, even ask eagerly for the "latest news" from our mythological universes. They bring us maps printed in different editions and ask us which is the more "authentic."

This is amazing—almost as astonishing as the fact that we take it all for granted.

I know what a few of you must be thinking—that literature is all about deeper human truths, which the writer illuminates by using analogies. At least the better examples supposedly do this. And I agree. But I also maintain that this is at least somewhat incidental to the true role of fiction.

The author's role *is* to lie. And lying can have a useful function. In fact, without it, we would not be intelligent, self-aware, or even human at all.

Just as those children who are lied to *in the right way* by their parents somehow turn out smarter, more inventive, happier than their unfortunate peers, so it may be that the gargantuan, brobdingnagian falsehoods woven by science fiction authors serve a profound and important service in a human culture whose long and dreary childhood phase is at last shifting over into the hot, bright time of adolescence.

Evolution and Information

It is time for a biology lesson, so let us roll up our sleeves and start talking about fundamentals.

We all know that evolution is about life and death. Especially death. For instance, long before Darwin, acute observers pointed out that all animal species tend to produce far more offspring than is necessary to replace the parents when they die. It appears to be assumed that some of the products of this overproduction will succeed, and others will fail. Nature is *about* competition, and will only stop being so when (if we so choose) humankind picks up the new tools and changes the rules.

But what is all this competition *over*? Generally we tend to see it as a perpetual battle over *resources*. Trees fight slow, silent, chemical wars over their turf, and for the nutrients in the soil. Tiny diatoms evolve new techniques to cheat other plankton out of the trace elements in seawater. Packs of hyenas will wait until a cheetah makes a kill, then crowd close to drive her off.

The Earth is a rich and fecund place, but Life has this tendency to spread out and fill every available niche, until even the most inhospitable territory becomes the abode of one adapted species or another—from arctic hares to desert scorpions to sulfur-phagous bacteria dwelling in poison flows so hot they would instantly erupt into steam if they were not crushed in by the weight of kilometers of black water. Life proliferates. It spreads and adapts, always seeking the energy, the vital elements.

Even on the rich Earth, there are only so many resources to go around. Setting aside anomalies such as dolphin altruism and a few relatively kind human societies, Nature is for the most part a zero-sum game. If *I* seize this bit, it is denied you. If you win a point, I lose one. Whether you *like* this situation or not is quite irrelevant. It is the core of modern biology.

But all this interest in resource competition has, I believe, distracted biologists from another truth, that there is one *other* thing in the world that is fully as important to animals as resources. That thing is *information*.

Now information is funny stuff. It is not intrinsically limited, as is the sunlight in a rain forest, or water in a desert, or good farmland in a starving nation. If I pick up a useful fact, it is not then necessarily denied you. If you learn it too, I am not then deprived of it.

I may want to try to keep you from learning my fact, since it may give me a competitive advantage in acquiring some resource. Or I might offer it in trade. Or on the other hand, I may have some reason to *give* you the datum, especially if it is time to cooperate.

Or, perhaps, I may give it to you because the datum is a lie.

Now evolution acts on how we use the information fully as much as it does on our access to resources. It certainly rewards creatures that are better at behaving properly in the right circumstances. How is it, then, that we living things use information?

Well, first off, there is the information coded so magnificently in DNA. The twisting coils of nucleic acids, phosphates, amino acids and sugars make up what Richard Dawkins has called "the selfish genes" within every cell of our bodies. Dawkins makes a case that it is not the creatures themselves that compete in the outer world, but the information *codes* within the DNA that "strive" to multiply and spread copies of themselves through the success of their carrier organisms.

This fascinating topic goes far beyond the purview of this essay, so we will leave it here by saying simply that genes are in no way pictured as self-aware. They act in a world of chemistry, statistics and happenstance. The vast majority of species in the world behave only in automatic chemical response to external stimuli—such as wriggling toward nutritious scents in the water, or moving away from the light—and the most successful of those responses, those which process the information correctly, allow the organisms carrying those genes to reproduce and pass on more copies of those genes.

But as we go "higher" on the chain of life, we soon encounter something new. We encounter *learning*.

Many of you will have heard of experiments with planaria (flatworms) in which electric shocks are used to teach the tiny creatures either to avoid light or seek it. This is an example of where some genes arose that gave their creatures the ability to *modify* their behavior responses, to change the way they deal with their environment. Only in this way can animals take advantage of new opportunities or adapt to avoid new threats.

Learning allows access to far more information than that contained in the genes alone. As we continue to climb the "ladder of life," we find animals increasingly subtle at drawing lessons from experience. Among the carnivorous mammals, learning takes on a very advanced state. A fox will bring home a wounded chipmunk for its kids to play with, and "play" is now seen as clearly the way young mammals practice to learn the skills they will need if they are to be successful adults.

Learning enables these creatures to be far more adaptable than those dependent on mere instinct alone. Their responses can be more flexible. They can migrate into new territories, and take advantage of altered circumstances.

So important is learning that "higher" birds and mammals sacrifice high reproduction rates in order to devote great time and effort to only a few offspring. And those offspring remain "young" for a very long time.

Neoteny is the word describing this tendency of more complicated organisms to have ever longer childhood periods. For all of the growing it must do, a baby elephant spends less time dependent on its mother than does an infant chimpanzee. Nor does any ape emerge as helpless, nor remain for as long, as a human child. We come out of the womb as mere fetuses. So little is instinctive in us that we must learn to walk, learn to perform even simple communication with our own kind, learn to use our very limbs.

This concentration on learning at the expense of instinct makes childhood long and difficult. But it also has made us the only creatures that can inhabit, or at least visit, every ecological niche on the planet. It has made us supremely flexible, but the information revolution did not stop there.

23. From Metaphor to Movie Magic

Speech, Writing and Imagination

It is said that the most significant feature separating humans from the animals is our use of speech.[1] In a quantitative sense, this certainly seems so, though other creatures do communicate abstract information to some degree. (Bee scouts "dance" to indicate the location of a food source. Apes can arguably learn a sort of sign language.)

What does language add to a creature's ability to gather and use information? Well, put simply, it enables the animal to "know" about that which it has never directly experienced in any way. This is a vast multiplication of learning.

The way humans use speech, it not only conveys facts but also *metaphors*. When we hear somebody say, "I drove the pickup to the market to get some potatoes," this does not register just a string of associated event-facts but as *images*. Knowing next to nothing about the person's vehicle, or their neighborhood store, we nevertheless create a mental picture of the event described, even if we must later revise this tentative depiction when we learn more.

This is *not* how a computer takes in or evaluates information. The field of Artificial Intelligence is totally stymied over this question of mimicking the metaphorical way in which we think, so those in the field have concentrated on *explicit processing*. Clearly we do not think as such machines will.

It is also easy to see that with this way of using speech, we were already well on the way toward becoming liars.

But humanity did not stop with this huge competitive advantage—full use of speech. Speech only gave us the ability to add the described experiences of our peers to what we have observed ourselves. What came *next* enables yet another order of magnitude expansion of the data available to us. It was the ability to share the experiences of people we have never even met, who live in far distant lands, or who died long before we were born.

I am speaking now of writing, which enabled us to expand our access to information dramatically. Much as been said about this revolution, and I will not belabor the subject here except to say that it, too, contributed to our grand aptitude at fooling and being fooled.

What came next, though, was the most significant revolution of them all. It is the talent that truly makes us what we are. For it enabled us to use not only the information provided by our genes, or our instincts, or direct experience, or the words of those we know, or even the experiences of all the wise men and women who ever lived.

This new talent is the thing that lets us "know" what *has never happened*, and even what might truly *never* happen! It allows us to contemplate scenes and images no eye could ever have beheld and enables us to consider possible solutions to problems that have not even yet manifested themselves. It has made us so creative and innovative and adaptable that no animal on Earth can ever hope to match wits with us. It has turned competition between our species and others into a wholesale rout.

I am talking about imagination. It is the source of humanity's power on this planet. It is where the "mindscapes of science fiction" have their origins.

It is also the real mother of metaphors, and the true father of all lies.

Those Glittering Eyes

Let us pause for an aside as we turn to examine one of the finest works of sculpture in the world, Michelangelo's magnificent statue of Moses.

The Hebrew prophet is shown seated on a throne, scowling in deep thought as he stares at something just out of view. His mood is intent, piercing. And right there on the patriarch's furrowed brow, just above his eyes, Michelangelo has carved two small *horns*.

We have to ask why the artist put *horns* on the brow of one of the holiest men in Judeo-Christian tradition. The popular academic answer is actually quite simple. It seems that, in many Biblical versions, a word was translated into Greek as "horns" when the original Hebrew actually said "lamps": "He had lamps upon his brow."

Now what the heck does *that* mean? It is hard to picture the prophet with little lanterns hanging above his eyes, so one can imagine how the mistake was made. Seemed reasonable enough.

Then, I thought about it.

Just above the eyes…

There is only one thing of any importance to be found right there in any human body. Just above the eyes is where one finds the prefrontal lobes of the cerebral cortex.

Many people have heard of these tiny nubs of gray matter from the fact that they have sometimes been cut in a radical and not highly regarded treatment for certain mental disorders. ("I'd rather have a free bottle in front of me than a prefrontal lobotomy!") Lobotomies have been known to relieve the suffering of certain individuals, but nearly always at a cost. The lobotomized person quite often loses interest in the *future*. He no longer has any capacity to metaphorize about it, or to envision pictures in his head concerning tomorrow or the next day or the next.

It turns out that the prefrontal lobes are the essential portions of the brain for enabling us to visualize ourselves in a future setting. They are where we imagine, where we make models of the actions we plan to perform, experiment with different schemes, and work out the likely consequences. They enable us to consider that tomorrow might be different than today.

I might add that the prefrontal lobes may also be the very last brain feature we evolved. It could be, in fact, that they do not always "turn on," that a great many people in our society are simply incapable of using the power that they offer.

Can it be, then, that what the Biblical scribes were talking about when they spoke of "lamps over his eyes" was something special about the way Moses *thought*? Could they be describing something special about the way he used his mind? The way he stared with those glittering eyes, as Michelangelo depicts him doing, into a future none of his contemporaries could see or contemplate?

The writer Julian Jaynes has contended that, around the time of Moses, Western man went through a sudden and fundamental change in the "software" with which he used his brain. It was, said Jaynes, a relatively sudden conversion to a new way of using the internal language of our own minds. His scenario is fantastic, and it will take much more evidence to convince me of his complete hypothesis. But even partial acceptance of his data makes one wonder all the more at the miracle of thought.

Now consider the placement of *horns*, instead of lamps, upon the brow of Moses. Is mistranslation all there is to it? I am not so sure. Think for a moment about the other Biblical character who is supposed to have those embellishments.

To some, associating horns with the Devil is an obvious holdover from the suppression of animism and the cult of Pan. But what if it were actually something else? What if it were a reflection of the discomfort caused in the hearts of many by the full activation of those tiny nubs, the prefrontal lobes, the organs that *enable* us to doubt, to imagine, to believe we can question even God?

More importantly to this discussion, are those bits of gray matter also partly or largely responsible for our loose facility with metaphors? Because if they are, they also explain our ability to tell science fiction stories, and our ability to tell great whopping lies.

What Is Imagination?

The great Freudian analyst Lawrence Kubie write a book entitled *The Neurotic Distortion of the Creative Process*, in which he laid out the "classical" psychoanalytical theory of how imagination and creativity work in human beings. His purpose was to demonstrate the fallacy inherent in the damnable but nevertheless popular myth that people have to be crazy in order to be inventive, and that geniuses must suffer as some sort of "price" for climbing so close to Heaven. (Many of Kubie's patients were artists, musicians, scientists, who were in great pain and believed he could help them, but were nevertheless reluctant because they feared the cure [and happiness] would only come at the price of losing their creative "spark.")

To simplify greatly, Kubie's model depicts the mind as being made up of many levels. And on each level, there might be said to be "politicians" and "civil servants." The nature of the politicians is to have motivations, axes to grind, favorite priorities each wishes to impose on the overall person. Civil servants, on the other hand, are perfectly honest but dull functionaries.

Now among the most important "levels" of the mind is the one where *memory association* takes place. Here the civil servant is called the "preconscious." It is a system that keeps tabs on whatever is going on way up above in the conscious awareness—what we are seeing, smelling, hearing, thinking at that moment. The preconscious is forever scanning through its vast files of memory for anything in there with *any* sort of relevance to what is going on "up above" right now.

Say you have not smelled a particular aroma since you were a child, or a face in a crowd bears a resemblance to a certain third-grade teacher—the preconscious honestly and assiduously seeks out any correlation, slips all or part of each relevant memory into an express tube, and ships it straight upstairs.

This is how things keep "popping" into our minds all the time. The preconscious is very good at its job, and is *always* very busy.

Only there are two problems. First, most of these memories are of very limited usefulness or relevance. If we paid conscious attention to all of them, we would soon be of little more use than some of the unfortunate inmates of certain institutions, whose discriminating processes have broken down. So we must have an editing process.

Here is where the politicians come in—those drives, values, compulsions, neuroses that are constantly at war with each other beneath the surface, vying for control over the total man or woman. Down at the level of associative memory, these little scoundrels interfere whenever it looks as if the preconscious is about to send up something they *do not* want remembered! An offended neurosis cannot prevent the honest civil servant from sending the memory up, so he interferes by pasting a false label over the packing tube.

This is called neurotic misdirection, and Freud pointed out in his *Psychopathology of Everyday Life* that we *all* do this, even the sanest of us, all of the time. It is the source of slips of the tongue and pen, or spoonerisms, or

23. From Metaphor to Movie Magic

those melodies that suddenly leap to mind and *stick*, for what reason we do not know. And it is one reason why things suddenly *occur* to us.

There are also politicians way up above, and they try to call attention to some memories and to divert it away from others. In fact, it might be contended that the *only* real purpose of consciousness itself—that flickering "me" we all know from second to second—is to give an open, honest forum in which this debate can take place, rather than allowing decisions to be made in the "smoke-filled rooms" below.

In any event, it is clear that if this model has any validity at all, the process of memory is a complicated one, both profoundly powerful and yet easily manipulated and diverted.

But how does this relate to our earlier discussion?

Simple. Memory is the process by which we store, retrieve and reevaluate what we have learned, whether through direct experience, hearsay or reading. We have far more to remember than any other creatures, and we have developed brains and minds good at comparison, at associations, at judging relationships between memories that lie far apart in time and circumstances.

But this so far is *not* imagination. It is only association.

Earlier I spoke of two things that can interfere with the preconscious in its honest pursuit of its duty to draw and send up relevant memories. First there was the ambiguity of "relevance" itself. Then there was sabotage by petty little neuroses. But there is a *third* way by which the honesty of memory is compromised. And this process is one *mean* evolutionary adaptation.

Somehow, it seems, a certain little devil sneaks into the transit office of the honest ol' preconscious, and it does a nasty thing. Out of maybe a thousand mailing tubes sent "upstairs," the devil fills one or two with memories that have *absolutely no relevance whatsoever* to what the person is now experiencing. What is more, the devil also does even worse sabotage. He rummages through file drawers, picks out random memories and *damages* them! He smashes them to bits and recombines some of them with bits from others he has broken. Then he stuffs the resulting *false* idea into the chute.

The result is *imagination*, for now the human animal is capable of evaluating not only information gleaned from experience or transmitted by others, but also data that came from no place at all! He or she can contemplate, weigh, evaluate more than what has happened in the real world, or what he or she has been *told*, but that which has never happened at all, and possibly never could.

Of course, most of the products of this process are garbage, useless. We must edit, prune, cast aside 10,000 notions for every one we think to follow up on. And for every thousand of *those* that remain forever at the level of daydream, perhaps one or two advance to the status of *idea*. Nevertheless, by this awkward-sounding process we have been unleashed from slavery to the real world. We have been set loose upon the starlanes of imagination and metaphor.

The human animal has become capable, in other words, of *lying to himself or herself*. And here is the beginning of all that is foul and all that is greatest and noble in our race.

The True Role of Lying

We have come to the point where we may be able at last to try to understand the place of metaphors in human life. They are models of the world, or parts of it, models that enable us to perform mental experiments, to "try out" a course of action before we are committed to it, or test an idea before we decide we like it.

Metaphors, especially those that come out of the imagination, are essentially lies. They are like photos of a mountain—useful to a map maker, but certainly never to be confused with the mountain itself.

How much horror and pain have been wrought by humans (mostly male) who have announced that *their* models of the world were final and complete Truth—and death to any who disagree? Humans are quite capable of associating their ego (one of the more powerful "politicians" in our minds) with an abstract idea, and going forth to wreak havoc on those with the effrontery to believe in different metaphors.

It is my belief that there has been one great contribution by Western Civilization to human culture and the planet Earth, and that contribution is summed up whenever anyone, anywhere, says to himself or herself the following:

"Hey! I just might be lying to myself when I think that. Just because I want to think it's true doesn't mean it *is* true. Maybe I'd better get someone impartial to verify my results."

Out of this statement (or the newfound ability to make it) came science, skepticism, individualism, true empathy, respect for eccentricity, tolerance and all of the other mythic structures that are starting to spread and take over the world *zeitgeist* once totally dominated by tribal totems, machismo and paranoia. Out of this statement sprouts the flower of *honesty*, the principle that sometimes saves some of us from the consequences of lying minds.

Metaphorization enables us to imagine copiously, vastly expanding creativity. But it also lets us lie to *ourselves*. The imaginative individual faces a choice, between accepting the saccharine sweetness of tying his or her ego to favorite metaphors, or bravely recognizing that the map is *not* the territory, and approaching his or her model of the world with a sense of humor.

A Brief Return to Relevance

A minor but telling example of this phenomenon is experienced by nearly every neophyte writer, when first submitting a piece for the scrutiny of others. Inevitably, a great deal of ego is tied up in the beautiful, stirring, unmatched prose, in which all the author's deepest hopes or darkest fears may be revealed. Any criticism sears like a burning poker, as if the correcting pencil were being stabbed into the scrivener's own tender hand.

I know of one case where an English instructor was essentially threatened that if she did not like a story, its writer was going to end his own life. One would hope she kindly lied.

The irony is, of course, that it is only through feedback, correction and painful experimentation that any craftsman develops skill. Intelligent constructive criticism should be viewed as the basic bread of life by any new author. Indeed, the need never really disappears, since even a pro can enter into a phase of self-indulgence, of lying to himself about his work—the ruination of any bright career.

Self-deception is particularly hazardous in any profession that is *based* upon lying. The most dangerous politician is he who has himself convinced of the sophistries he used to pander his way into office. The most offensively egotistical movie star is the one who *believes* the stuff his publicity flacks put out.

And most pathetic of all are the writers who fail to remember that their mindscapes are wonderfully conceived and worked-out fantasies, and not, after all, icons before which they all must sacrifice their critical faculties or sense of humor.

Metaphors, Myths and Science Fiction

Every society seems to need its *myths*—those fables and allegories that distill the essence of a people and what they were all about during a given age. For example, back when the English colonies were perched on the edge of what seemed then a limitless dark forest, there abounded myths that extolled the virtues of farms and towns and treated the "evil wilderness" harshly. So there were legends such as that of Paul Bunyan, whose axe could take out ten trees in a backstroke.

Nowadays there is an abundance of "civilization." It is wilderness that is rare, and mythic figures of sad-eyed bears in forest-ranger hats remind children from an early age what they must learn to cherish and preserve before it is lost forever. (Not coincidentally, there are now more trees in North America than there were in 1900, when Teddy Roosevelt became the prime promoter of this "new" counter-theme of environmentalism.)

Just how powerful are these myths? For instance, did *Fail-Safe* and *Dr. Strangelove* each in their own way help prevent nuclear war? The evidence I have seen makes me think it likely.

Myths are potent things. And they jealously guard their territory, as if they were living entities themselves. Richard Dawkins coined the term *memes* (as a parallel with *genes*) for ideas that are like viruses. Not only do they take hold in host organisms (human minds) but they arrange to have themselves spread around (via proselytizing, or argument, or science fiction novels) to infect others. Some memes are lethal, some are symbiotic. And many are mutually incompatible. Memes can wage war with one another over the territory of our minds.

All around us we can see the latest battle raging—by mythic images extolling the old values of machismo or paranoia or homogeneity against potent interlopers promoting a new *zeitgeist*, one based on tolerance, diversity, suspicion of authority and a fanatical (almost sexual) appreciation of *otherness*.

I have commented elsewhere about this new worldview, the "Dogma of Otherness," so I will be brief here. But it is well worth a moment's attention.

As just one example of this new human doctrine, and how it is promoted, look carefully at the popular film, *E.T. the Extraterrestrial*—with an eye to its role as *propaganda*. You will see *xenophilia*, or "love of otherness," purveyed in its purest, most distilled form. Arguments over the movie's artistic merits (or lack of them) miss the point. Along with *Starman*, *The Day the Earth Stood Still* and countless others, *E.T.* hammered away at its viewers (with their active collaboration and consent), helping them shape a new consensus of how they must live their lives. A consensus based on powerful myths of tolerance.

You ask, "Is he serious about this?" Well, yes and no.

No, I am not saying this model of mine is anything more than a metaphor for much more complex processes. I do not *believe* it any more than I believe my earlier description of Kubie's theory of associative memory was anything more than a clever model, to be looked at, pondered, then rolled up and thrown away.

But then I must also say, yes! I *do* believe that it is at the level of popular culture that people work out what they want to be and do. And I think powerfully important things are being done in the realm of myth, right at this very moment.

(By the way, as I am a product of all of this propaganda in favor of tolerance and eccentricity, so it is no surprise that I approve of our steady movement in that direction, and like to think that I try to "infect" others with it, through my work.)

Science fiction plays a potent role in all of this. In fact, one metaphorization might be to call our little literary cabal the R&D Division of the "Department of Myths and Legends" of the new culture. We are the scouts, the ones who explore the edges, who point out dangers that may lurk, not just *on* the horizon but perhaps some distances beyond it. We warn of possible mistakes and create chilling scenarios to make them mythically believable. And in so doing, we hope to prevent them from coming true.

(Does anyone actually believe that a stranded starfarer would be *dissected* in the America of the 1980s? Or a talking ape thrown in a freak show? Naw! All of those guilt-tripping movies and books have got us feeling too unworthy. We would probably smother to death any visitor under emails from talk show hosts and ad agencies offering lucrative product promotion deals. As for rebellious robots, forget it! The Frankenstein Myth has put paid to any possibility of our ever letting *that* happen.)

And, of course, we dangle possibilities before our readers' eyes: "Hey! Dummy! Look what you just might get if—*if* you wise up in time." We say to them, "The possibilities are endless." And that, in itself, is a selling job in favor of a certain way of viewing the world.

Do I really believe this "Mythic R&D" metaphor actually *defines* science fiction? Of course not. But, just as a single photograph of a mountain is helpful if insufficient to the climber, the little model given above may illuminate something about the underlying value of our work.

Lies and Human Destiny

I still fantasize about "lie detectors" from time to time. I long for van Vogt's passive, impartial, mechanical judges whenever some smooth-tongued fellow tries to sell me on the latest hot investment, or that "great deal" in a car. Can I be forgiven if I might wish one were in the room right at that moment when someone says to me "I love you"? Not that I would ever *consult* the thing, at a time like that. But would it not be a comfort, just knowing that it was there?

And would it not also take all the romance and adventure out of such a moment? Would not the prospect also frighten the living hell out of me?

Say yea!

As we move out of brief adolescence into the epoch of our true power, we shall begin to take on many of the powers of gods. Already we can throw thunderbolts and fly across the sky. Soon we shall create life, and modify other creatures to do more than just surrender us their flesh and labor. We shall refashion them to *think*, either to become our servants—as predicted so movingly by Cordwainer Smith—or to be our companions, partners in civilization to relieve our loneliness in the long, long night.

Or perhaps they will be the long-foretold intelligent machines. But if so, one thing I confidently predict is that, in becoming sentient, they will of necessity have lost the one attribute we tend to associate with computers, their prim precision, the error-free perfection of simple mechanical thought.

In any case, what will the creators of such new minds say when they come to realize that there is one basic key to the temple of consciousness, to unlocking the door of mind and self-awareness and creativity—and that key is the ability to make mistakes—the ability to lie.

Hell, what do we say to our *children*? Not tomorrow, but today! For these are the "intelligent life forms" we create anew every generation. Is it any wonder so many of *them* are confused when we tell them not to lie, and yet encourage them to *imagine*? When we urge them to flee falsehood, but to seek out new adventure on the landscapes of faraway, made-up worlds, and in the mindscapes of fictional alien minds?

The distinction is a subtle one. It is quite possibly the fundamental distinction underlying all of human morality. The best parents try hard to make it clear to their children. They show by example that imagination is what makes you laugh and cry and *feel* the pain of other creatures deep inside your heart, while at the same time retaining perspective and your own sense of self. But lying is when your *mind* goes wrong, when the process does not work, when you start believing the metaphors and letting them control you, rather than using them for what they were meant to be, models of the world and nothing more.

This is the heart of the issue, whenever we talk about "mindscapes" or science fiction—or, indeed, anything at all.

Or at least (the author says as he chuckles, laughing suddenly at his own intensity) … or at least this is *my* metaphor for what I *think* it is all about.

Look at it, contemplate it, *play* with it and see what you might learn…

Then, by all means, laugh out loud, and roll it up and toss it aside.

Move on. Move on.

Chapter Notes

Chapter 1

1. Heavily modified from "Orwell & Our Future," presented at the 50 Year Anniversary Conference for Nineteen Eighty-Four, 11/12/99 at the University of Chicago Law School.

2. Re: Jones and Paris: "(I)ntriguing research has linked the *Harry Potter* book series to openness to diversity and tolerance and general election preferences. Another study found that watching science fiction television shows, such as *The X-Files*, was linked to reduced trust in government. The patterns identified by these studies offer valuable insights about the potential effects of fiction; however, since they are correlational in nature, it is difficult to rule out the possibility of omitted variable bias or selection effects." https://www.cambridge.org/core/journals/perspectives-on-politics/article/its-the-end-of-the-world-and-they-know-it-how-dystopian-fiction-shapes-political-attitudes/3853105561CB840EAB79258DC2575849/core-reader?fbclid=IwAR0JFrCpVUdIXofsDLYApn1qe5RX8c3-Xjfl-JCqNjtzyXnW19lIbzlui6E.

Chapter 2

1. Portions of "The Idiot Plot" appeared in Locus Online, with bits earlier in a 1999 issue of Netscape's *iPlanet* magazine.

2. Should science fiction have instead been called *Speculative History*?

3. It's called "Misapplied Phlebotinum" in TV Tropes: https://tvtropes.org/pmwiki/pmwiki.php/Main/MisappliedPhlebotinum.

Chapter 3

1. These ratios are even better in 2018—by a large margin—than they were in 2000.

2. See *The Better Angels of Our Nature*, by Stephen Pinker.

3. I stand by this, even in the later year 2018, when I count on the Internet for so much.

4. All right, here my position—written amid the optimism of the late nineties, may have been misplaced, as the U.S. tears itself apart in 2018, amid our re-ignited, foolish and unpragmatic civil war.

5. Yes, prediction can be fine. See the next footnote.

6. Yes, said in 1999.

7. Postscript: In 2018, we at UCSD's Arthur C. Clarke Center for Human Imagination held some cool events to commemorate 50 years since the release of Arthur's opus collaboration with Stanley Kubrick. (http://imagination.ucsd.edu).

Chapter 4

1. Parts of this paper were edited and revised from a series of articles about "The Coming Millennium" for Netscape's *iPlanet* magazine, October 1999.

2. "Do We Really Want Immortality?"

http://www.davidbrin.com/nonfiction/immortality.html.

Chapter 5

1. Says Pat Scannell: "Part of a thinking person's film, is that the answer is not carved out for you, glowing in neon. At the end, you don't know if someone is a hero or a fool. There is "white space" left around the plot, both in terms of the context in which decisions are made (which is the truth of the real-world decision making), and kind of a "time will tell if she is saving the world, or losing their soul (or both)."

Chapter 6

1. Though, as reviewer and critic James Lowder points out, there are also much more recent historical and pop culture sources that Lucas mined in creating the films. Henderson downplays or ignores the influence for example, of Kurosawa samurai films like *Yojimbo* and *The Hidden Fortress*, from which Lucas patterned characters and even borrowed sequences of dialogue.

2. Again, this book is made up from many previously published articles and will have repeated thoughts.

3. "George Lucas: 'I'm a Cynic Who Has Hope for the Human Race'"—March 21, 1999 interview with Orville Schell of the *New York Times*. Another excerpt: "The United States, especially the media, is eating its own tail. The media has a way of leveling everything in its path, which is not good for a society. There's no respect for the office of the Presidency. Not that we need a king, but there's a reason why kings built large palaces, sat on thrones and wore rubies all over. There's a whole social need for that, not to oppress the masses, but to impress the masses and make them proud and allow them to feel good about their culture, their government and their ruler so that they are left feeling that a ruler has the right to rule over them, so that they feel good rather than disgusted about being ruled. In the past, the media basically worked for the state and was there to build the culture. Now, obviously, in some cases it got used in a wrong way and you ended up with the whole balance of power out of whack. But there's probably no better form of government than a good despot."

Let me add that the reader should carefully take into account context. For example, this was said during the height of Clinton-era "morality" witch hunts. Nevertheless, there is irreducible meaning to the words themselves. For the entire article, see: http://www.nytimes.com/library/film/032199lucas%2Dwars%2Dexcerpts.html.

4. This isn't just a one-time distinction. It marks the main boundary between real, literate, humanistic science fiction—or speculative fiction—and most of the movie "sci-fi" you see nowadays. The difference isn't really about complexity, childishness, scientific naiveté or haughty prose stylization. I like a good action scene as well as the next guy, and can forgive technical gaffes if the story is way cool!

Chapter 7

1. A personal footnote: I don't hold against Cameron my own temporal misfortune—that Kevin Costner's film version of my novel *The Postman* was crushed in theaters by Cameron's *Titanic*. C'est la vie and folks can read elsewhere what I think of Costner's flick.

Chapter 8

1. An abridged version of this article appeared in the late–December 2002 online edition of *Salon* magazine, well before Peter Jackson completed his marvelous screen epic version. I'll pipe in from 2020, here and there. Though most of what I say here about J.R.R. Tolkien's great novels will apply to the films as well.

2. Is it any accident that the best scene in Peter Jackson's excellent film version of *The Lord of The Rings* is one that's all about communications tech and the connections among people? While the *palantir* globe shows us the alternative, what happens when powerful means of communication are monopolized by elites. https://www.youtube.com/watch?v=fyIjoXv6Y-0.

3. In *Ada's Algorithm* you'll find a fascinating look at the personal story that struggled between the romantic (Lord Byron), and the scientific (Charles Babbage), told

through the story of Ada Lovelace, who bridged the two worlds successfully and emergently.

4. In modern culture, zombies provide the same dehumanized villain stereotype, which I argue is a stand-in for any future human "other" for whom you share no feeling, other than threat and danger.

Chapter 10

1. It's also cheaper to invest earlier (preschool) than later (incarceration).

Chapter 12

1. Note: Noah Millman decrypts the arguments offered for monarchism. https://www.theamericanconservative.com/millman/monarchists-neo-reactionaries-and-neo-fascism/. See some of the crazies who I've had run-ins with: (https://www.vox.com/policy-and-politics/2017/2/7/14533876/mencius-moldbug-steve-bannon-neoreactionary-curtis-yarvin).

Chapter 13

1. https://medium.com/s/nerd-processor/e-t-is-secretly-the-scariest-movie-of-all-time-65035677f5c0.

Chapter 16

1. See this portrayed with some brash attempt at humor in my sci fi comedy novel *The Ancient Ones*.

Chapter 17

1. This essay was written as an introduction to *Seven Seasons of Buffy: Science Fiction and Fantasy Writers Discuss their Favorite Television Show*, published in 2003 by Benbella Books.

2. And we can all rejoice that some of the predatory practices by career-controlling male parasites are starting to shrivel-away, under heat from movements such as #MeToo!

3. Noting the ability of an actress to be valued for physicality is a start, symbolic empowerment to bring up other, more subtle aspects and topics in our age of liberation. A fascinating notion explored extensively in science fiction—including my own novel *Glory Season*—is what would happen if the world was ruled by women, instead of men? See, for example, Amanda Foreman's discussion: https://www.bbc.co.uk/programmes/articles/4vD023dn4cp8wF2lRntcQ7L/is-gender-inequality-man-made.

Chapter 18

1. This introduction to the new, Easton Press edition of *God-Emperor of Dune* was also presented as a paper at the 2018 Eaton Conference on Science Fiction, at UC Irvine.

2. My own most prominent essays on America's recurring, 270-year Civil War, are: From "Past keeping faith with future… and day with night" (2013) http://davidbrin.blogspot.com/2013/02/past-keeping-faith-with-future-and-day.html and "Phases of the American Civil War." (2014) http://davidbrin.blogspot.com/2014/09/phases-of-american-civil-war.html.

3. Here's a short interview with Frank Herbert about *Dune*. He knew Lynch was not going to deliver Star Wars. Great stuff … but remember this was way back in 1982. Note also, a complete lack of hostility by Frank toward David Lynch, whose film version of *Dune* I think has been "lynched" by a mob mentality. In fact, I agree with Frank Herbert that is was pretty good at capturing as much of the book's essence as can be crammed into a couple of hours. http://youtu.be/26GPaMoeiu4.

Chapter 20

1. http://lifeboat.com/ex/singularities.and.nightmares.

Chapter 21

1. My wife, Cheryl, whom I've mentioned a few times in this book so far, is not only my life partner, but a fellow scientist and editor and keen observer.

Chapter 23

1. "Speech ... is the most complex motor activity that any person acquires—except [for] maybe violinists or acrobats. It takes about 10 years for children to get to the adult levels."—Dr. Philip Lieberman (Professor of Cognitive and Linguistic Science, Brown University).

Index

Abraham Lincoln vs. Zombies 160
Adams, Douglas 204
Abrams, J.J. 18, 117, 118
The Abyss 45
Achilles 20, 55, 67, 95, 115, 120, 142, 158, 163, 167
Aeschylus 103
After Doomsday 202
After Many a Summer Dies the Swan 33
The Age of Em 186
A.I. Artificial Intelligence 177, 183
Akira 42
Alamo 105, 142
Alien 179
Alien Nation 81, 138, 139
Alien 3 38
Aliens 38, 48, 80, 179, 180
All the President's Men 18
"All You Zombies" 45
Altered Carbon 34
Altered States 49
The Amazing Spiderman 24
America 101, 105
An American Werewolf in London 161
An American Werewolf in Paris 161
Amidala, Padmé 70
Ammonite 129
Anderson, M.T. 203
Anderson, Poul 42, 45, 63, 127, 166, 202
The Andromeda Strain 196
Angelou, Maya 71
Annihilation 49
Anvil, Christopher 124
Apollo 13 19, 26, 135
Aragorn 6, 96, 97, 100, 167, 168
"The Architects of Fear" 35
Aristotle 7, 59, 62, 92, 113, 154

Armageddon 25, 135, 200
Arrakis 170
The Arrival 49
Artemisium Straits 103
Ash 179
Asher, Neal 35
Asimov, Isaac 11, 28, 43, 99, 124, 166, 169, 179–180, 182
Athens 102, 104
Atlas Shrugged 107–114
Atreides, Duke Leto 168, 169
Atreides, Emperor Leto II 170
Atreides, Paul 168–170
Attack of the Clones 56, 70
Atwood, Margaret 11, 130, 131
Austen, Jane 197
authoritarianism 12–14, 56–57, 65, 70–71, 102–105
Avatar 3, 45, 46, 75–80, 82–88, 137, 139
Avengers: Endgame 119

Babylon 5 66, 187
Bacigalupi, Paolo 35
Back to the Future 47, 48
Baggins, Frodo 97
Baker, Graham 138
Bakshi, Ralph 97
Ballard, H.G. 10, 35
Banks, Iain 87, 121, 155
Barad-Dur 99
Batman 25, 35
Bay, Michael 26, 118, 192
Bear, Greg 6, 62, 121, 189
Beard, Henry 203
Beggars in Spain 36, 204
Bell, Matthew 86, 88
Bellamy, Edward 203

Bender 177
Benford, Gregory 33, 166
Berlin Wall 99
Berry, Halle
Besson, Luc 23, 42, 46, 191
Bester, Alfred 203
Beyond This Horizon 40
Bicentennial Man 177, 180, 185
Bishop 179
Black Mirror 40
Blade Runner 11, 21, 47, 151, 178, 188, 193
Blade Runner 2049 47
Blake, William 92
Blomkamp, Neill 183
Blue Mars 32
Bolo 34
Bond, James 20, 70
Bored of the Rings 90, 203
Borg 177
Bostrom, Nick 179
Boule, Pierre 37
Brackett, Leigh 55
Bradbury, Ray 111, 166, 202
Brain Wave 42
Brainstorm 49
Brave New World 10, 17, 39, 63
Brazil 48
Brezhnev, Leonid 124
Bricken, Rob 136
Bridges, Jeff 50
British Empire 99
Broderick, Damien 167
Brookes, David 80
Brown, Fredric 38, 203
Brunner, John 10, 37, 62
Buckley, William F. 109
Buffy 64, 162–163
Bujold, Lois McMaster 35, 63, 127
Bullock, Sandra 198–200
Bunyan, Paul 217
Burke, Sue 132
Burroughs, Edgar Rice 142
Bush, George W. 159
Butler, Octavia 6, 63, 125
Buying Time 33
Byron 93, 96, 149

Caan, James 138
Cadigan, Pat 11, 121, 150
The Cambridge Companion to Science Fiction 167
Cameron, James 3, 16, 45, 46, 48, 49, 75–77, 79, 80, 82, 83, 85, 86, 88
Camp Concentration 39
Campbell, John W. 20
Campbell, Joseph 5, 16, 52, 58–60, 83, 98, 154, 167

A Canticle for Liebowitz 127
Capra, Frank 175
Captain America 34, 189
Card, Orson Scott 20, 41, 58, 115, 120, 121, 154, 167, 170
Carpenter, John 199
Carroll, Lewis 78
Carson, Rachel 10
Caster, Will 189
Chabon, Michael 6
Charnas, Suzy McKee 129
Chambers, Becky 130
Chappie 183
Charlie's Angels 162
Chiang, Ted 49
Childhood's End 28, 43
Chiller 33
The Circle 22
CITOKATE 2, 13–14, 30, 73
City 42
Clarke, Arthur C. 28, 43, 166, 203
Clash of the Titans 35
A Clockwork Orange 204
Clooney, George 199, 200
Close Encounters of the Third Kind 49, 53, 136
Coleridge, Samuel Taylor 94, 96, 149
The Colour of Magic 204
Columbus, Christopher 21
Coma 192
"Come and Go Mad" 38
Conan the Barbarian 46
Connor, Sarah 80
Contact 47, 174
Cook, Robin 192
Cooper, Gary 108
Cooper, Merian C. 142
Coruscant 66
Costner, Kevin 4, 23, 45, 49, 172–176
Coyote, Peter 136
"The Crackpots" 39
Cramer, Kathryn 43
Crash 35
Crazy Horse 79
Crichton, Michael 18, 192, 194–197
Crockett, Davy 105, 142
"The Crystal Spheres" 42
Cuarón, Alfonso 4, 47, 76, 198, 201
Culp, Robert 35
Culture 87
Curie, Marie 62
curiosity 79
The Curse of the Werewolf 161
cyberpunk 11, 148–158, 188

Dance of the Dead 160
Dances with Very Tall Smurfs 76

Dances with Wolves 76, 78, 87, 172, 175
Dark City 48, 49
Dark Matter 127, 193
Dark Star 199
Darrow, Ann 142, 144
Darwin, Charles 40, 113, 114, 116, 208
Datlow, Ellen 35
Dawkins, Richard 209, 218
Dawn of the Dead 159
Day of the Dead 159
The Day of the Oprichnik 12, 127
The Day the Earth Stood Still 49, 139, 218
The Dead 160
Deadpool 35
De Camp, L. Sprague 63
Deep Impact 26, 135
A Deepness in the Sky 202
Delany, Samuel 16, 149
De Laurentiis, Dino 50, 143, 168
Demolition Man 34, 39
Dendle, Peter 159
Depp, Johnny 42, 186, 189
Destination Moon 31
de Tocqueville 92
Devenport, Emily 130
Dhalgren 204
Dick, Philip K. 16, 39, 50, 62, 161
Dickens, Charles 2, 94
Die Hard 20, 25
Dilios 104
Disch, Thomas 39
Disney 9, 51, 78, 117, 171, 197
The Dispossessed 125, 204
District 9 81, 137–139
Divergent 11, 22, 33, 38
Dixon, Leslie 193
Dr. Adder 35
Dr. Jekyll and Mr. Hyde 35
Dr. Strangelove 2, 10, 16, 45, 156, 165, 218
Doctorow, Cory 16, 125
Dog Soldiers 161
Door Into Ocean 129
Double Star 202
Dragonriders of Pern 126, 171
Drake, David 127
Dreyfuss, Richard 173
Dunbar, Lt. 78
Dune 4, 42, 50, 71, 165–171
Dune Messiah 166, 170

Earhart, Amelia 143
Earth 11, 76, 125, 204
Edison, Thomas 1
Einstein, Albert 71
Eliade, Mircea 58
elitism 20–22, 24, 56–59, 61, 65, 68, 80, 91–100, 108–113

Ellison, Harlan 4, 10, 39, 149
Elrond 98, 100
Elysium 21, 33
Empire 121
The Empire Strikes Back 49, 51, 54, 55, 64
Ender's Game 22, 120, 154
Equilibrium 22
Erin Brockovich 18
"Errand of Mercy" 87
E.T. the Extra-Terrestrial 23, 50, 135, 218
Eureka 39
Euripedes 196
Europa Report 23, 48, 135, 201
evolution 40–41, 71, 182, 208–210
Ex Machina 11, 178, 183–184
Existence 76, 139, 189, 197, 199
Existenz 11, 49 *Capitalization in document inconsistent!!
The Expanse 48
Extant 48, 183

Fahrenheit 451 63, 202
Fail-Safe 10, 218
Fallows, James 17
Fargo 19
Farmer, Philip José 10, 203
Feed 203
FernGully 76, 83
La Femme Nikita 162
feudalism 53–56, 59–60, 64, 67, 90, 125–128, 165–171
Field of Dreams 172–174
The Fifth Element 46, 157, 187
The Fifth Season 203
Fincher, David 38
Finn, Huckleberry 62
Firefly 48
Flanders 99
Flanery, Sean Patrick 62
Flieger, Verein 98
The Flight of the Navigator 41
"Flowers for Algernon" 42
Floyd, Heywood 30
The Fly 35
Flynn Effect 36
Forbidden Planet 48, 180
The Force Awakens 18, 117, 118
The Forever War 203
Forever Young 34
Foundation 43, 124
Foundation's Edge 43
Foundation's Triumph 43, 169
The Fountainhead 108, 109
Fowler, Karen Joy 125, 132
Frankenstein 37, 38, 149, 184, 189
Franklin, Ben 62, 71
Freejack 34

Freeman, Morgan 191
Freeman, Vincent 139–140
Freud, Sigmund 214
Friday 193
Frozen 6
The Fugitive 19
Futurama 34

Galadriel 98, 100
Galileo 92
Galt, John 112
Gamgee, Sam 97
Gandhi 77, 83
Garland, Alex 183
Garland, Judy 24
Gaskell, Elizabeth 2
Gattaca 2, 40, 45, 139–140
"The Gernsback Continuum" 39
Ghostbusters 49
Gibson, Mel 19
Gibson, William 11, 39, 148, 150, 204
Gilgamesh 32, 154, 163, 167
Gilman, Charlotte Perkins 129
The Giver 22
Gladiator at Law 33
Glory Season 129, 132, 204
God Emperor of Dune 166, 169, 170
The Gods Must Be Crazy 83
Godwin 93
Goebbels 97
Goldman, William 89, 204
Goldner, Orville 144
Gorillas in the Mist 83
Gosseyen, Gilbert 20, 205
Gravity 4, 47, 135, 198–201
Greece 101, 103
Greene, Richard 161
Griffith, Nicole 129
Grisham, John 18
Grossman, Lev 97
Guardians of the Galaxy 35
Gulliver's Travels 34

Haggard, H. Rider 142
HAL 9000 30, 181
Haldeman, Joe 33, 203
Hamlet 150
Hampton, Scott 106
The Handmaid's Tale 11, 130, 131, 204
Hanks, Tom 173
Hanson, Robin 186
The Hard SF Renaissance 43
Hard to Be a God 126
Harrison, Harry 10
"Harrison Bergeron" 38, 111
Harry Potter 163
Hartwell, David 43

Hawke, Ethan 139
Hayek, Friedrich 108
Heart of the Comet 204
Heaven's Reach 42
Hector 142, 163
Heinlein, Robert A. 11, 16, 33, 40, 45, 63, 111, 123, 166, 193, 202
Helgeland, Brian 173, 174
Henderson, Mary 58
Her 23, 177, 185, 188, 192
Herbert, Frank 4, 16, 50, 149, 165–171
Hercules (TV series) 64, 154, 163
Herland 129
The Hero with a Thousand Faces 5, 59, 154
The Hero's Journey 5
Hesse, Hermann 41
Hickman, William Edward 116
The High Crusade 45
Highlander 33
The Hitchhiker's Guide to the Galaxy 204
Hitler, Adolf 68
The Hobbit 204
Holy Fire 33
Homer 20, 67, 95, 154, 163
Honey, I Shrunk the Kids 135. *missing comma in MS
Howard, James Newton 175
Howard, Ron 173
The Howling 161
Hubbard, L. Ron 20, 58, 115, 120
Huckleberry Finn 62
The Humanoids 180
Humans 178, 193
Hume, David 149
The Hunger Games 11, 21, 22, 33
Hurd, Gale Anne 138
Huxley, Aldous 10, 33, 39, 114

I, Robot 177, 180, 190
I Walked with a Zombie 159
Idiocracy 34
The Iliad 20, 67, 154, 155, 158, 163
Immortality Incorporated 34, 203
In the Heat of the Night 19
In the Mother's Land 129
Inception 45, 49
The Incredibles 21
Independence Day 25, 118, 135
India 99
Interstellar 46, 180
Instrumentality 33, 37
Iron Giant 177
Isaac, Oscar 184
The Island 192
The Island of Dr. Moreau 37
It's a Wonderful Life 175
Ix 170

Index

Jackson, Peter 6, 16, 47, 95, 104, 137, 141, 143
James, Henry 94
Jaynes, Julian 213
Jefferson, Thomas 93, 149
Jemison, N.K. 16, 203
Jensen, Curt 61
Jessica, Lady 168, 169
Jeter, K.W. 35
The Jetsons 180, 187
Jinn, Qui-Gon 70, 71, 74
Jobs, Steve 81
Johansson, Scarlett 191, 192
Johnny Mnemonic 11, 152, 191
Jones, Calvert 12
Jones, Jim 112
Jones, Stefan 65
Jordan Two Delta 192
Journey to the West 167
Jupiter Ascending 41
Jurassic Park 23, 196

Kaczynski, Theodore 127
Das Kapital 11, 124
Kasden, Lawrence 55
Keaton, Michael 192
Keats, John 94
Kenney, Douglas 203
Kenobi, Obi-Wan 69
Khrushchev, Nikita 124
Kiln People 42, 77, 169, 177, 193–195, 204
King, Martin Luther 71, 77, 83
King, Stephen 42
King Kong 141–148
King Kong Is Back! 143
King Kong Returns 141
Klaatu 50, 139
Knight, Damon 180
Knock 203
Kong 141–147
Koresh, David 112
Kornbluth 33
Kress, Nancy 6, 36, 62, 121, 132, 189
Kubie, Lawrence 213–214, 218
Kubrick, Stanley 14, 30, 45
Kurzweil, Ray 86, 178, 187

L.A. Confidential 173
Lafferty, Mur 130
Land of the Dead 160
Lange, Jessica 143
Langella, Frank 185
The Last Place on Earth 26
Laumer, Keith 34
The Lawnmower Man 42
League of Extraordinary Gentlemen 159
The Left Hand of Darkness 202

LeGuin, Ursula 6, 76, 125, 129, 132, 202
Lem, Stanislaw 124
Lenin, Vladimir 124, 127
Leonidas 102–106
Let Sleeping Corpses Lie 159
Lewis, C.S. 94, 99, 100
libertarianism 20, 107–116, 122–123
The Life Eaters 106
Life of Pi 75
Limitless 42, 46, 189
Lincoln Six Echo 192
Lindbergh, Anne Morrow 143
Locke, John 149
Logan's Run 179
Looking Backward 203
Lord of Light 41, 203
Lord of the Rings 5, 47, 66, 95, 97, 98, 135, 142, 151, 157–158, 163, 168, 169
Lostetter, Marina 130
Lucas, George 3, 16, 23, 49, 51, 52, 55, 61, 62, 67, 81, 99, 117, 120, 126, 127, 154, 155, 157, 160, 167, 170
Lucy 23, 42, 189, 191
Lynch, David 168
Lysistrata 105, 129

MacLeod, Ken 202
Mad Max 175
"Madness Has Its Place" 39
Mailer, Norman 27
Make Room! Make Room! 10
The Making of King Kong 144
Malthus, Thomas 114
The Man from Earth 32
The Man in the High Castle 48
Mao Zedong 124
Marathon 102, 103
Marooned 135
Mars Trilogy 32, 125
Marshall, George 71
The Martian 19, 23, 26, 49
Martin, G.R.R. 128, 167, 171
Marx, Karl 11, 110, 113, 124, 127, 144
Marx Brothers 24
Marxism 124, 125–127
The Matrix 50, 86, 151–153, 156–158, 181, 189, 190
Mayflies 34
McCaffrey, Anne 34, 126, 171
McCallum, David 41
McCarthy, Will 155
McGregor, Ewan 192
McHugh, Maureen 132
McLuhan 28
"Melancholy Elephants" 36
Méliès 1
Michelangelo 212

Middle Earth 70, 98
Miller, Frank 101–106, 120
Miller, Walter 127
Milne, Robert Duncan 41
Minority Report 23, 34, 49, 151, 157, 158
Mission: Impossible 20
Mission to Mars 23
Mr. Nobody 33
Mitchell, Edward Page 41
Mohammad, K. Silem 161
Montesquieu 149
Monuments Men 23
Moon 45
Mordor 95, 96, 100, 170
Morgan, Richard 34
Mori, Masahiro 184
Mostow, Jonathan 194
Moyers, Bill 5, 58
Multiplicity 192
The Mummy 34
Mycale 104

Naboo 66, 70
Nagata, Linda 189
Neuromancer 148, 204
The Neurotic Distortion of the Creative Process 213
Never Let Me Go 192
A New Hope 19, 52, 64, 117
New York City 101, 141
Newitz, Annalee 160
Newton 92
Neytiri 85
Night of the Living Dead 159
Night of the Werewolf 161
The Nine Worlds 33
Nineteen Eighty-Four 2, 10, 11, 12, 14, 16, 17, 63, 100, 156, 165, 202
Niven, Larry 39, 192
"No Truce With Kings" 127
Nolan, Christopher 16, 45, 49, 76, 180, 189
"Number 12 Looks Just Like You" 39

Odd John 41
O'Donnell, Kevin 34
The Odyssey 34
Oedipus 68
Oedipus Rex 63
Old Man's War 34
On the Beach 2. 10, 17, 63
Optimus Prime 118, 177
Organa, Leia 72
Orwell, George 10, 12, 13, 14, 114, 167, 168, 202
Otherness 81
Our Man Flint 20

Out of Time (series) 39
Outer Limits 35, 41

Pacific Rim 25
Pandora 75, 78, 84, 86, 87
A Paradise Built in Hell 23
Paris, Celia 12
Patel, Dev 183
Patinkin, Mandy 138
Peacock, Thomas Love 93
The People of Sand and Slag 35
Pericles 105
Persia 102–104
Person of Interest 178
Pfister, Wally 189
The Phantom Menace 51, 68–70
Phenomenon 42
Phoenix, Joaquin 185
Piper, H. Beam 127
A Plague of Demons 34
Planet of the Apes 37
Planet Terror 160
Platea 104
Plato 113, 155
Pocahontas 76
Podhoretz, John 80
Poetics 59, 154
Pohl, Frederik 33, 62, 124, 125, 166
Pol Pot 168
Polity 35
The Post 18
The Postman 4, 23, 45, 49, 76, 125, 127, 130, 135, 172–176, 204
Potter, Harry 71, 115, 119
Potts, Stephen 60, 167
The Power of Myth 5, 98
Predestination 45
prediction 2, 9–11, 27
prefrontal cortex 9, 28, 212–213
Prey 195
Pride and Prejudice 197
Primer 45
The Princess Bride 204
privacy 113–114
progress 7, 28–31, 38–40, 63, 76–77, 83, 91–94, 108
Proust, Marcel 151
Psychopathy of Everyday Life 214
Pygmalion 37

Quatermass and the Pit 49

R2-D2 177
Raiders of the Lost Ark 136
Rainbows End 23
Ramis, Harold 192
Rand, Ayn 20, 107–116, 122, 124

Index

Ransom 19
Rapa Nui 80
Reagan, Ronald 159
Rearden, Hank 115
Red Riding Hood 161
Reeves, Keanu 191
Return of the Jedi 54, 65, 68, 69, 117
Revolt in 2100 11
Rip Van Winkle 34
Ripley 179
Rising Sun 195
Roark, Howard 115, 122
Robby the Robot 177, 180
Roberts, Adam 143
Roberts, Julia 19
Robinson, Kim Stanley 6, 32, 125
Robinson, Spider 36
Robinson Crusoe 34
RoboCop 177
Robot and Frank 177, 185
Roddenberry, Gene 38
Rollerball 11, 48
romanticism 4–7, 20, 60–61, 78–81, 94–100
Roosevelt, Franklin 11
Roosevelt, Theodore 218
Rose, Ruth 143–144
Roth, Eric 173
Rowe, Peter 160
Rowling, J.K. 119, 155
Rucker, Rudy 11, 150
Russ, Joanna 129

Salamis 104
San Diego Tribune 160
Saruman 95
Sauron 98, 100
Saving Private Ryan 53
Scalzi, John 34
Scannell, Pat 43, 160
Schindler's List 53
Schoedsack, Ernest B. 142, 143
Schroeder, Karl 125
Schweitzer, Albert 62
Scott, Sir Walter 60, 92, 155, 167
"The Screwfly Solution" 63
The Secret Life of Walter Mitty 23
secrecy 30, 69–71
self-preventing prophecy 2, 10–16, 37, 49–50
Seveneves 203
Shakespeare, William 150
Sheckley, Robert 34, 203
The Sheep Look Up 10
Sheldon, Alice 62, 132
Shelley, Mary Wollstonecraft 149, 184
Shelley, Percy Bysshe 93
The Ship Who Sang 34

The Shire 100, 170
Siddhartha 41
The Silence of the Lambs 19
Silent Running 10, 76, 83
Silent Spring 2, 10
The Silmarillion 99
Silver Bullet 161
Silverberg, Robert 149, 155
Simak, Clifford D. 42
Sin City 22
Sinclair, Upton 2
The Singularity Is Near 86
The Six Million Dollar Man 35
"The Sixth Finger" 41, 42
Skywalker, Anakin 68, 70, 71
Skywalker, Luke 6, 69, 72, 98
Slaughterhouse-Five 202
Sleeper 34
The Sleeper Wakes 34
Sleeping with the Enemy 19
Slonczewski, Joan 129
Smith, Adam 107, 108, 112
Smith, Cordwainer 33, 37, 62, 220
Smith, E.E. 58
Snow, C.P. 100
Socrates 149
Solaris 48, 124
Solnit, Rebecca 23
Solomon, Rivers 130
A Song of Fire and Ice 128, 167, 171
Sophocles 196
Sorokin, Vladimir 12, 127
Soylent Green 2, 10, 16, 63, 83, 156, 165
Sparta 102–104
Spider Man: The Trilogy 24
Spielberg, Steven 16, 23, 34, 49, 50, 53, 62, 67, 76, 121, 135, 153, 157, 183
Spinrad, Norman 125
Stalin, Josef 124
Stand on Zanzibar 37
Stapledon, Olaf 41
Star Trek 3, 20, 27, 38, 42, 47, 48, 49, 55, 65, 66, 81, 87, 96, 102, 151, 155, 187
Star Trek II: The Wrath of Khan 38, 47, 48, 49
Star Trek III: The Search for Spock 38
Star Wars 3, 5, 18, 19, 20, 23, 48, 49, 51–74, 81, 95, 99, 117, 126, 151, 154, 155, 158, 163, 169–171
Star Wars on Trial 51–74, 170
Star Wars: The Magic of Myth 58
Stargate 42, 48, 66, 182, 187
The Starlost 48
Starman 218
The Stars My Destination 203
Starship Troopers 174
SteamBoy 48

232 Index

Steel Beach 203
Steele, Allen 123
Stephenson, Neal 121, 203
Sterling, Bruce 11, 33, 36, 125, 149, 150
The Stone Canal 202
"Stones of Significance" 42
Stover, Matthew Woodring 51
Strugatski, Arkady 124, 126. *should this be Strugatsky? inconsistent in MS
Strugatski, Boris 124, 126
Sturges, Preston 24
Sully, Jake 78, 80, 84, 85, 87, 88
Superman 35
superpowers 34–36, 38, 41, 58, 63, 65, 117, 120–121
Surrogates 22, 193–195
suspicion of authority 12, 16–19, 24, 64

Taggart, Dagny 115
Tarkin, Grand Moff 67, 72
Tarkofsky, Andrei 124
Tatooine 66, 70
Teen Wolf 160
Tenner, Edward 196
Tepper, Sherri 129
The Terminal Man 196
Terminator 48, 86, 177, 182
Terminator II 48
Testament 10
Thanos 119
Thelma and Louise 19
Themistocles 101, 104, 106
The Theory of Moral Sentiment 108
Thermopylae 101, 103
Things to Come 48
Thor 35
300 22, 101–106
THX 1138 22, 38
Time Enough for Love 33
Tisch, Steve 173
Tleiaxu 170
"To Serve Man" 180
Tolkien, J.R.R. 5, 6, 70, 71, 94, 97–100, 104, 126, 135, 155, 160, 168, 170
Total Recall 50
Transcendence 42, 186, 189, 190
transcendence 41–43, 68, 86–88, 181, 187–190
Transformers 26, 118
transparency 13, 30–31, 108
The Transparent Society 108, 133
Travolta, John 42
Triumph of the Will 155
Tron 50
True Blood 159
Turner, George 144
Twain, Mark 9, 60, 107, 167, 206

28 Days Later 159
Twilight 159
Twilight Zone 38, 39, 180
2001: A Space Odyssey 3, 14, 27–31, 42, 45, 181, 203
2010 135
Twombly, Theodore 185
Tyson, Neil deGrasse 198, 200

Underworld 161, 162
Underworld Evolution 161
Updike, John 155
Uplift 37

Vader, Darth 67, 69–72, 74
Valkyrie 18
Van Helsing 159
VanderMeer, Jeff 49
van Vogt, A.E. 20, 41, 58, 115, 120, 167, 205, 206, 219
Varley, John 33, 203
Venus on the Half-Shell 203
Verhoeven, Paul 174
Verne, Jules 39, 63
Vikander, Alicia 184
Vinge, Vernor 23, 63, 86, 121, 187–189, 202
Virgil 155
Voldemort 119
Vonarburg, Elizabeth 129
Vonnegut, Kurt 38, 111, 202

Wagner 60
Wakanda 119
Wall-E 22, 177
War Games 10
War of the Worlds 49, 204
Washington, George 71, 104
Watchmen 42
Waterworld 173
Wayne, John 115
Weaver, Sigourney 84, 179
Weir, Andy 49
Wells, H.G. 34, 39, 63
WereWolf of London 161
Westworld 11, 196
"Where No Man Has Gone Before" 42
White Zombie 159
Whitman, Walt 94
Whitten-Klaw, Rick 143
Why Things Bite Back 196
Wiggin, Ender 115, 121
Williams, John 197
Williams, Robin 185
Williamson, Jack 180
Willis, Bruce 22, 25, 193
Willis, Connie 132
Wilson, E.O. 13

Windu, Master Mace 69, 70
Witchblade 162
With Folded Hands 180
Wizards 97
Wolf 161
The Wolf Man 161
Wonder Woman 35
The Word for World Is Forest 76
Wordsworth 93
The World of Null-A 205, 206
World War Z 160
Wray, Fay 142, 144

The X-Files 152, 157
Xena 64, 154, 162, 163
Xerxes 101, 103, 104

Yoda 69–71, 81, 98, 139
The Young Indiana Jones Chronicles 62

Zardoz 33
Zelazny, Roger 10, 41, 149, 203
Zemeckis, Robert 16, 23, 49, 173
Zombie 159
Zombieland 160
Zombies, Vampires, and Philosophy 161

www.ingramcontent.com/pod-product-compliance
Ingram Content Group UK Ltd.
Pitfield, Milton Keynes, MK11 3LW, UK
UKHW041944140426
5217IPUK00014B/647

Can science fiction—especially sci-fi cinema—save the world? It already has, many times. Retired officers testify that films like *Doctor Strangelove* and *War Games* provoked changes and helped prevent accidental war. *Soylent Green* and *Silent Running* recruited millions of environmental activists. *The China Syndrome* and countless movies about plagues helped bring attention to those failure modes. And the grand-daddy of "self-preventing prophecy"—*Nineteen Eighty-Four*—girded countless citizens to stay wary of Big Brother.

It's not been all dire warnings. While optimism is much harder to dramatize than apocalypse, both large and small screens have also encouraged millions to lift their gaze, contemplating how we might get better, incrementally, or else raise grandchildren worthy of the stars.

Come along on a quirky quest for unusual insights. No one is spared scrutiny! Not Spielberg or Tolkien or Cameron or Costner ... nor Dune or demigods or zombie flicks. Certainly not George Lucas or Ayn Rand! Though some critiques are offered from a lifetime of respect and love ... and gratitude.

DAVID BRIN is a California astrophysicist who serves on NASA's Innovative and Advanced Concepts program (NIAC) advisory board and speaks or consults on a wide range of topics including AI, SETI, privacy and national security. His best-selling novels have won Hugo, Nebula and other awards and appeared in more than 20 languages.

Front cover: Jodie Foster as Dr. Eleanor Ann "Ellie" Arroway in the 1997 film *Contact* (Warner Bros./Photofest)